THE PECULIAR SANITY OF WAR
Hysteria in the Literature of World War I

THE PECULIAR SANITY OF WAR

Hysteria in the Literature of World War I

Celia Malone Kingsbury

Texas Tech University Press

This book was set in Adobe Garamond. The paper used in this book meets the minimum require-ments of ANSI/NISO Z39.48-1992 (R1997). ∞

Printed in the United States of America

"'The Novelty of Real Feelings': Restraint and Duty in Conrad's 'The Return'" previously ap-peared in *Conradiana* 32.1 (Spring 2000), 31–40.
"'Infinities of Absolution': Reason, Rumor, and Duty in Joseph Conrad's 'The Tale'" previously appeared in *Modern Fiction Studies* 44.3 (Fall 1998), 715–729.

Design by Brendan Liddick

Library of Congress Cataloging-in-Publication Data
Kingsbury, Celia Malone.
   The peculiar sanity of war : hysteria in the literature of World War I / Celia Malone Kingsbury.
     p. cm.
Includes bibliographical references (p.   ) and index.
   ISBN 0-89672-482-4 (alk. paper)
   1. English literature—20th century—History and criticism. 2. World
War, 1914-1918—Literature and the war. 3. American literature— 20th century—History and criticism. 4. World War, 1914-1918— Psychological aspects. 5. War neuroses—History—20th century. 6. Hysteria in literature. I. Title.
   PR478.W65 K56 2002
   820.9'358—dc21   2002001868

02 03 04 05 06 07 08 09 10 / 9 8 7 6 5 4 3 2 1

Texas Tech University Press
Box 41037
Lubbock, Texas 79409-1037 USA
1-800-832-4042
ttup@ttu.edu
www.ttup.ttu.edu

For Chuck

Contents

Illustrations

Foreword

Celia Kingsbury's eloquent and moving book on the First World War—known in its time as the Great War or the War to End All Wars—brings together war and madness in unexpected ways. Beginning with a phrase from Joseph Conrad, she diagnoses the condition of a culture gone awry, a "peculiar sanity" induced by the shameless and distorting forces of wartime public opinion. She cites Robert Graves, who, home on leave, found the civilians to be odder than any soldiers: "We could not understand the war madness that ran about everywhere, looking for a pseudomilitary outlet. The civilians talked a foreign language; and it was newspaper language" (p. 107). We might associate the combination of war and madness with rage, as in the berserk frenzy attributed to the Vikings; with the cruelty and craziness of pillage, rape, and slaughter after battle, as seen in Callot's etchings of the Thirty Years War, or in the brutalities of Nanjing; with hostilities begun over football matches, severed ears, or the precise nature of salvation, with doomed charges and hopeless last stands; with unreined loathing or an unslakable craving for revenge; or with the flight of reason in the face of horror and fear. Dr. Kingsbury attends to all these associations, especially the last, but she sets them against a vision of sanity as vulnerable and inconstant—sometimes malleable, sometimes brittle, always contingent. Her subject, then, is consensual foolishness, sanity defined in bad faith. Among the writers she considers are Edith Wharton, Willa Cather, H. D., Rebecca West, H. G. Wells, Ford Madox Ford, Virginia Woolf, Rudyard Kipling, and, of course, Conrad. It is one of this study's many merits that she sees the intricacy and uncertainty of their positions: neither safe from the imaginative diseases of their time (as if their art could make them immune) nor so infected as to be helpless.

In a remarkable passage of the *Agricola,* the biography of a Roman governor of Britain, Tacitus allows a voice to the British resistance. He translates the words of Galgacus, who said of the conquerors: "Ubi solitudinem faciunt, pacem appellant" ("Where they make a wilderness, they call it peace"). Writing of events that happened almost nineteen hundred years later, Dr. Kingsbury exposes a similar discrepancy between words and deeds and a similar awareness that warfare is neither simply physical nor simply textual but involves words about combat and combat about words. Novels, histories, memoirs, reportage, stories, poems, speeches, editorials, plays, not to mention photos, paintings, monuments, and movies from the First World War and its aftermath all conditioned, and continue to condition, what people thought and think about military events, but so did the physical effects of howitzers, flamethrowers, bayonets, gas generators, machine guns, bombs, barbed wire, and rifles—twisted words and broken people. This is a book admirably alert to complexity and contradiction. Always judicious, Dr. Kingsbury is careful to insist, for example, that the falsity of some atrocity stories does not inevitably mean that all of them were false. We have to acknowledge the cynical promotion of lies and exaggerations by the press and the authorities without falling into the delusion, either cynical or naïve, that rapes and barbarous and illicit killings simply did not happen.

To do their work, atrocity stories need accomplices. Many of the narratives discussed in this study deal with, and sometimes embody, the collusion of propaganda with gossip and rumor. Whatever its pleasures, currently aided by a sycophantic press, gossip can be meanminded, prejudicial, and coercive—a kangaroo court in permanent session. Wonder or amusement at human frailties slides easily into contempt or hatred for the alleged frailties of particular groups—those with the wrong opinions, the wrong anatomy, or the wrong clothes. When this kind of malicious disparagement then combines with the favorite clichés, the received ideas of the day, the result is noxious in peace or war. Dr. Kingsbury's especially illuminating analyses of Willa Cather's *One of Ours* and Ford Madox Ford's tetralogy *Parade's End* bring out the richness of these underread works in just such terms, as do her readings of Rebecca West's *The Return of the Soldier,* Kipling's "Mary Postgate," Conrad's "The Tale," and many more.

There are good reasons, Dr. Kingsbury argues, for seeing the constraints, anxieties, denials, hatreds, and inconsistencies of the 1914–18 period as acute intensifications of peacetime thinking rather than as completely new states of mind. In her reading, the culture of the prewar years both in the United Kingdom and the United States was inflected by convention, conformity, and a habit of lying about anything that might embarrass or expose the status quo. The English-speaking countries suffered from an epidemic of what the existentialists would come to call bad faith.

Cultural conditions elsewhere in the world suggest a similar diagnosis. From Italy, for example, Sibilla Aleramo's *Una Donna* (1906) shows the forces of patriarchy, male and female, closing ranks against any suggestion that life might be lived more richly; from Japan, Natsume Soseki's *Botchan* (also 1906) satirizes a conspiracy of provincials and educational tradition-alists against everything new and cosmopolitan. Begun before the war and finished after, Thomas Mann's *The Magic Mountain* presents case after case of hysteria only just restrained by the rules of polite behavior, rules which are not, in the end, enough to check the murderous hostility be-tween Naphta and Settembrini.

A strong and lively argument will survive a little balking at the details. Some scholars, for instance, have identified an Edwardian mindset, a Brit-ish or English frame of mind. Others describe a much more turbulent scene. Dr. Kingsbury leans toward the first position, so that the obfusca-tions of Ford's Dowells and Ashburnhams characterize a whole society. Yet between the death of Queen Victoria and the death of the Archduke Ferdinand, British society was far from singleminded. The militant wing of the women's suffrage movement turned to bombs and window-breaking; striking Liverpool dockers confronted machine-guns, and striking Welsh miners the cavalry; in alliance with a hundred Labour MPs, the Liberal government of 1906 proposed an ambitious program of welfare legislation provoking the strenuous opposition of Tories in the Commons and a fierce constitutional conflict with the Lords; at political rallies, supporters of the government gave spirited renditions of "God Gave the Land to the Peo-ple"; leading members of that government were accused of flagrant insider trading in Marconi shares; British officers in Ireland threatened to mutiny rather than allow Home Rule; almost half a million Irish Protestants, male and female, pledged themselves to resist Home Rule "using all means which may be found necessary." In cultural and political terms, the idyllic Edwardian summer beloved of some memoirists was subject to hail, high winds, the threat of thunderstorms, and sudden blizzards. If the hypocri-sies of *The Good Soldier* epitomize the character of the prewar years, so too do the intense debates of D. H. Lawrence's *The Rainbow* and the political militancy of Robert Tressell's *The Ragged-arsed Philanthropists*.

One could make similar points about the United States, with its strug-gles over race, women's rights, and immigration, its controversies sparked by the new status as an imperial power. None of these reservations, how-ever, seriously weakens the power of Dr. Kingsbury's argument. The rigid attitudes she identifies continued firm among the military and social elites; as Arno Mayer demonstrates in *The Persistence of the Old Regime* (1981), at the outbreak of the war these European elites still held immense power. Arguably, power in the United States was more diffuse but was concentrated in the hands of businessmen and political magnates with a vested interest in defining "American" values by their own. In both countries, moreover, the churches and the popular press were likely to encourage consensus rather than debate. The more the opinion makers felt the threat of social crisis, the more noisily they appealed to whatever they claimed to be obvious fact or common sense. The war itself brought many challenges to these obvious facts—women, for instance, proved perfectly capable of doing a "man's job"—but the war also provided many excuses, many opportunities to discipline heterodox opinion. To quote Dr. Kingsbury, in wartime "any kind of aberrant behavior can be deemed treason" (p. 84).

Was the First World War unique in its "peculiar sanity"? Certainly other wars provoked comparable behavior. The savagery of Cromwell's war in Ireland was provoked by religious and political fanaticism coupled with wildly exaggerated rumors about the numbers of Protestants massacred or tortured during the Catholic rising of 1641. The Peloponnesian War led Athens into seriously compromising the moral and cultural values that were supposed to be its glory. The wars of the Manchu dynasty against the millenarian Taiping rebels were a prolonged contest between two forms of extreme social control. Nevertheless, the First World War stands out as exemplary and probably unique. Despite heavy censorship and management of news, it was widely reported, painted, photographed, and even filmed. Lords of the press such as Northcliffe boasted of making or breaking the reputations of generals and ministers. In no previous and no subsequent wars have so many intellectuals and so many academics lined up to assert the rightness of their own country's cause. In no previous war had music halls and football stadiums become such ready grounds for sergeants trolling for recruits. For the first time in several centuries some Britons were convinced (by a short story in a newspaper) that angels had come to the aid of the British army. It is hard to think of any other war whose conclusion brought about such a rush of pacifist art and pacifist statements or which killed so many poets. The profusion of justifications had been astonishing: it was a war for God, King (or Emperor), and Country (or Empire); it was a divinely approved war of civilization against barbarism (fought, inter alia, with poison gas and flamethrowers); it was a war for the rights of small nations (especially those of Belgium, the master of the Congo, but not those of Ireland); it was a war to purge the deplorable fatness of peace and comfort (soldiers would go to battle "as swimmers into cleanness

leaping," wrote Rupert Brooke); it was a war to end wars whose final disposition of border, territories, and people continues to be vexed.

Although virtually everyone had the details wrong, it was also one of history's most anticipated wars. Instead of swift cavalry actions and immediately decisive naval actions, there were battles across the globe and on
many fronts the interminable misery of the trenches. The immense literature of future war stories that proliferated between 1871 and 1914 raised
fears and expectations that intensified every time a new alliance was
formed or a new colony annexed. A war was expected but not this one.
Most of these stories came from writers bent on sensation or a particular
cause such as the need for conscription or the threat of foreign spies. Fiction fed on rumor; rumor fed on fiction.

It is one of history's ugly ironies that General Sherman's summary of his
Civil War experiences—"There is many a boy here to-day who looks on
war as all glory, but, boys, it is all hell"—has been twisted by editorialists
and couchbound tacticians into the argument: "Sherman said that War Is
Hell, therefore anything goes, and we don't have to be squeamish or punctilious about our own atrocities." This dubious syllogism has in our own
time been dragged out to justify everything from the killing of prisoners to
the use of phosphorus shells or napalm. Introducing a reprint of *Parade's
End* in 1950, Robie Macauley, who had been a student of Ford's before the
Second World War, observed: "Perhaps in this edition we can take a second look at the Tietjens story and discover that it is less about the incident
of a single war than about a whole era, more about our own world than
his." Macauley's point still holds. When the slaughter of reluctant conscripts is called a turkey-shoot, when villages must be destroyed to save
them, we are not in a morally steady position to patronize the "peculiar
sanity" of the First World War. Wisely resisting the pleasures of sanctimo-
niousness or the privilege of the grandstand, Dr. Kingsbury writes, "It is
not the purpose of this book to malign any writer for writing propaganda,
performing war service, or enlisting in active service. On the contrary, by
examining the sometimes illogical behavior of those who do write about it,
we may come to a greater understanding of what war is and why it so thoroughly stirs our emotions" (p. xxi). It is fitting that she should end her
book with a discussion of memory and oblivion, for thinking about the
First World War and other wars honestly, carefully, and compassionately
is the best we can do about them.

LAURENCE DAVIES
Dartmouth College

Acknowledgments

I would like to thank Hunt Hawkins for his support during the completion of this book. He encouraged my participation in the conferences of the Joseph Conrad Society of America that resulted in the publication of parts of this project. I am also grateful to all the members of the Conrad Society for welcoming me so warmly into the academic community, especially to Bruce Harkness for helping create in that organization an atmosphere amiable to new scholars and to Jane Ford for making specific suggestions on how to begin my project. In addition, I would like to thank the members of my doctoral committee, Stan Gontarski, Eric Walker, Karen Laughlin, and Bill Cloonan, for making that academic endeavor an enjoyable process, and the English Department at Florida State for providing a collegial atmosphere in which to work. I am also indebted to Donald Rude at Texas Tech for putting me in contact with Jackie McLean, my editor at Texas Tech University Press, whose conviction, commitment, and enthusiasm have remained constant and have been indispensable. I am, in addition, grateful to my anonymous readers at the Press for their astute observations and advice. Finally, I would like to thank my husband Chuck Martin, whose constant love, encouragement, and patience have made this work possible.

Introduction

Growing up in a small Southern town has given me firsthand knowl-edge of the force of gossip and rumor. My extended family was very con-scious of what "they" said. As far as my paternal grandmother was concerned, the worst thing that could be said of someone, usually a man, was that he "drank a good bit of beer." Women in this milieu, of course, did not drink. One of my early memories of the way the fear of rumor shaped the lives of my family occurred after the death of my father in the late fifties. People in mourning still wore black then, and when my mother went back to her job in the local bank, she dressed accordingly. But her hair, largely untended during my father's illness, needed a perm. So soon after becoming a widow, she did not dare go to the beauty salon to get it done. Instead she arranged for a woman who "did hair" in her home to do it. Even with this circumspect arrangement, her very Victorian father took exception. People, he declared, would say she was "primping up," which implied she was already on the hunt for another husband or, even worse, that she was looking for a good time.

In the first decade of the new millennium, such concerns may seem out-dated. But the lessons I eventually learned about the power of gossip as a social force were invaluable. First, as Joseph Conrad reminds us in *Heart of Darkness,* we live "in the holy terror of scandal, and gallows, and lunatic asylums."[1] That we fear scandal as much as gallows speaks to the power of gossip's hold over us. (To my mother's credit, she got the perm, but I'm sure she spent some restless nights over it.) Second, and much more sinis-ter, gossip generally bears little resemblance to the truth. While this is no revelation to many of us now, to a rebellious teenager it was ammunition. Tongues were going to wag no matter what I did, therefore . . . and so the argument goes. But the force of gossip became far more serious when, several years later, a young woman, who already had one strike against her because her parents were divorced, was forced to leave town in the aftermath of a silly—and by current standards innocent—indiscretion on a church hayride. She kissed another young woman's date. And still later, as a response to the sixties' dissent, locals looked to the lunatic asylum as a place for those who disregarded moral convention.

I refer to these moments of personal history because they prepared me for this study of World War I propaganda, for the inevitable extension, in the name of patriotism, of gossip's tongue into the political arena. From the onset of the Great War, gossip and rumor isolated, threatened, terrorized, and even destroyed individual lives. Already bound up in convention, gossip and rumor became ready tools for enforcing jingoism and heightening paranoia. They became propaganda tools. They became the harbingers of the often rabid behavior I will later define as peculiar sanity.

For the term *peculiar sanity,* I am indebted to Joseph Conrad. His genius echoes throughout this book. As I began gathering material on the war, his 1916 story "The Tale" caught my attention because it so clearly links behavior of a particularly irrational and deadly kind with gossip and rumor. I was swept away by the story and decided to present a paper on it at the Conrad Conference that year in Philadelphia. Researching the paper which now forms part of my fourth chapter, I found the term *peculiar sanity,* which Conrad uses in his 1905 essay "Autocracy and War." My application of the term to the behavior of the Commanding Officer in "The Tale" was the core of my project. Conrad's understanding of the changes war wrought on combatants and noncombatants alike surpasses that of any other writer. He alone seems to have seen the complex sources of his own participation in it. His letters from the war years reflect his fear for his son Borys, who was at the front, and his hope that the war might ultimately bring about Polish independence. But beyond that, the letters reveal a depression and cynicism that left him physically ill much of the time. "The Tale" is his only fictional work dealing with the war, and it is set in a hypothetical world in which rumor is the chief source of information and even the most steadfast and rational souls act upon it.

The aim of this study, then, is to analyze what happens to otherwise sane people who nonetheless may be prone to gossip, or fear its far-reaching effects, when war breaks out. It reexamines assumptions about commonplace and daily involvement in the Great War, and takes a closer look at lives out of kilter in ways those living them and writing about them don't quite understand and can't quite control. Finally, it considers shell shock, the condition most commonly associated with war neuroses. War literature, even the most cynical, reflects a deep pathos that grows out of the acknowledgment of human frailty and impotence in the face of communal disaster. But wars are much easier for humans to start than they are to stop. We are creatures of momentum, and the fervor of war often carries us further into the fray than we may have planned. Recent studies of war literature are often reluctant, in light of post-Vietnam cynicism, to recognize war fervor in writers who are otherwise held in high favor. Feminist critics in particular are sometimes reluctant to admit to eager participation in war on the part of those who are traditionally left behind. Although all the writers I consider in these pages recognize and write about propaganda and jingoism, many also wrote propaganda, some of it jingoistic. It is not the purpose of this book to malign any writer for writing propaganda, performing war service, or enlisting in active service. On the contrary, by examining the sometimes illogical behavior of those who do write about it, we may come to a greater understanding of what war is and why it so thoroughly stirs our emotions.

Perhaps the most significant of World War I studies is Paul Fussell's 1975 work, *The Great War and Modern Memory.* Fussell argues that the irony that grew out of an understanding of the war allowed those who participated in it to retrieve and, in a sense, to organize their memories of it. That irony has of course also informed much of twentieth-century literature. The Battle of the Somme in 1916, in which 60,000 were killed on July 1 alone, serves for Fussell as the defining moment of the War, the moment at which those involved "fully attained the knowledge of good and evil."[2] According to Fussell, that day, "one of the most interesting in the whole long history of human disillusion, can stand as the type of all the ironic actions of the war."[3] Fussell's analysis of the war has indeed put much of war literature and the war itself into perspective for us.

Fussell sees the war as resulting from a single and simple moment in history in which "two persons, the Archduke Francis Ferdinand and his Consort, [were] shot."[4] Contemporary historians, however, have become loath to identify a single action as the cause of the war, arguing that many other factors, economic and political, also came into play. Fussell also draws a heavy line between pre- and postwar literature. *The Waste Land,* for instance, came about only later, but one of Eliot's other major works, "The Love Song of J. Alfred Prufrock," which reflects the same cynicism, was begun in 1910. Ford Madox Ford's great ironic work *The Good Soldier* was published during the opening months of the war. And when Fussell cites Conrad as one of the authors who writes of "traditional moral action delineated in traditional moral language,"[5] he does an injustice to the great ironic voice of Charlie Marlow, and to much of Conrad's short fiction, including "The Tale" and "The Return," to which we shall soon turn.

Fussell, in addition, seems nostalgic about pre–twentieth-century modes of warfare. Objecting to the use of the word *battle* to describe World War I combat, he argues that "[t]o call these things *battles* is to imply an understandable continuity with earlier British history and to imply that the war makes sense in a traditional way."[6] Wars have never "made sense," nor have they ever, except perhaps in the most rhetorical and obtuse political way, been logical. War has always meant death and destruction, though on varying scales. But to call such an event as Passchendaele a battle is, in Fussell's words, "to try to suggest that these events parallel Blenheim and Waterloo not only in glory but in structure and meaning."[7] However, Tolstoy's battle scenes from Napoleonic wars in *War and Peace* illustrate as well as any later writer the futility of war, the inability of either general or soldier to see, much less "control," the course of a battle. There is no intention here to diminish in any way the devastating effect of the Great War, either on those who participated in it or on the subsequent history of the twentieth century, nor to diminish the ultimate value of Fussell's study. It is not necessary to glorify previous wars to point out the magnitude, the universal tragedy of the Great War. And although irony has become an essential part of modern consciousness (and later wars as well), irony is only one aspect of it. As Francis Ford Coppola illustrates in *Apocalypse Now,* his remake of *Heart of Darkness* set in Vietnam, madness is certainly another.

In 1988, Sandra Gilbert and Susan Gubar published the first of their three-volume series *No Man's Land: The Place of the Woman Writer in the Twentieth Century.* In it, the authors examine the battle of the sexes as represented in twentieth-century literature. Using the trope of the "no-man," that is, the maimed, deformed, or otherwise impotent male, they analyze what they believe to be the male response to heightened female endeavor. The Great War becomes, for Gilbert and Gubar, a symbol of masculine anxiety. Dug in on the frontiers of no man's land, the soldier "saw that the desert between him and his so-called enemy was not just a metaphor for the technology of death and the death dealt by technology, it was also a symbol for the state, whose nihilistic machinery he was powerless to control or protest."[8] That public powerlessness becomes private impotence that turns into anger directed at women, "as if the Great War itself were primarily a climactic episode in a battle of the sexes that had already been raging for years."[9] In their discussion of a poem by D. H. Lawrence, "Eloi, Eloi Lama Sabachthani?" (Christ's *My God, my God, why hast thou forsaken me?*), Gilbert and Gubar question the poem's suggestion that women are responsible for male suffering—questions that ultimately inform their interpretation of war literature. "Can this be," they ask, "because the war, with its deathly parody of sexuality, somehow threatened a female conquest of men? Because women were safe on the home front, is it possible that the war seemed in some peculiar sense their fault, a ritual of sacrifice to their victorious femininity?"[10]

The problem with interpreting the war from a single perspective lies not so much with the perspective itself, but with the limitations imposed by such a specific interpretation of a complex event. Few feminists doubt the basic notion that some men may feel threatened by the emergence of female autonomy, or that literature, and perhaps even public policy, may reflect that fear (war or no war); but to suggest that the "battle between the sexes" informs the responses of all men, especially those struggling to keep themselves alive under enemy fire, oversimplifies the human response to the threat of death and to war in the same way that Fussell's assertion that the war grew out of the Archduke Ferdinand's assassination oversimplifies the political cause of the Great War. Yes, the assassination was part of the turmoil leading to war, and yes, some men may have resented women for staying home, but the nature of battle, of killing and being shot at, alienates anyone who participates in it from anyone—regardless of gender—who does not. Many women, Vera Brittain among them, resented staying home and became VADs, members of the Voluntary Aid Detachment, or the Red Cross, or the YWCA's work corps that went to Europe to perform civilian war service. Response to war is seldom logical or predictable. Part of war's madness lies in the way it elicits the irrational response; "the stress of moral and physical misery" stretches the human psyche to its limits in battle and on the home front, and we must not anticipate a single response.[11]

While Gilbert and Gubar focus solely on gender in their study of modernism, they rely on the cultural and historical context of literary works to support their arguments, a critical method also adopted by such critics as Trudi Tate, Claire Tylee, and other feminists who have examined the roles of men and women during the Great War and later wars as well. In the preface to the first volume of *No Man's Land,* Gilbert and Gubar establish their critical perspective by declaring that their study is "based on two assumptions: first, that there is a knowable history and, second, that texts are authored by people whose lives and minds are affected by the material conditions of that history."[12] Such a statement is necessary to address the tendency of many critics, in their literary studies, to obliterate history and the individual lives within it. Although Gilbert and Gubar's focus remains, by

design, limited, those two assumptions sustain the most appropriate
method of examining material written during and about the Great War.

Trudi Tate's work on the First World War is extensive. In *Modernism,
History and the First World War,* she sets out to establish a connection between the Great War and literary modernism. In her authoritative study,
Tate looks at a number of modernist texts alongside journals written during and about the war. Placing these texts side by side allows Tate to see
modernism as "a peculiar but significant form of war writing."[13] Tate's literary history raises questions about "[w]ho is witness, and what is it that
has been witnessed,"[14] questions of perspective and perception.[15] Claire
Tylee in *The Great War and Women's Consciousness: Images of Militarism
and Womanhood in Women's Writings, 1914–1964* also examines the novels and diaries of women who endured the Great War, women who like
Brittain "went to war" with a high degree of idealism fostered by propaganda, despite Edwardian social restrictions. Those restrictions, Tylee believes, contributed to the widening rift between the sexes. Tylee argues
that, contrary to Brittain's suggestion that the war and its horrors came between men and women, "it was the construction of the reality of the War
that came between men and women."[16]

Like Tate, Tylee, and to a lesser extent, Gilbert and Gubar, I will be
looking at "nonliterary" as well as literary sources. To document the cultural context of the war, I will rely heavily on propaganda materials: books,
pamphlets, posters and broadsides, newspaper and magazine advertise-
ments, popular songs, and children's stories. All these sources, of course,
conclude that the allies are good and that "Prussians" are evil. All assume
that Germany was guilty of horrendous and multitudinous atrocities documented in publications such as the Bryce Report, a collection of testimonials from Belgian civilians and soldiers who fled or escaped occupied
territories. Peter Buitenhuis, in his 1987 study *The Great War of Words,*
documents the extent of the propaganda war in England and in the U.S.
Buitenhuis points out that the information contained in the Bryce Report
is largely suspect, "a tissue of invention."[17] Along with often unfounded
atrocity stories, propaganda made great use of two actual events—the sinking of the Lusitania and the execution of Red Cross nurse Edith Cavell.
The debate over the Lusitania concerned whether or not the ship was carrying arms, a charge the Allies flatly denied. Anti-German propaganda arising from this incident portrays Germans gloating over drowning mothers
and babies. In Germany a coin that on one side depicted the sinking and on
the other death as a ticketing agent was minted, although not officially. The
Bristish government copied the coin and issued it as a piece of propaganda.

The execution of Edith Cavell also was used for the duration of the war to stir up hatred for Germany. Cavell was a Red Cross nurse in occupied territory who was accused of helping French and Belgian soldiers escape, an accusation to which she apparently confessed. She was duly shot, in spite of efforts to have her execution stayed, and immediately became a martyr. James M. Beck, in a propaganda book, *The War and Humanity,* concedes that Cavell should have been detained for the duration of the war but maintains that "the history of war, at least in modern times, can be searched in vain for any instance in which any one, *especially a woman,* has been condemned to death for yielding to the humanitarian impulse of giving temporary refuge to a fugitive soldier" and calls the incident "a black chapter of Prussianism."[18] Propagandistic use of this incident focused largely on the fact that Cavell was a woman and that only barbarians shoot women, or drown them and their children. In Willa Cather's *One of Ours,* Claude Wheeler's friend Leonard Dawson tells Claude that he has enlisted for three reasons, "Belgium, the Lusitania, and Edith Cavell."[19]

Accusations of atrocities are sometimes hard to document. In light of German atrocities committed during the Second World War and repeatedly documented, it is difficult not to assume Germany's guilt during the First. Nevertheless, the purpose of this study is not to determine Germany's innocence or guilt, but to consider how the accusations themselves and the way they were used inflamed Allied nations against the enemy, and additionally, to analyze how writers of "literary" material also made use of them.[20]

My first task, then, is to define the term *peculiar sanity,* which makes use of gossip and rumor and their extensions, propaganda, jingoism, and paranoia. Next, I shall examine texts selected from a huge body of writings from the Great War that most strikingly illustrate the concept of peculiar sanity as it emerged on the home front and came to dominate the lives of virtually everyone who was touched by the war.

Chapter 1
SUPERFICIALITY AND REPRESSION
Peculiar Sanity In Prewar Conventions

Peculiar Sanity

Long before events in Europe embroiled most of the world in World War I, Emily Dickinson wrote on the question of madness and the extent to which definitions of that state can be subjective:

> Much Madness is divinest Sense—
> To a discerning Eye—
> Much Sense—the starkest Madness—
> 'Tis the Majority
> In this, as All, prevail—.

Unfortunately, this reversal of definitions becomes most pronounced during wartime, and the Great War certainly is no exception to that phenomenon. Lawrence LeShan, in *The Psychology of War: Comprehending Its Mystique and Its Madness,* suggests that humans' perceptions of themselves are different in war and peacetime. This change in our worldview "involves a shift in the perception of reality, an essential change from our structuring the world in our customary way to our structuring it in the ways of a fairy tale or a myth."[1] Good and Evil are clearcut: we are good and our enemy is evil. God is on our side, and our victory will forever change the world for the better. Psychological projection plays a large role in this shift, and LeShan is not the first writer to point this out. Sam Keen, in *The Faces of the Enemy,* uses Jungian archetypes to detail the psychological gymnastics accompanying aggression—that is, our enemy is a psychological projection of our worst traits, those we prefer not to acknowledge;[2] this projected demon arises out of the area of the psyche Jung referred to as "the shadow," "the dark side of our nature."[3] German naturalist Konrad Lorenz in *On Aggression* examines what he calls militant enthusiasm, a complex union of instinctive aggression and social norms.[4] Lorenz, Keen, LeShan, and other writers dealing with aggression may disagree on the location of the departure from rational behavior in wartime, but all agree that such a departure occurs.

Michel Foucault, looking at the question of madness itself in *Madness and Civilization,* returns to what he refers to as "that zero point in the course of madness at which madness is an undifferentiated experience, a not yet divided experience of division itself."[5] In the Middle Ages and in the Renaissance, while perceptions of madness did vary, unreason was considered an integral part of human nature. Madness was very often a source of human "truth" as well as a symbol of human misbehavior. The Age of Reason was the locus of the division we now know, the moment when the insane became one of the "problems of the city,"[6] and were confined in hospitals; it was also the moment in history when we developed a vocabulary for describing madness, much of which is still in use. In examining this evolution, Foucault reminds us of the subjective nature of such definitions and of the unavoidable connection between unreason and reason. José Barchilon refers in his introduction to Foucault's work as a "tale of . . . relative values, and delicate shadings . . . [that] re-establishes folly and unreason in their rightful place as complex and human—too human— phenomena."[7] The current dichotomy between madness and reason, according to Foucault, allows no dialogue between the two states, a dialogue which existed in the Middle Ages and in the Renaissance. We perceive madness and reason as well-defined opposites. If we were to place madness and reason on a continuum, it would exist only with a wide and largely empty middle.

Within the realm of this dichotomy, then, that perceptual shift which occurs during war, seen on a continuum, shifts or slides across the empty middle toward the kinds of action normally associated with madness; unreason now occupies the previously empty middle and insanity as it would have been previously defined moves rapidly toward what was once unthinkable. Oddly enough, when the will to participate in the "group madness" of war falters, when the trauma of atrocity becomes too appalling and, in response, the human psyche shuts down, war neurosis, or more commonly shell shock, arises. Insomnia, loss of appetite, hallucinations, memory loss, and loss of sensory function and mobility appear to a greater or lesser degree. *Shell-Shock and Other Neuropsychiatric Problems* reports 589 case histories from soldiers of the Great War, and these symptoms and others occur repeatedly.[8] In peacetime, these are symptoms associated with neurosis and psychosis. Associated with shell-shock during the Great War, these symptoms were considered signs of weakness, of moral turpitude, and depending on the physician, of shirking or malingering, not of insanity. Shell-shock victims were often feminized, treated with Weir Mitchell's rest cure, which had been used to treat or subdue "hysterical" females. As Foucault points out, we have always treated "the insane" as outcasts even when they reflect our own more finely tuned responses to reality. In the case of war neurosis, the psyche's attempt to protect itself from total disintegration is "punished" with the stigma of cowardice. Even when this response is not articulated, shell-shock neurosis is considered a "problem," one which must be dealt with in order to get the soldier back to the front or the civilian back to his or her job. The specific role of war in the breakdown is never analyzed.

Although Foucault's intention in *Madness and Civilization* is to consider the division between the states of madness and reason, to examine the process through which we have acquired our perceptions of the two states, and to discover our methods of dealing with madness, his historical treatise may lead us to another way of examining the phenomenon of war by teaching us that definitions of madness are relative and subjective. Wars are instigated as acts of reason; they usually are entered into formally with documents signed by monarchs and prime ministers and presidents. But the implementation of these decrees becomes another thing altogether. When we are at war, we—combatants and noncombatants alike—do things that would otherwise be perceived as mad, and we do them as naturally as we eat, sleep, and bond with those in our own group. We treat madness as the most heightened form of reason and do so without questioning our behavior. If madness, in its broadest definition, is a part of the human psyche, the always present dark side of reason, then certainly war triggers the mechanism that brings that dark side to the surface. Call it instinct, call it the collective unconscious, call it patriotism—when war is declared, humans become different animals. Seen in this way, the Great War leaves us in an unfamiliar territory, one which the Commanding Officer in Joseph Conrad's "The Tale" describes as "a world of seas and continents and islands" which is like earth, but is not the familiar world we normally inhabit.[9] We have fallen down a rabbit hole, or more accurately, into a shell hole, but the strangeness we see is far from a wonderland.

In "Autocracy and War," the prophetic 1905 essay analyzing the Russo–Japanese War, Conrad writes of this shift from sanity to insanity as experienced by troops. "It seems that in [opposing] armies," he explains, "many men are driven beyond the bounds of sanity by the stress of moral and physical misery. Great numbers of soldiers and regimental officers go mad as if by way of protest against the peculiar sanity of a state of war."[10] Conrad is referring to battlefield exhaustion and shell shock, but the moral misery provoked by war reaches well into civilian life. Extended to include noncombat behavior, Conrad's term "peculiar sanity" accurately describes those perceptions and the kind of aggression that Keen, LeShan, and Lorenz describe in their studies of human behavior—specifically, the sudden vilification of "the enemy," the suspicion that friends and neighbors are enemy sympathizers, and the fervent desire of civilians to kill or maim the villains. The atmosphere of peculiar sanity that exists in wartime cloaks rabid behavior in the garments of normalcy, and shell shock becomes a logical response to horror. During the Great War, civilians settled comfortably into bigotry, making Germans, some of them relatives, into barbarians of the worst sort; they then turned their gaze toward their neighbors. In Great Britain, the Defense of the Realm Act (DORA) threatened basic civil liberties. In America, neighbors spied and informed as easily as they bought consumer goods, or tilled their Victory Gardens in order to "Can the Kaiser" [fig. 1.1] Gossip, atrocity stories, and propaganda fuel group mania, and this mania feeds on itself until ordinary citizens find themselves in a frenzy of hatred and suspicion. Gossip, as I pointed out in my introduction, is an entrenched method of social control, the origin of the scandal we fear as much as the gallows. The peculiar logic of war encouraged intellectuals who might rationally have observed the way the evils of gossip influenced the nature of war politics, if not of war itself, to become part of the groundswell of jingoism.

Almost an oxymoron, the phrase *peculiar sanity* dissolves the barrier between reason and madness; it helps explain war fanaticism. Removed from the context of war, however, Conrad's term also accurately characterizes the social forces in operation in prewar Europe and America, as recounted in my introduction, and helps trace their evolution into war mania. Although Conrad's use of the term suggests that peacetime life is sane and war is insanity, we can find peculiar sanity in Victorian and Edwardian life—in its hypocrisy and superficiality, in the ubiquity of rumor and gossip, and in the dissociation that occurred with the onset of the twentieth century. It is to that highly structured social milieu, the decades that precede the war, then, we shall now turn.

Fear and Morality

Although its beginning in 1914 places the Great War well into the second decade of the twentieth century, most of us tend to look at the war as the moment when the twentieth century really began, when, to paraphrase

Fig. 1.1. Front cover of the 1919 Victory Edition of *Home Canning and Drying,* a cookbook asking women to continue in their efforts to conserve food for a still starving Europe

Yeats, things fell apart. And in a sense it was. The battlefield saw the first uses of the modern machine gun, the grenade, and gas. Air attacks on civilian populations became possible because of the development of the zeppelin, and, of course, the new airplane made combat in the air a reality. Almost an entire generation of English and French males lost their lives; altogether, over nine million combatants died and perhaps five million noncombatants.[11] Eighty-eight years later, the violence of the war still astonishes us.

Still, we must acknowledge the truth that Samuel Hynes and other historians point out—that most of the signs of social upheaval that became manifest after the war had already appeared before it. Many Modernist writers had already begun publishing before the war: Lawrence's *Sons and Lovers* appeared in 1913; *Blast*, Pound's little magazine, was already printing Joyce's work, among that of others; a young T. S. Eliot had written, if not published, *The Love Song of J. Alfred Prufrock;* and Ford Madox Ford, then Hueffer, had an established literary career. His "great auk's egg," *The Good Soldier*, a masterpiece of Modernist "structure," was begun in late 1913. What we refer to as modern art first appeared with a vengeance in the United States in New York at the Armory Show of 1913. Americans were slower to accept what their British counterparts had come to tolerate. Samuel Hynes reports in *The Edwardian Turn of Mind* that by the Second Post-Impressionist Show in London in 1912, modern art was, at least in that city, "no longer regarded as a loathsome disease."[12] Emerging from the constraints of Edwardian society, the avant-garde illustrates the extent to which the old ways and the new differed, as well as the extent to which the old ways no longer worked. Although entrenched conventions resist change, the twentieth century would quickly demand adjustments, some of which came at a high price.

Transitional in many ways, the Edwardian era provided a brief and appropriate link to the past, to the vast reign of Victoria which dominated the previous century and much of the world. But for Edward, the propriety that had been the bulwark of his mother's reign had been largely ceremonial. The distinction between the public and private self, always a part of Victorian morality, took on even greater significance. Hynes begins *The Edwardian Turn of Mind* with a description of a portrait of Edward VII and his wife Alexandra, impeccably dressed, formally posed, "an emblem," in Hynes's words, "of the Edwardian Age: a present, dominated by King and Queen, symbols of the established order—rich, punctilious, and unoccupied."[13] But as history and popular culture point out, Edward was far from the clean-lived monarch his portrait suggests. He was a celebrated womanizer, and his family bore the brunt of vicious gossip. Rumors raised the possibility that his son, Prince Albert Victor, Eddy as he was called, might actually be the serial killer, Jack the Ripper, a rumor based on the notion that Eddy had contracted syphilis from a prostitute and killed for revenge. Scott Palmer suggests the prince was out of town at the times of the murders, but as we know, truth never squelched a rumor. [14]

Yet, it is undoubtedly no coincidence that Hynes's description of Edward VII's foibles reads in fact very much like Ford Madox Ford's descriptions of the good people in *The Good Soldier,* and particularly like that of Teddy Ashburnham, as we shall see. The king favored, Hynes explains, "racing, gambling, shooting, and sailing; journeys to continental spas filled much of his time. . . . His moral views . . . were . . . a contradictory mixture of public propriety and private indulgence."[15] Because Edward was so well known for his "private" peccadillos, his hypocrisy becomes a part of his persona; the gap between the public and private self has become institutionalized.

And of course, Edward was not Victoria's only offspring serving at the helm of a modern state. As Martin Gilbert points out in *The First World War: A Complete History,* in the years before the war, "almost every European Head of State was related by marriage to every other."[16] Edward was succeeded at his death in 1910 by George V, his son and Victoria's grandson. Kaiser Wilhelm was also Victoria's grandson and cousin of George V. Two days before the Archduke Ferdinand was assassinated in Sarajevo, the Kaiser hosted a regatta at Kiel at which a squadron of British warships was honored. Ironically, Wilhelm, as an Admiral of the Royal Navy, wore a British uniform.[17] Gilbert wonders why these connections were not enough to stave off the threat of war, and goes on to explain essentially that family ties could not stop "the continual building up of armies and fleets, the development of the new science of aerial warfare and the national rivalries of the European powers [that] contained ominous overtones."[18] The war takes on the tone of a large-scale family squabble. Beyond the diverse causes of war Gilbert cites, we may look to a decadent, slightly incestuous monarchy that was becoming largely ceremonial and that was unable to function because the twentieth century was rapidly outgrowing archaic systems of governance. While the Kaiser and his cousin by marriage, the Russian czar Nicholas, in 1914 still wielded a certain amount of power, their days were also numbered. Appearance became the "substance" of the European upper class, although many continued to believe that their way of life, as Dowell asserts in *The Good Soldier,* was "the most desirable type of life in the world,"[19] that their era was still very much a golden age. But as

Hynes points out, "the forms of values had become the values; institutions had become more important than the ideas they embodied. If propriety expresses the forms of morality without conviction, then the Edwardian period was an Age of Propriety."[20]

The intense conflict between old and new, heightened by accelerating discoveries in science, medicine, and technology, and the level of hypocrisy evidenced in this monumental gap between the public and private self, provide fertile ground for the development of peculiar sanity, even without the added stress of war. Beyond spawning the usual neuroses arising out of the conflict between eras, between worn-out beliefs and changing ways of life, the stresses of social transition work in some ways as the stress of war does on civilians. Because the fear of losing a way of life may cause some to cling all the more ardently to it, and because those threatening the old ways thus become easily identified as the enemy, a social war ensues. For those who pretended that nothing had changed, the war became a holy crusade to crush the forces of immorality apparent in books, on the stage, in scientific research, and in the streets. Walter E. Houghton, in *The Victorian Frame of Mind*, describes the transition from the Victorian to the modern era in this way:

> First, men believe sincerely in the established truths. Then, as those truths are undermined by new knowledge or new political forces, the conservatives pretend to believe the old creeds and evade the difficulties: doubt and "hypocrisy" are born together.[21]

The social war—located in Edwardian hypocrisy, in the gap between pretension and reality, form and conviction, public persona and private self—was fought on both sides of the Atlantic and on many fronts. Groups concerning themselves with the regulation of behavior, mostly sexual, were so prevalent during Edward's reign that they formed an alliance in 1910, the Conference of Representatives of London Societies Interested in Public Morality. And in the same year, the National Social Purity Crusade organized a Public Morals Conference, the purpose of which was to "educate public opinion and to arouse the social conscience by bringing together recognised representatives of Religion, Education, Hygiene, the Home, the School, the Press, the Law, and Rescue Work to contribute by papers and speeches to a constructive policy of Prevention, and to promote a more effective effort to combat existing evils and temptations."[22] These purity crusaders, composed largely of clergy and a few politicians, were, according to Hynes, "at war with the twentieth century."[23] Hynes astutely links their fear of immorality to a fear of what he calls "the threat of Europe."[24] In the minds of the old guard, moral strength and military strength were one and the same. A decline in morality, therefore, signaled a decline in the ability to fight, a belief put forward on both sides of the Atlantic during the war, and one very much a part of the propaganda campaigns waged against Germany. Interesting parallels exist between the crusade against "inappropriate" literature and behavior, and later wartime laws such as the Defense of the Realm Act (DORA) in Great Britain and the Sedition Act in America. Movements such as Britain's National Social Purity Crusade, begun in 1901, sought basically to ensure uniformity of thought and action and to pillory those who did not comply, a goal shared by anti-sedition laws.

To those who touted the strongest connection between moral strength and military strength, sexual morality, as it related to the replenishment of potential soldiers, became doubly important. Sexual purity, they argued, bred the strongest soldiers. Conformity and genetic superiority ran on parallel tracks. C. W. Saleeby, in "Education for Parenthood," his contribution to *The Nation's Morals,* the published proceedings of the Public Morals Conference, uses the term *racial instinct* to refer to sexual desire. Saleeby explains his use of the term in the following way:

> The advantage of the name, which I have been in the habit of using for some years, is not only that it can freely be employed without offence before a mixed audience, but that it asserts definitely, from the first, *that for which the instinct exists.* . . . It is not merely the cause of a vast amount of the evil of human life, it is not merely the fundamental fact . . . of the evil against which we are here assembled, but—a point which frequently escapes the moralist—it is also the necessary condition of all the good and beauty of existence.[25]

Saleeby means, of course, parenthood, and goes on to promote an almost Nazi-like attitude toward breeding. James Marchant in his pamphlet *Social Hygienics* (1909), uses the term *racial instinct* as well.[26] Hynes believes the use of the term expresses "a fear that society will change so radically under these [sexually] liberating pressures as to remove it from the authority of the established order and of the abstractions that that order depended on: property, the family, Christianity, class, the dominance of men."[27] First, Saleeby and Marchant are drawing battle lines which place in the enemy camp those who do not conform to the Crusade's standards, and ultimately barbarize them. Second, their efforts against evil are wholeheartedly directed against "immoral" sexual behavior, not other evils of the day, such as greed and political corruption. Saleeby then establishes his belief in a connection between sexual morality and national defense in the paragraphs he quotes from *Parenthood and Race-Culture,* his book on eugenics. "[P]arenthood," he asserts, "necessarily takes its place as the

supreme factor of national destiny," and therefore, "true patriotism must
. . . concern itself with the conditions of the quality of parenthood."[28]
Saleeby here goes well beyond questions of propriety into the realm of social control. It is ironic that such a campaign arose during Edward's reign
and at a time when British imperialism—itself morally questionable—still
dominated the globe.[29] The Purity Crusade in and of itself constituted peculiar sanity because it condoned numerous violations against democratic
principles, ostensibly in the name of British democracy. Fear of the future
and preserving the status quo—principally, winning the war against the
enemy of twentieth-century culture, art, and literature—took precedence
over civil liberties.

Of the methods adopted by the purity crusaders, censorship played a
prominent role in the attempt to stave off the forces of the new morality. A
sort of manifesto for the Purity Crusade before the Public Morals Conference, *Public Morals* was first published in 1901 and then reissued in 1908.
James Marchant, who edited both texts, quotes his Editor's Note from the
first edition and suggests that the book has "in a small measure" achieved
its desired ends, which were

> arousing the sluggish conscience of the nations to respond to the urgent demand
> for improved national and international laws for the protection of the innocent,
> for purer homes for the people, safer streets, more wholesome papers and pic-
> tures, a sweeter atmosphere in places of amusement, and an equal and higher
> standard of morals for men and women.[30]

Vague and idealistic, Marchant's words clearly do not address questions
of morality beyond those of a sexual nature, nor do the essays themselves, a
point admitted by Percy William Bunting in his article "Morality and Literature."[31] The third essay in the collection, "Law and Morality," written
by William Alexander Coote, the Secretary of the National Vigilance Association, reveals a kind of creative illogic when it turns to the question of
censorship. In the section titled "Immoral Books and Obscene Pictures,"
Coote focuses on one of the continuing problems of censorship, the definition of obscenity. He declares that "[w]hile the English law makes ample
provision for the punishment of those who publish, sell, or expose for sale,
immoral books or pictures, in no place does it define, either by analogy or
comparison, what are the constituent legal elements of indecency."[32] But
then having elucidated the problems of enforcing laws under such circumstances, Coote suggests a three-point amendment to the law which gives
magistrates even more power to use their own discretion in defining and
suppressing "obscene" material. Bunting, in "Morality and Literature,"

frankly states that "there is no possible legal definition of indecency. It is the question of the effect of a production as judged by responsible men accustomed to the ways of the world and deciding by their common sense."[33]

Both writers are advocating the enforcement of laws that are not clearly defined and are therefore left to individual discretion for enforcement. In a more sweeping gesture, the Public Morals Conference adopted as one of its three resolutions to be delivered to the Home Secretary a statement asking that he "introduce further measures of control over the production and circulation of indecent books and papers."[34] All three documents advocate the devotion of court and legislative time and process to questions of "personal" behavior, and in the case of literature, taste. Such arbitrarily enforceable laws lay the foundation for later sedition laws that relied for their application on such subjective measures as gossip and rumor. Both kinds of laws operate on the same assumptions—behavior will be homogeneous or it will be punished. Conformity has become a matter of law for Edwardians; later, it will become a matter of national defense. H. Grattan Guinness, writing on lust in "Men in Relation to the Problem of the Social Evil," like Seleeby connects purity to national strength. Guinness, a medical doctor, writes, "[w]e have heard lately the shout of patriotism and imperialism, and it is well; but, if these cries are not to be mere empty sounds, they must be backed by such personal purity and self-restraint as will leave a benediction in national and imperial life."[35] Guinness does not address the question of imperialism or the evils associated with its pursuits, or of the effects of imperialism on individual and national morality.

The Purity Crusade offers a clear example of the social war that erupted during the first decade of the twentieth century. Hynes's assessment of the movement points out the emptiness of such struggles:

> The whole movement [had] a parochial quality about it; it did not offer a moral judgement of Edwardian life in the light of clear moral principles; rather it sought to marshal the vague moral pieties of a past life against the social anxieties of a fearful present.[36]

Instead of falling under the crusade's control, sexuality becomes foregrounded in much of Modernist art and literature. Addressing the question of *The Good Soldier*'s concern with the topic, Ford biographer Max Saunders also looks at Edwardian social conflicts and what he calls "the conservative defense of the family."[37] As for *The Good Soldier*, "[p]art of the novel's fascination is that it reads as a compendium of the anxieties and disturbances afflicting Edwardian England."[38] We have seen what those anxieties and disturbances were, and have located their source in the death of Victorian traditions. We have also identified the phenomenon of peculiar sanity in the contradictions of the purity movement's actions. In *The Good Soldier,* we see the hypocrisy inherent in clinging to traditions that retain only superficial value, and the pitfalls of ignoring what Saunders calls "the mismatching between monogamy and desire."[39] In Saunders's words, "*The Good Soldier* gets to the heart of [those] contemporary contradictions and uneasiness. What is more, Ford shared the belief that the regulation of sexuality was a thoroughly political issue."[40] Indeed the Purity Crusade made social control through the regulation of sexual behavior a legitimate matter for legal and legislative concern. That it did not get very far indicates the extent to which it largely constituted moral posturing, but during the war DORA and the American Sedition Act carried the true force of law, and in the United States, the Prohibition Amendment, a product of the Temperance Movement, banned the legal sales of liquor, an action the "moral" British would never have stood for.

Peculiar Sanity in the Manor House: Ford's *The Good Soldier*

The "contradictions and uneasiness" that Saunders sees as inherent in Edwardian England, and the emptiness and insanity of Edwardian pretensions are in fact apparent in Ford's *The Good Soldier.* Ford began this novel on his fortieth birthday, in December 1913, and completed it in the fall of 1914, after the start of the war on August 4. All crucial events in the novel occur on August 4. Critics disagree on whether the importance of that date to the outcome of the novel is coincidental. Saunders is among those who believe Ford's choice was coincidental, citing, along with other evidence, the fact that the first section of the novel had been published in *Blast* in June 1914.[41] Ford begins the third chapter of section one with a reference to August 1904, but not precisely to August fourth, making the choice of date seem an improbable coincidence. Nevertheless, while these arguments may prove fruitful for other discussions of the novel,[42] our focus might be better directed toward Ford's accomplishment, which was to present in minute detail the tensions and hypocrisies of Edwardian society's last days or, as Robert Green explains, the "world-vision of a class faltering through an epoch of social convulsion."[43] An astute observer of humanity, Ford experienced ambivalent feelings about the social disintegration he anticipates in *The Good Soldier,* and expressed that ambivalence through the narrator John Dowell. Biographer Arthur Mizener calls Ford's own life "the saddest of stories" because it encompasses both the anachronistic idealism of Teddy Ashburnham, the novel's good soldier, and the cynicism of John Dowell. "Part of him," Mizener writes, "believed in the honorable and simple life of the Tory gentleman . . . so intensely that he could not imagine that it was unachievable, and part of him was the skeptical observer who was reduced to hopeless inaction by his common-sense recognition that it was."[44] *The Good Soldier* focuses on this conflict in the narration of Dowell, who loves Ashburnham to the extent that he only obliquely admits to Teddy's failures, to his inability to be the good soldier he feels he is obliged to be. Ashburnham's belief in the life of the Tory gentleman, in the feudal system (the term Dowell uses to describe Asburnham's way of life), is betrayed by the failure of that system and by his own human weaknesses. Rendered untenable by Britain's movement, at least in England proper, toward more democratic institutions, feudalism is a dying, but not yet dead, way of life in the first decade of the new century. Ashburnham's weakness for women is so closely allied to his idealism and to the feudal system that the two become indistinguishable.

John Dowell sees the failure of Ashburnham's idealism, but he never rejects the aristocratic way of life. His narrative is full of contradictions; observations which indict their limited way of life are often undercut by disclaimers, by an often repeated "I don't know." Speaking of the nine years he and his wife Florence have spent in the company of the Ashburnhams, Dowell concludes that "by God, it is false! It wasn't a minuet [de la coeur] that we stepped; it was a prison—a prison full of screaming hysterics, tied down so that they might not outsound the rolling of our carriage wheels as we went along the shaded avenues."[45] But immediately the nostalgia for his old life brings Dowell full circle, and he declares, "And yet I swear by the sacred name of my creator that it was true," and by the end of his observation, pulling back again, says "I don't know" (9). Submerged in Dowell's vacillations is the contradiction inherent in Edwardian hypocrisy, the psychosis inherent in masking the private self with a completely conflicting public persona. Beneath the polite veneer of society lies a social and emotional chaos which emerges in spite of Dowell's wish to deny it. While the trenches of the social war may have been dug elsewhere, the battle rages in the lives of the "good people," and Dowell knows that theirs is a doomed way of life. Very early in the novel, before we learn the tragedy of Dowell's nine seasons with the Ashburnhams, we are given the idea that indeed this story may serve as a requiem for western civilization. Explaining why he is telling this story to his imagined listener who sits with him beside a fire, Dowell tells us that

> it is not unusual in human beings who have witnessed the sack of a city or the falling to pieces of a people to desire to set down what they have witnessed for the benefit of unknown heirs or of generations infinitely remote; or if you please, just to get the sight out of their heads.
>
> Someone has said that the death of a mouse from cancer is the whole sack of Rome by the Goths, and I swear to you that the breaking up of our little four-square coterie was such another unthinkable event. (7–8)

This falling to pieces of a people, this break up of their "four-square coterie," later manifests itself in the peculiar sanity of the Great War and, if it culminates at all, culminates in the war's aftermath.

As the Purity Crusade clearly establishes, the old order's method of staving off the falling to pieces, of forestalling the apocalypse, becomes the cosmetic and visible action of regulating sexual behavior. Max Saunders, in his lengthy analysis of the novel, draws on Ford's response to a negative review of *The Good Soldier* in which Ford says, the book is a "serious . . . analysis of the polygamous desires that underlie all men."[46] This generalization becomes problematic, as Saunders suggests, and raises as many questions as it answers. Unquestionably, the novel, subtitled "A Tale of Passion," revolves around the infidelities of Edward Ashburnham and Florence Dowell, and the consequences of their actions. And yet, to limit our examination of *The Good Soldier* to Edward's and Florence's peccadillos seems to reduce a novel of social nuances to an Edwardian version of "men (and women) behaving badly." The social nuances, the conventions and repressions left over from Victorian morality offer a feasible explanation for that bad behavior. We can see how sexuality becomes the most appropriate way to rebel against the old order and to express in fiction a changing social structure.[47]

But we could also raise questions about morality in general, or the extent to which sexuality becomes a metaphor for morality. If Ford's assessment that "the regulation of sexuality [is] a thoroughly political issue" is correct, and our investigation of the Purity Crusade suggests that it is, we may still wonder about the tentative hold morality in general has over human behavior. Edwardian sexual restraints were at best stifling and at worst unreasonable. Many spokespersons for the Purity Crusade held that relations between married couples were only appropriate when their intention was reproduction—sex as recreation, even in marriage, was a definite taboo. If such an unreasonably restrictive morality, one often rightfully ignored, is an emblem for morality in general, then the progression to a more general immorality might seem logical. Immorality may be inherent in this hypocritical and political moral system. As Conrad's Marlow points out, in the absence of the policeman on the corner, morality does tend to dissolve.

But in *The Good Soldier,* the application of the law itself becomes questionable. A landowner and magistrate, Ashburnham is the policeman on the corner, which leaves morality on truly shaky grounds. Even in terms of postwar morality, the morality Hemingway thinks of when he describes his code hero—that is, someone who doesn't do things that make him feel guilty the next morning—Ashburnham fails because he knows he is misbehaving. He feels bad about it, but he does it anyway. Like the monarch who so notoriously misbehaves in private, Ashburnham upholds one set of standards for the county, but he does not apply them to himself. But as long as Ashburnham and the king abide by the external expectations of the good soldier, as long as he throws himself overboard ship to save his men and keeps his drunken tenants out of jail, as long as he does not kiss servant girls on trains, he need not restrain his private sexual urges with married women of his own class. As long as he subscribes to the public limitations of "public morality," he remains a good citizen. To reiterate, within this gap between public and private behavior lies the tension out of which arises the peculiar sanity of prewar society, or in Saunders' words, "moral chaos." *"The Good Soldier,"* he tells us,

> makes it clear that [the] sense of how little stands between high civilization and barbarism, insanity and squalor is, curiously, a perception which pre-dates the war or which could be said to anticipate it. . . . Rather than trying to categorize *The Good Soldier* as a pre-war book or a wartime book, we should recognize how it comes out of many of the same tensions and forces which produced the war.[48]

High civilization resides on the brink of insanity in *The Good Soldier,* or for our purposes, the brink of peculiar sanity. The old ways are so deeply entrenched, the good people cannot see beyond them, cannot sense the approaching conflagration. As he relates to us the details of Ashburnham's relationship with the courtesan, La Dolciquita, the affair which gives Leonora eventual control of Ashburnham's estate, Dowell declares that Ashburnham believed "salvation [could] only be found in true love and the feudal system" (176). But La Dolciquita, who is not feudal, believes in the power of money, specifically twenty thousand pounds to buy a pearl tiara. Since Ashburnham's wealth is largely feudal, he resorts to loan sharks for the cash to buy the love he desires, believing that once she is in his possession, she will at least become his "sympathetic confidante" (176). She does not. This event proves crucial to the outcome of the novel, and it illustrates one of the novel's central ironies. Ashburnham's pursuit has nothing to do with true love, and his action places his feudal estate in the hands of Leonora, whom H. Robert Huntley in *The Alien Protagonist* describes, along with Dowell, as more modern types who are "replacing older types like Ashburnham with his feudal heritage of passion, idealism, aristocratic responsibility" (171). The problem with this theory is that Ashburnham's feudalism is a sham to begin with, and Ford, in his choice of names, illustrates that sham. La Dolciquita is very close in sound to Dulcinea, the name of Don Quixote's "true love." Like Don Quixote, Ashburnham may wish he were a medieval knight or lord but, also like Don Quixote, he isn't. However much he may wish to deny it, feudalism's days are numbered, as are the days of Victoria's numerous descendants who by 1914 occupied most of the palaces of Europe.

Forms and institutions, both without content, rule the good people. The tension between their public actions, which express Edwardian morality, and their private desires, which contradict it, lays the groundwork for the kind of madness we will refer to as peculiar sanity. Emotions are so taut beneath the practiced civility of the good people, they finally snap. What Dowell refers to as a "minuet de la cour" [sic] ends in two suicides and a bona fide case of madness which emerges after Nancy Rufford learns that Edward and Leonora's marriage is not the sacred union she had imagined it to be and after she learns of Edward's suicide. Nancy falls prey to madness, through which Saunders suggests she "gains her faith, and possibly her salvation," because she has not yet learned the cynicism which allows the four adults in the novel to profess one way and behave another.[49] For Teddy and Florence, even cynicism fails when they must confront the logical progression of events which grows out of their carefully constructed lies. Human communication, human connection, human sympathy, which might redeem the lives in question, do not exist because they are not built into Edwardian morality. As T. S. Eliot points out in his introduction to Djuna Barnes's *Nightwood,* this kind of morality assumes that "the decent man need have no nightmares."[50] In *The Good Soldier,* their lives are nightmares of restriction and isolation. All members of Dowell's "little four-square coterie," including Dowell himself, are riddled with repressed desires, not all of them sexual (8). Not one of the four adults seems capable of expressing honest emotion or affection. Hynes, in "The Epistemology of *The Good Soldier"* addresses the question of isolation in all five. "Alienation, silence, loneliness, repression," he explains, "these describe Ashburnham and Leonora and Nancy, and even 'poor Florence' as well as they describe Dowell. Each character confronts his [or her] destiny alone."[51] Nancy's mute madness at the end of the novel becomes an apt metaphor for this alienation, and interestingly enough, forms a comparison with certain forms of shell shock which will appear during the war. This "prison full of screaming hysterics" which threatens to break loose at any moment, will be particularly susceptible to war mania (9). Committed to conformity at all costs, the good people are not likely to question the forces of propaganda, nor are their repressed souls likely to resist the desire for action, or the need to feel connected.

The demand for public propriety in the lives of the good people is overwhelming on a number of levels which reflect both superficiality and repression. First, the regimen of their daily lives leaves little room for variation. While the regimen of the spa itself determines for instance that those with "hearts" remain in their beds in the afternoon for "the hour and a half prescribed by the Kur authorities," diet and leisure time seem to be regulated by a set of unwritten laws, or the laws of convention (59). Next, "along . . . the lines of . . . public functions" as Dowell puts the matter to Leonora, the rules are very well understood (105). About Edward's position as landowner, Dowell says Edward possessed a "violent conviction of the duties of his station," duties which involve keeping his tenants out of jail and free from financial burden (62). Finally, and in a sense the most crucial point, as we have seen, the emotions are also under strict regulation. This is the British stiff upper lip; across the Atlantic, it is called Puritan self-control. In all these areas, there is little room for individual interpretation or expression. While Hynes argues the importance of the "interaction" between passion and convention,[52] we must wonder if the good people actually experience passion, if their passions have been repressed beyond redemption. Dowell insists that Florence "had not the hot passions of these Europeans" (76); she was instead a "cold sensualist with imbecile fears" (102). Teddy Ashburnham, Dowell tells us, is a sentimentalist, whose trouble in the Kilsyte case arises not out of passion but out of chivalry. "[W]hen he . . . kissed [the servant girl]," Dowell explains, "he had desired . . . to comfort her" (62). Dowell later reiterates that Ashburnham "immediately felt that he had got to do something to comfort [the servant girl]. That was his job in life. He was desperately unhappy himself and it seemed to him the most natural thing in the world that they should pool their sorrows" (164). About Teddy's affair with Mrs. Basil, Dowell says, "it was old Mr. Mumford—the farmer who did not pay his rent—that threw Edward into Mrs. Basil's arms" (184). In each of these cases, Edward seems to be confusing passion with his feudal duties.

Nancy Rufford is, according to Dowell, "the real passion of [Edward's] life" (63), and about Nancy much must be said. Saunders goes so far as to suggest that Nancy may actually be Edward's illegitimate daughter,[53] and if that were the case, then *The Good Soldier* would become a novel of the psychology of perversity rather than a novel of passion and convention. As it is, Edward's love for her stretches the bounds of reason, and to an extent reflects peculiar sanity. For Edward, Nancy represents the moment when the tensions stretch to the breaking point. His role as feudal lord is threatened by the taint, real or metaphorical, of incest. When he insists on playing the role of the good patriarch in spite of his urges, he perishes.

Superficiality: Ford's *The Good Soldier*

The propriety which is expressed in *The Good Soldier* is largely superficial, a propriety, like that of the monarchy's, based on manners and deportment. On the surface, the Dowells and the Ashburnhams are perfect couples, subjects, no doubt, of much envy and admiration. Even John Dowell is fooled by the placid beauty of the surface of their lives, largely because he wants to believe in it. When he learns of the deceit and betrayals to which he has been subjected by his wife and his "best friend," Dowell still clings to the idea that his life was a good one. In one of the novel's most apt and often quoted metaphors, Dowell compares his world to an apple rotten at the core. If, he asks, "[I] discover its rottenness only in nine years and six months less four days, isn't it true to say that for nine years I possessed a goodly apple?" (9). Of course Dowell's marriage is never a goodly apple. Florence lies to him to pursue her liaison with the blackmailer Jimmy before their honeymoon ship to Europe picks up steam. Dowell thinks little, that we know of, about having a marriage that is never consummated. Doing so would be ungentlemanly, an insult to what he believes to be his wife's poor health. Florence's fake heart condition has its origins in her Uncle Hurlbird, whose heart condition is discovered to be nonexistent only after his death from bronchitis. That Uncle Hurlbird, a bastion of New England responsibility, should nurse a false ailment which unwittingly perpetuates an illicit affair for his niece, offers yet another appropriate metaphor for the emptiness, the rottenness, of Edwardian morality. Here once again, the surface truth is a lie, and the rottenness of the core spreads to the heart of conventionality. While Uncle Hurlbird is a kind old soul who gives away California oranges to everyone he meets, his staunch belief in the concealment of the truth coupled with a belief in a double standard of behavior for women encourages Florence to dupe Dowell. Herein, it would seem, lies one of the novel's sad paradoxes. Dowell believes that if he had embraced Florence in her room on the evening he elopes with her, none of the novel's tragedies would have occurred. The question which must be raised here is this: why does Florence choose an illicit affair with the smarmy Jimmy over a relationship with Dowell, even considering his restraint? The answer must lie both in concealment and in the double standard. Florence is a bright woman, a Vassar graduate for whom the conventions, the superficialities, are a bore. What better way to amuse herself, to ripple the smooth surface of her privileged life than by engaging in sexual conquest? The superficialities, the assumptions, as we have seen, promote it.

The specificity of Edwardian conventions is, when viewed from a distance of nearly a hundred years, stunning. In the area of daily activities, assumptions determine the diet and bathing habits of the good people; in their hotel, they must dine at the same table, day in and day out. When Florence Dowell offers to share their table in the hotel dining room with the Ashburnhams, her response for a moment belies the propriety of their lives, hints that the core of this "goodly apple" is in fact rotten. "Why shouldn't we all eat out of the same trough" (34), she asks, and then goes on to qualify her words as "a nasty New York saying" (35). Suggesting that they are all animals underneath their impeccably tailored clothing, Florence's words are quickly buried under the "minuet" which begins when they all order roast beef, "underdone, but not too underdone" (37). Dowell believes "an atmosphere of taking everything for granted" (37) underlies the behavior of the good people. Choice is never involved in any of the small details of their lives. Even the landscaping at the Englischer Hof is carefully calculated; Dowell stands on the steps waiting for Florence to come out of the baths and observes "the carefully arranged trees in tubs upon the carefully arranged gravel whilst carefully arranged people walked past in carefully calculated gaiety" (24). Those calculations determine that the women drink white wine spritzers with their meals, and the men drink brandy after dinner, rather than a sweet "womanish" liqueur; nor do gentlemen drink beer. At no point does it occur to any of them to do otherwise. Dowell chafes at the assumptions but carefully qualifies his words first. "Mind," he interjects, "I'm not saying that this is not the most desirable type of life in the world; that it is not an almost unreasonably high standard." He then goes on to say that

> it is really nauseating, when you detest it, to have to eat every day several slices of thin, tepid, pink india rubber, and it is disagreeable to have to drink brandy when you would prefer to be cheered up by warm, sweet Kummel. And it is nasty to have to take a cold bath in the morning when what you want is really a hot one at night. And it stirs a little of the faith of your fathers that is deep down within you to have to have it taken for granted that you are an Episcopalian when really you are an old-fashioned Quaker.
>
> But these things have to be done. (40)

At this level, repression must beg a certain amount of rebellion somewhere, but it does not occur. Dowell does not sneak Kümmel into his room or add hot water to his bath; the idea that the servants would know prevents him from sinning along these lines.

At the public level, feudalism, or the class structure, determines behavior, and here some disagreements arise as to what is appropriate. Edward and Leonora quarrel bitterly over how the Branshaw estate should be managed. Leonora resents Edward's leniency toward his tenants largely because she comes from a family of Irish landlords, what Dowell refers to as "a hostile garrison in a plundered country" (160). Leonora's father, Colonel Powys, has been shot at by his own tenants and thinks Edward would be better off if he got rid of his English tenants and imported workers from Scotland. But Edward's policies are based on an older feudal tradition of kinship and responsibility, on his sense of his heritage. For years Edward has allowed old Mr. Mumford, the farmer earlier alluded to, to pay only half his rent. When he is unable to pay it at all, Leonora is furious. Once Leonora gains control of Edward's estate after the affair with La Dolciquita, she evicts the old man from his farm, and gives him a cottage rent free, along with seven shillings a week. In India, when Edward learns what Leonora has done, he falls, as we have seen, into the arms of Mrs. Basil. On the surface, Edward's actions toward his tenants are laudable, but ultimately they are destructive because they support an outmoded system. Edward runs his estate the way it has been run for hundreds of years. He may be a good landlord, but he could as easily be a Colonel Powys. What is needed here are new ways, but the performance of superficial duties prevents innovation, and ultimately, even forces Edward into actions which should conflict with his ideas of justice. Once back in England after Florence Dowell's suicide, Edward defends his gardener's daughter, who is accused of murdering her baby. Keeping his tenants out of jail is one of his duties as a county magistrate. In a classic example of Dowell's ambiguous narration, this woman is first referred to as "a poor girl, . . . who had been accused of murdering her baby" (31). Later, Dowell says that "Edward spent a great deal of time, and about two hundred pounds, for law-fees on getting a poor girl . . . acquitted of a charge of murdering her baby" (213). By the end of the novel, Dowell tells us that "he took all that trouble over getting off the gardener's daughter who had murdered her baby" (273). This revelation casts doubt on Edward's purported love of children and raises questions about his own character, if we believe Dowell's declaration that the gardener's daughter is in fact guilty. Edward will not admit that feudalism, which never served the needs of anyone beyond the landowner, is certainly not appropriate to the needs of the twentieth century.

Leonora, whom Dowell at one point calls the "villain of the piece" (260), knows that Teddy is not what he should be. In a conversation with Dowell, she agrees that "there could not be a better man on the earth. There would not be room for it—along those lines" (105). The lines to which she refers are those of the duties of his station, that is as a soldier and a magistrate. But Leonora goes on to ask Dowell if he believes those are the only lines that count, and Dowell suggests that those lines must carry over to Edward's behavior as a husband and guardian. They don't. And yet Leonora herself is not the same woman in private that she is in public. Entirely conventional, very religious, very conscious of keeping up appearances even when they are relatively poor in India, Leonora behaves as badly as anyone else in the novel, if not worse. She is like Edward along those lines, and so is Rodney Bayham, whom Leonora marries after Edward's death. Dowell suggests that Bayham will cheat on Leonora just as Teddy has done, but he will not take his infidelities seriously as Teddy has done. He is not a sentimentalist, and therefore will not endanger his marriage by falling in love with his mistresses. Dowell bitterly grants that deceit, which maintains appearances, is a part of "normal" marriages, a part of "normal" life. Judging the outcome of the Ashburnham tragedy, Dowell considers Leonora's role in the affair and at this point, calls Nancy and Edward the villains, Leonora, the heroine, "the perfectly normal, virtuous, and slightly deceitful heroine—[who] has become the happy wife of a perfectly normal, virtuous, and slightly deceitful husband. She will shortly become a mother of a perfectly normal, virtuous, slightly deceitful son or daughter. A happy ending, that is what it works out at" (273). The oxymoron here, virtuous and slightly deceitful, reflects the hypocrisy of the Edwardian and early Georgian ages. The deceit will hide those little behavioral anomalies, which, when hidden, needn't be accounted for. This easily slips into peculiar sanity when the urgencies of war allow certain kinds of bad behavior, betrayals and persecutions among them, to become public.

Repression: Conrad's "The Return"

Emotional repression is perhaps the most dangerous of Edwardian conventions. The necessity for concealment, not just public but private, virtually guarantees neuroses. It might be well to digress briefly from *The Good Soldier* to an 1897 story by Joseph Conrad called "The Return." Published before the Ford/Conrad collaborations began, "The Return" relates the break-up of a "perfect" marriage. Protagonist Alvan Hervey, who arrives home early one evening to find that his wife of five years has made an abortive attempt to elope with another man, tells her that "[s]elf-restraint is everything in life, you know. It's happiness, it's dignity . . . it's everything."[54] In much of Conrad's work, restraint is the key to personal decency and social stability. In *Heart of Darkness*, Marlow reminds us that Kurtz's lack of restraint functions as a primary factor in his downfall. But restraint itself becomes the key to Hervey's downfall. Crushed when he discovers that his wife has almost left him for a poet and editor with large teeth, a "rank outsider" of "no class at all," a man who is not one of the good people, Hervey thinks only of maintaining appearances, a criticism Marlow levels at the manager who accompanies him on his search for Kurtz. Preserving appearances, Marlow tells us, is "his restraint."[55] Hervey, like the manager and unlike Marlow, misapplies the concept of restraint.[56] He chooses and marries his wife without emotion because he believes emotion is not appropriate to his status. His wife's pedigree and bearing determine his choice. We are told that he "thought of her as a well-bred girl" (128). Bound by his misinterpretation of restraint, Hervey cannot go beyond public understanding of love. In his description of Hervey's courtship and marriage, Conrad carefully avoids any mention of "real feelings." Hervey "declare[s] himself in love" (120) because "it is very well understood that every man falls in love once in his life" (119), and he always does what is expected. At no time does he express warmth for "the girl," who is never named. Love is a "poetical fiction" not an emotion, a thing to be feared "more than fire, war, or mortal disease" (120).

Written four years before Victoria's death and the ascension of Edward VII to the throne, "The Return" deals with the demise of an upper-middle-class marriage bound up in the social conventions of the late Victorian period. Caught on the cusp of the ensuing social transition, Alvan Hervey's marriage looks backward toward the old era for its foundations, while looking ahead in its thoroughly modern façade—a fashionable West End home and literary friends. Within four years of the completion of "The Return" and less than a year into the new century, the modern era would be ushered in with Victoria's death, and much of England would express concern about its future. According to his biographer Leon Edel, Henry James, whom Conrad had met shortly before writing "The Return," was distressed by the Queen's death. Victoria, he believed, had been a "safe and motherly old middle-class queen" who in her later years "thr[ew] her good fat weight into the scales of general decency."[57] As James sees it, general decency may come somewhere near its literal definition, but as we have seen it under the guise of Victorian idealism, anachronistically expressed by James Marchant and his colleagues in the Purity Crusade, decency means public morals, which as we have seen is a euphemism for sexual morality, a morality which excludes sexual pleasure from marriage. This is the "idealism" strongly entrenched in that bastion of middle-class propriety, the Victorian marriage. It is precisely that Victorian idealism and its inherent hypocrisy, as embodied in the institution of marriage, that Conrad examines in "The Return."

The marriages in *The Good Soldier,* of course, are long on hypocrisy, and with the exception of Ashburnham, short on idealism. The Hervey's marriage is built on both, but Hervey's idealism provides the foundation for his hypocrisy. In a chapter devoted to this question in *The Victorian Frame of Mind,* Walter E. Houghton considers three factors, "conformity, moral pretension, and evasion," which he calls "the hallmarks of Victorian hypocrisy." First, the Victorians sought conformity at all costs. Second, they were not as well behaved as they claimed to be, and third, they refused to see the truth if it did not conform to their ideas of what was correct, or of what should be.[58] Houghton argues that the Victorians "lived in a period of much higher standards of conduct—too high for human nature. As men were required to . . . accept the moral ideals of earnestness, enthusiasm, and sexual purity, the gap between profession and practice, or between profession and the genuine character, widened to an unusual extent."[59] Earnestness, enthusiasm, to an appropriate degree, and sexual purity are all ideals that Alvan Hervey accepts, and thus the gap between profession and character, or in his case perhaps the overlap of the two, becomes crucial to the story's outcome. In his depiction of Hervey, his pretensions, pomposities, and hypocrisies, Conrad exposes the failures of Victorian morality, and in doing so, looks ahead to the turbulence of the Edwardian age which culminates in the apocalypse of the Great War.

Often neglected among Conrad's stories, "The Return" still receives some notice, if only for its divergence from much of Conrad's other work, or for its shortcomings.[60] The story is almost Jamesian (perhaps a reflection of their recent meeting), and it ventures into an area not entirely familiar to Conrad, that is the middle-class suburb and its domestic accouterments. Zdzisław Najder points out that Edward Garnett most likely suggested the idea for the story, but the distaste for bourgeois morality and materialism reflected in the story is purely Conrad's.[61] Conrad wrote of the story repeatedly in letters to Garnett. Almost all reveal Conrad's frustration with the story, but many also reveal at least some of

Conrad's intentions in creating a character like Alvan Hervey. "My dear fellow what I aimed at," Conrad writes Garnett on September 29, 1897, "was just to produce the effect of cold water in every one of my man's speeches. . . . I wanted to produce the effect of insincerity, or artificiality. . . . I wanted the reader to *see him think* and then to *hear him speak*—and shudder."[62] Later on October 11, writing to Garnett about the possibility of Chapman & Hall publishing "The Return" at Christmastime, Conrad jokes in parentheses, "I nearly fell off my chair in a fit of laughter. Can't you imagine the story read by the domestic hearthstone in the season of festivity?"[63] While Meyer and Moser argue that "The Return" reflects Conrad's problems with relationships, perhaps his own sexual dysfunction rather than the desire to debunk bourgeois conventions which he expresses in his letters,[64] the story itself suggests otherwise, as we shall see.

Aside from its content, "The Return" is also faulted at times for its craftsmanship. Conrad himself expressed mixed feelings about it, some perhaps defensive. In a letter to Unwin about its publication in *Tales of Unrest,* Conrad says, "'The Return' is not a tale for puppy dogs nor for maids of thirteen. I am not in the least ashamed of it."[65] One of the problematic elements of the story is its tone, which Ted Billy calls "corrosive satire," and other critics refer to as simply irony.[66] But as Billy aptly points out, the tone is not consistently satirical, especially at the story's conclusion.[67] And yet "The Return" has much to offer. While Conrad might have been out of his element in his portrayal of the Herveys, he did understand the concepts of duty and restraint and the adverse effects blind reliance on them can produce.

In the Author's Note written for *Tales of Unrest,* Conrad expresses his doubts about "The Return." Writing long after the defensive letter to Unwin, he calls the story a "left-handed production," and goes on to describe being seized by a "material impression" when rereading the story, an impression of sitting in the rain under a "large and expensive umbrella. . . . In the general uproar," he explains, "one could hear every individual drop strike on the stout and distended silk."[6] Conrad did not intend this remark to be read as praise for "The Return," and in the context of his other work, perhaps it isn't. We do not relish being pelted with rain, which falls in this story as a deadening mist, a more typical Conradian touch. But with each one of the story's worrisome splats, we are forced into Hervey's umbrellaed world in a way that compels us to see what we might ordinarily miss. In his Author's Note, Conrad reveals an important element involved in the way the story works—that is its impressionism. "The story consists for the most part," he says, "of physical impressions; impressions of sound and sight, railway station, streets, . . . reflections in mirrors and so on, rendered as if for their own sake and combined with a sublimated description of a desirable middle-class town-residence which somehow manages to produce a sinister effect."[69] This is not the Conrad of "seas and continents and islands,"[70] but "The Return," through these impressions, and through its biting tone, conveys to us the dark side of restraint, the problem of relying solely on the opinions of others, and the hazzards of sublimating "real feelings." The physical impressions may indeed be rendered for their own sake because they constitute the reality of Alvan Hervey's life. Here, style and theme overlap; Hervey's superficiality is what we are to see and fear, to shudder at.

Two of these physical impressions, set against the description of the Herveys' London neighborhood and their suburban home, form the locus of the story. The first, in the train station, locates Hervey in the new world of middle-class commuters. When he emerges from the fashionable West-End station, Hervey emerges with a horde of other men, identically dressed, "almost as if they had been wearing a uniform" (118). They are—the impeccably tailored uniform of the proper gentleman. Hervey, and they are all Herveys, or mirror-images of him, would no sooner violate the dress code than he would dance on the pavement in the rain. But these men are alike in other ways as well. Hervey and his colleagues share the same demeanor, a kind of composed expression of indifference, of emotional objectivity, of separateness. These are men whose "indifferent faces . . . somehow suggested kinship, like the faces of a band of brothers who through prudence, dignity, disgust, or foresight would resolutely ignore each other" (118). Alone in their conventionality, they wear "the same stare, concentrated and empty, satisfied and unthinking" (119). While he may ignore the presence of the others on the train, each man is well aware of the social force implied in the daily ritual of dressing, speaking, eating, and working in tandem, of being part of a herd. In his description of the men as they disperse, Conrad continues to rely on images of superficiality located this time in motion which almost calls to mind the movement of insects. Emerging into the street, the men "scattered in all directions, walking away fast from one another with the hurried air of men fleeing from something compromising; from familiarity or confidences; from something suspected and concealed—like truth or pestilence" (119). Foreshadowing Hervey's desire to conceal the truth of his wife's betrayal, this passage also reveals Conrad's lack of respect for Hervey's superficiality, for what Ted Billy calls his "status in the workaday world."[71]

But Hervey's conventionality and Conrad's ridicule do not stop after Hervey separates from the pack. As he walks to his newly built home, among other newly built homes, the neighborhood itself becomes a reflection of his superficiality, of his restricted existence. Even the trees lining the streets are "tame-looking" and grow in "respectable captivity behind iron railings" (123). At home in his beautifully appointed residence, Hervey steps into the dressing room lined with mirrors. Here, in the second of the defining physical images Conrad lays before us, all the repetitions we see are literally Hervey. The mirrors, mounted on wardrobe doors and at his wife's dressing table, "multipl[y] his image into a crowd of gentlemanly and slavish imitators, who [are] dressed exactly like himself; [have] the same restrained and rare gestures; . . . and [have] just such appearances of life and feeling as he thought it dignified and safe for any man to manifest" (124). Just like the men who ride the commuter train with Hervey, his own mirror images betray no emotion, no recognition; they exemplify restraint. And because the mirrors reflect at various angles, Hervey's doubles are fragmented versions of himself, at least as it appears on the surface. Hervey is in a "convincing illusion of a room," a carnival fun-house which is about to become a house of horrors (125). When he reads the farewell letter his wife has left on her dressing table, all the images reflect "wild eyes" that he feels are spying on his "pain and his humiliation" (129). These are the self-appointed enforcers of Hervey's moral code who allow no room for folly or emotion. Because his wife's actions cannot be explained by logic, Hervey cannot fit them, just as he cannot fit the initial sight of the unexplained envelope, into his scheme of things.

Hervey's first "emotion" is anger at losing something that had "been so much his property" (135). His actions—stamping his feet and tearing the letter into tiny pieces—suggest a childlike response to loss, but his anger immediately turns ugly. Unable to cry because men do not cry, Hervey realizes that not only do foreign men cry, they resort to murder, which under the circumstances may be condoned in other societies. Violence is perfectly justified, Hervey believes, if only it were a part of social convention. But English law does not permit outraged husbands to murder their wives, and Hervey finally wishes that his wife had simply died. Appropriate responses to death are included in his moral code, and he longs for the comfort of those carefully orchestrated feelings; he longs for his old life, "that sane and gratifying existence untroubled by too much love or by too much regret" (129). The intrusive letter has made this life impossible. Hervey's rage, which continues to grow, reveals the danger of living as he does a life of unquestioned restraint, of living according to "the gospel of the beastly bourgeois" (*Letters* l: 393). Remembering his earlier walk home, Hervey wonders about the lives of other people, his doppelgängers, who live behind the walls of the other houses in his neighborhood. The middle-class residence which should be a source of comfort and safety, becomes now a place of walls which may be hiding "abominations—meditated crimes" (135). The residence, its "closed doors and curtained windows," becomes emblematic of Victorian hypocrisy, the location of all the evils that cannot be spoken of in public (135). Hervey thinks with horror of the "grim, *impenetrable* silence of miles of walls concealing passions, misery, thoughts of crime" (136, italics mine).[72]

Conrad continues, once Mrs. Hervey returns, to link the closed Victorian dwelling to violence and concealment, and to Hervey's search for comfort in the complicity of his "band of brothers." Still in the mirrored dressing room, Hervey advances toward his wife, and while he does not openly admit that he may have very nearly killed her, he understands that the "violence of the short tumult within him had been such as could well have shattered all creation" (145). Again the house and all the identical houses on his block immediately become connected with his action. Hervey has come within a hair's breadth of murder, and nothing in the physical world has changed; the house "had not fallen. And right and left all the innumerable dwellings, standing shoulder to shoulder, had resisted the shock of his passion, had presented, unmoved, to the loneliness of his trouble, the grim silence of walls, the *impenetrable* and polished discretion of closed doors and curtained windows" (145, italics mine). Functioning in the same way as the mirrored images of Hervey himself, the houses ultimately condemn him with their unforgiving rigidity. The houses, like the iron railings that hold the trees in captivity, become prisons, even for one who sees himself as a "severe guardian of formulas" (156). Conrad finally ties together the mirror images of Hervey and the houses which mirror his as Hervey continues to admonish his wife. He gestures and

> three exact replicas of his face, of his clothes, of his dull severity, of his solemn grief, repeated the wide gesture that in its comprehensive sweep indicated an infinity of moral sweetness, embraced the walls, the hangings, the whole house, all the crowd of houses outside, all the flimsy and inscrutable graves of the living, with their doors numbered like the doors of prison-cells, and as *impenetrable* as the granite of tombstones. (156, italics mine)

The irony of this passage is lost on Hervey, and here perhaps we see one of Conrad's lapses in tone, but the connection between Hervey, the crowd on the train, and the multitude of houses becomes clear. All are inextricably bound by Victorian convention and by Victorian hypocrisy.

Images of the house as a tombstone or prison among many tombstones or prisons, both of men and the truth, continue as the Herveys descend to the dining room in a charade designed to keep the servants from suspecting anything is wrong. In one of the story's most satiric moments, Hervey congratulates himself on his decision to go through with dinner. "It seemed to him necessary," he explains, "that deception should begin at home" (170). Once again the idea of secrecy is "discreet like a grave," and the walls are "faithful walls that would stand forever between the shamelessness of facts and the indignation of mankind" (170). But even when the servants leave the room, Hervey continues his deception for the walls themselves. Unwilling to betray himself to the very room they dine in, which, like his reflections and the neighborhood, has become an antagonist, he "remain[s] carefully natural, industriously hungry, . . . as though he had wanted to cheat the black oak sideboard, the heavy curtains, the stiff-backed chairs into the belief of an unstained happiness" (170).

This dinner scene, which seems to Hervey and perhaps to the reader to go on forever, is reminiscent of *The Good Soldier.* Dowell, while much less judgmental than Hervey, reflects his love of convention. But Dowell views the world with the late Edwardian's cynicism even though, like Hervey, he might wish to see the world as a place of clearly defined values. In Dowell's world, deception most certainly begins at home and the structure of this deception becomes painfully apparent at the dinner table. The Ashburnhams and the Dowells dine together for nine seasons at Nauheim and never once reveal the nature of the entangled relationships that exist, or don't exist, behind locked bedroom doors. But one of the crucial scenes of the novel also occurs at the dinner table. Dowell learns one evening that Nancy, whom at this point he wants to marry, is leaving the next day for India to be with her father. What Dowell does not know is that Nancy is being shipped off to thwart the affair with Ashburnham. Teddy, who is now madly and inappropriately in love with Nancy, at this news "went on eating his pheasant." Dowell wonders why he has not been warned of this eventuality, but believes that it "was only English manners—some sort of delicacy that I had not got the hang of" (220–1). In both "The Return" and *The Good Soldier,* the dinner table serves, as do the rows of uniform houses, to illustrate the ultimate sacrifice ill-placed restraint demands. Dowell wonders if, instead of behaving so impeccably, "it would have been better in the eyes of God if they had all attempted to gouge out each other's eyes with carving knives. But they were 'good people'" (270). Such violence does occur to Alvan Hervey, as we have seen, but the conventions of "good people," rather than concern for human suffering, demand his restraint. In

Hervey's mind, human suffering belongs only to "the ignoble herd that feels, suffers, fails, errs—but has no distinct value in the world except as a moral contrast to the prosperity of the elect" (171).

Combining physical impressions with this kind of satirical tone does produce a sinister effect. Living in "the perfect security, as of an invincible ignorance" (152–3), Hervey does not evoke our sympathy. At every step, his reliance on the rules condemns him, and while we understand his condemnation, he never does. Hervey chooses his wife because she is "well connected, well educated and intelligent" (119–20). In another moment of irony, we are told that among her other "charms," Hervey's intended "had not a thought of her own in her head" (120). But this is a mistake on Hervey's part, because he also knows that she is bored in her parents' home where she cannot exercise her "individuality" (120). During the five years of their marriage, Hervey thinks her philanthropical work exercises that individuality, but the poet/editor finds a void in her personality that his attention fills. Longing for affection which Hervey cannot and does not wish to offer, Mrs. Hervey bolts, at least temporarily. Her sense of duty to her husband finally renders her unable to carry out the elopement and compels her permanently to abandon the needs and individuality that Hervey now rejects.

Among critics who compare "The Return" with the later World War I story, "The Tale," Jeremy Hawthorn also places part of the blame for Mrs. Hervey's defection on her husband's lack of emotion,[73] as does Ruth Nadelhaft in her feminist analysis of the story. When his wife returns home, Hervey self-righteously asks her, "Did you want me to write absurd verses; to sit and look at you for hours—to talk to you about your soul? You ought to have known I wasn't that sort. . . . I had something better to do" (148). Each has disastrously mistaken the other's intentions because their moral code does not allow for the "novelty of real feelings, . . . that know nothing of creed, class, or education" (131). While Hervey deplores the possibility that he will never know his wife's intentions again because her life has now become one of lies (172), in his outrage at her behavior, he celebrates the lie repeatedly. Before his wife returns, Hervey looks toward lies to "sustain life, to make it supportable, to make it fair" (134). Marlow, who knows the difference between restraint based on inner strength and restraint based on principles alone, detests lies, believes that "[t]here is a taint of death, a flavour of mortality in lies" (82). Hervey, on the other hand, equates failing to conform with death. "If you don't conform to the highest standards," he tells his wife, "you are no one—it's a kind of death" (157). When his wife fails to conform, to live the lie, their marriage does in fact die. Hervey's neurosis, a word Hawthorn also uses,[74] grows out of this conflict between the public persona and the private self. Because Hervey's world is one of surfaces without depth, his public persona has become his private self, profession and character have become one. Hervey's surface becomes fragmented, as we see in the mirrored dressing room, and since his surface is his substance, he cannot cope. Like Marlow who understands that "principles [alone] won't do," Hervey does learn that "morality is not a method of happiness" (183). Lacking Marlow's inner strength, however, Hervey is shattered by this revelation.[75] Seeing himself as "an exiled forlorn figure in a realm of ungovernable, of unrestrained folly," where "[n]othing could be foreseen, foretold—guarded against," Hervey leaves the room, and his wife, never to return (159-60).

Not a story for puppy dogs, the subtlety and beauty of "The Return" lies in the juxtaposition of bland surface impressions and biting irony. On the surface, "The Return" may appear to turn Conradian values—the respect for restraint and duty—upside down in its effort to ridicule them, but what Conrad actually ridicules here is excess and invincible ignorance. Alvan Hervey is no Kurtz, at least not yet, but he is no Marlow either. Hervey embodies the worst of an age, the worst of a culture which Conrad sees clearly. Through Hervey's blindness and inflexibility, Conrad shows us the real danger of middle-class conformity—his stated goal in writing "The Return." Hervey is to be for us, perhaps, another kind of horror.

Conrad may not have been particularly proud of "The Return" because it is a story of surfaces. But those surfaces, expressed some sixteen years before *The Good Soldier,* lend an insight into the emotional strangulation experienced by the Dowells and the Ashburnhams, who do allow creed, class, and education to determine at least what they are supposed to feel. In the years elapsed between "The Return" and *The Good Soldier,* the world has advanced toward Armageddon, toward that "realm of ungovernable, of unrestrained folly." The gap between what the good people should feel and what they do feel has widened, and the dangers of such pretense become even more apparent. Dowell comes closest to Alvan Hervey's self-restraint, but even he slips now and then.

Dowell is troubled by the extent of his own self-restraint, at least in the area of desire. When he compares himself to the more "manly" Edward Ashburnham, he calls himself a eunuch (14), and certainly Dowell behaves that way toward Florence and toward Leonora and Nancy, whom he claims to love. Ever the Philadelphia gentleman, Dowell seems to embody the Edwardian spirit of chastity and cleanliness. But Dowell's placid demeanor, like that of Alvan Hervey, conceals resentments and anger which appear, not in sexual misbehavior, but once again in the form of violence. When Dowell elopes with Florence, he commits an act of violence which frightens Florence so much that she is afraid he will kill her if he finds out she is not what she is supposed to be. Dowell's old servant, Julius, who is to be left behind at Florence's insistence when the two leave for Europe, drops Florence's medicine case because he is distraught at being abandoned. Furious and perhaps guilty, Dowell blacks one of his eyes and would have strangled him if it had not been for the commotion Julius makes on the ferry. This action gives Florence a "pretty idea of [his] character" (101), and instills in her a fear for her own life. Whether or not Dowell is capable of the kind of violence Florence fears, we know he is capable of the great cruelty he describes here, that is, of abandoning and then striking his old servant. Dowell also admits that had he known Leonora was jealous of Florence on the day she touched Edward's wrist in Martin Luther's bedroom, he would have "turned upon Florence with the maddest kind of rage" (72). The assault on Julius, coupled with his earlier undemonstrative behavior in Florence's bedroom, defines the character of their marriage. Later, after Florence is dead, Dowell admits that he has not loved her for much of their relationship, a claim supported by his immediate desire to marry Nancy Rufford. Standing virtually over Florence's corpse, Dowell says to Leonora, "Now I can marry the girl" (116). Dowell's words describing his feelings for Florence retain a tone of resentment; she was "something burdensome," a wife of no "intrinsic value," whose dresses he doesn't even like (100). Although he cloaks his resentment of Edward, that too breaks occasionally to the surface. After his death, Leonora refers for the first time to the affair between Edward and Florence, which Dowell claims not to know about. Dowell's response to the news leads us to believe that he has some understanding of human psychology as it emerged in the early part of the century. "I don't suppose I felt anything," he says, "unless maybe it was with that mysterious and unconscious self that underlies most people. Perhaps one day when I am unconscious or walking in my sleep I may go and spit upon poor Edward's grave. It seems about the most unlikely thing I could do; but there it is" (116). For this act even to occur to Dowell suggests that he does have feelings which are submerged in his concept of appropriate behavior. His violence toward Julius, his obvious resentment of Florence, voiced in the petty criticism of her clothing, and his imagined desecration of Edward's grave, all point toward Dowell's overzealous self-restraint at times when that mysterious and unconscious self should have been let go. But like Alvan Hervey whose violence remains completely submerged, Dowell does not think emotional displays are becoming to a gentleman. While the intention here is not to suggest that only repressed people misbehave, or that a certain amount of repression is not necessary as an integral part of civilization, it seems incontrovertible that too much repression, as Freud tells us, is dangerous.

The outwardly circumspect Leonora Ashburnham also commits violence of the verbal kind against Edward and Nancy and of course, in an act tying her to Florence Dowell, slaps Maisie Maidan. Of the two kinds of violence, the verbal is more damaging to its victims. Edward and the ultimately innocent Nancy suffer at the hands, or more appropriately, tongue, of Leonora. According to Dowell, "having been cut off from the restraints of her religion, for the first time in her life, she acted along the lines of her instinctive desires" (222). Afraid to go to confession because she is afraid she will be blamed for deceiving Dowell (211), Leonora can only harangue those near at hand. True, Edward is guilty of numerous betrayals, but Leonora virtually crucifies him, and Nancy does not even understand the nature of adultery until she reads about the Brand divorce in the newspapers. But Leonora resents Nancy's youth and Edward's love for her to the extent that she, like Dowell, fantasizes violence of a particularly sadistic kind. She wanted, we are told, "to bring her riding whip down across the girl's face. . . . She imagined the pleasure she would feel when the lash fell across those queer features; the pleasure she would feel at drawing the handle at the same moment toward her, so as to cut deep into the flesh and to leave a lasting wheal" (229). Leonora does drive Nancy to the point of madness, but it is Edward's suicide that finally pushes her over the edge. The contrast between the daylight Leonora and the nighttime Leonora is considerable. During the day, the social niceties prevail. While Edward and Nancy are racing toward madness and death, Dowell asserts that "those three presented to the world the spectacle of being the best of good people" (267).

But under cover of darkness, after the servants have gone to bed, Leonora becomes an emotional vampire. Scuttling between Edward's room and Nancy's room, Leonora for a time has Nancy convinced that she must submit to Edward's desires because he is dying of love for her. Leonora even offers to divorce Edward, which Nancy knows Leonora cannot do. After telling Nancy about all Edward's affairs, Leonora then says, "You must save Edward's life; you must save his life. All that he needs is a little period of satisfaction from you. Then he will tire of you as he has of the others. But you must save his life" (262). Browbeaten, Nancy goes to Edward's room in a white kimono and offers herself as a sacrifice. Of course, Ashburnham refuses the girl's offer, but once again, the gap between what he wants and what is tenable widens. Dowell tells us that Ashburnham actually considers the possibility of accepting Nancy as a lover because he believes she would "remain his forever" (263). Herein lies the scandal of Edward's behavior. Through his initial carelessness on the night of Florence Dowell's suicide, Edward has committed himself emotionally to a girl who is virtually or, if we are to believe Saunders, literally, his daughter. Edward's emotional immaturity underlying his public persona dupes him into this misplaced affection and allows him to be sucked into Leonora's nocturnal violence, which eventually destroys him and the girl as well. When the appropriate action is finally taken and Nancy is shipped off to India, it is far too late to save her sanity or Edward's life.[76] Edward's only escape from this "prison full of screaming hysterics" is death. He is too connected to the land and to the dying feudal system to consider any other. But for many, the war's emergence from the ashes of Edwardian society provided a way out, a place where many of the constraints of home disappeared and, for good or ill, their own repressed personalities flourished.

Chapter 2
INTO THE RABBIT HOLE

Madhouse to Charnel House

Placed in the environment of war or of colonialism, good people need not exercise restraint. With an enemy specifically defined and vilified, good people may act on their repressed urges. At the risk of relying too heavily on Freudian dogma, we also know from experience or from popular psychology that repressed feelings will find a way to the surface. Before the war, peculiar sanity is submerged, conducted under the cover of darkness, protected by the stone walls of the manorial estate, and perhaps dangerously intensified by being repressed. With the declaration of war, peculiar sanity becomes especially evident, in anti-German behavior as irrational as killing German breeds of dogs, as silly as calling sauerkraut victory cabbage. But between the peculiar sanity of home and the peculiar sanity of war, we may find a means of escape. For those not quite willing to take the extreme measure of suicide, as does Edward Ashburnham, war offers a place to escape the restraint and superficiality of home, to engage in risks not afforded within the narrow confines of conventionality. Since propaganda conceals the peculiar sanity of war from recruits, soldiering can seem at first like a lark, like a great adventure, until its true nature becomes apparent.

Escaping the rules of convention while seeming to support them may also be one of the attractions of colonialism. Edward Ashburnham goes to India to recoup his fortune and to get out from under the taint of the Kilsyte case. The farthest reaches of empire offer the same freedom from constraint offered in the trenches, the same escape from the peculiar sanity of home. But like the trenches, the colonial outpost develops its own peculiar sanity. In its tropical climates and its absence of order, madness emerges full blown. Two novels, Willa Cather's *One of Ours* and Joseph Conrad's *Heart of Darkness,* show both the potential for escape and the potential for madness in war and colonialism. In *One of Ours* we will see

Claude Wheeler gain the self-respect he has never had at home. Trans-
ported from the suffocating environment of Nebraska to the cultural para-
dise of France, Claude finds existential release and emotional peace before
he sacrifices his life. In *Heart of Darkness* the infamous Kurtz finds the edge
of his own sanity, and all his morality cannot keep him from going over it.
In both cases, the peculiar sanity of home quickly intensifies: for Claude it
becomes the illogic of carnage, for Kurtz, the illogic of megalomania.

Temperance and Tin Cans: Morality in America

Superficiality and repression as sources of peculiar sanity were by no
means limited to the English side of the Atlantic. Rural small-town America, the subject of much scrutiny in American fiction, becomes a likely setting for the clichés and irrationality which arise during national conflicts.
America, like Great Britain, experienced its share of culture shock as the
new century firmly established itself. In America where questions of morality have always been a matter for public concern, the temperance movement gained power. Previously linked to the abolition movement and still
linked to the suffrage movement, the temperance movement focused on
the idea that the Demon Rum in general and saloons in particular weak-
ened American moral fiber. According to social historian J. C. Furnas, if
women were granted the vote, reformers believed they would "clean up
politics, wipe out prostitution, [and] suffuse American life . . . with the
bright light of womanly purity and idealism."[1] And in fact, much of the
American reform movement did look to women as a source of salvation, although the Prohibition Amendment was ratified before the Nineteenth
Amendment that gave women the right to vote.[2] Apart from the crusade to
ban the production and sale of alcoholic beverages, other women's movements expressed the belief that women could improve the moral standards
of the country largely within the home environment. Laura Shapiro, in her
incisive study, *Perfection Salad: Women and Cooking at the Turn of the Century*, examines the movement generally known as the "domestic science"
movement. This "movement" sought to educate women in the new science
of nutrition, to engage industry to produce laborsaving, nutritious food
products, and to establish, in her words, "the link between science and
housework."[3] Shapiro argues, and propaganda texts bear her out, that
women were believed to be responsible for the moral well-being of the
American character. Old-fashioned housewives who refused to take advantage of modern conveniences, she maintains, "bore the responsibility for

the failings of the American home, failings that seemed to lead directly to poverty, disease, alcoholism, unemployment, and all the other social miseries apparent at the turn of the century."[4] What the British tried to accomplish through moral evangelism, Americans would seek in the germ-free modern kitchen, in Kellogg's Corn Flakes, which appeared in 1906, and in canned food. Conformity and conventionality wear the garments of science and progress.

Domestic science continued well into the century and appears full blown during the Great War in propaganda posters, books, and magazine articles asking women to conserve food. Here, women are held responsible not only for the moral salvation of the country through housekeeping but, in echoes of the Purity Crusade, its military salvation as well. Herbert Hoover, in an appeal published in the August 1917 issue of *Ladies' Home Journal*, speaks directly to American women about food shortages in Europe and ways to rectify them at home. "Every woman," he writes, "should feel herself definitely engaged in national service in her own kitchen and in her own home."[5] Alluding to the new domestic science, Hoover goes on to insist, "[t]he intelligent woman of America must make a proper study of food ratios, so that the most nutritious foods will appear in their proper proportions on the home table."[6] Hoover's entreaty is followed by an article on baking bread from wheat substitutes. Hoover and the U.S. Food Administration also targeted school children with a book, *Food Saving and Sharing*, which was sponsored by the National Education Association and intended as a textbook to be used in "the instruction of American children."[7] Among its contributors were the editor of the *Journal of Home Economics*, and a professor of food chemistry at Columbia University. *Food Saving and Sharing*, like the *Ladies' Home Journal*, asks children to contribute to national security and world health by saving food. According to the most recent information on nutrition, the five food groups are represented by imaginary booths at a food market that intelligent children visit with a shopping basket. Children are instructed in domestic science and world politics at the same time; in both publications, domestic science becomes a method of engaging women and children in the war effort.

Even before the war, however, the domestic science movement took on the zeal of peculiar sanity. In *The Margin of Happiness: The Reward of Thrift*, published in 1917 but written before America's entry into the war, Thetta Quay Franks asks for women's participation in a nationwide endeavor just as Hoover does. Insisting that women have vast powers in matters of national importance, Franks asks, "How many women realize the dignity and value of their position as guardians of the national health, spenders of the national wealth? Much of the power and influence of a nation lie within the keeping of its women. How many American women have learned to think nationally?"[8] Among what Franks lists as "some of the nation's most urgent problems" that she believes women can solve are "the high cost of living, the increasing death rate from organic disease, and the rising divorce rate" (3–4). Poor housekeeping, according to Franks, is responsible for the increase in the divorce rate in the United States, which in 1909 was 73 per 100,000 inhabitants (22). Franks quotes an article from the *Newark Evening News* of March 28, 1916, that states, "Women's ignorance and neglect of homemaking arts were pointed out as a leading cause of family desertion, at a conference yesterday afternoon of social workers" (27). The "proof" for this conclusion is a statement made by a Mr. Gascoyne who declares, "much of the blame for the delinquent husband rests on the undesirable home conditions caused by the presence of an untrained wife" (27).

Franks goes on in her book to instruct women in the ways of intelligent housekeeping by suggesting that all packaged food be stored in glass jars with etched or painted labels (118) and that a grocery list be prepared on the typewriter and maintained in alphabetical order (134). In considering the question of budget allotments, Franks's belief in homemaking as a "social service" is repeated. A budget allotment for "betterment," including books and the theater, she believes, "has ethical as well as economic values," because "[l]ove of home and all that home stands for is the only safeguard for the nation against the growing tendency to evade the responsibilities of home life" (114). In this interesting example of circular reasoning, Franks, like the authors of *Public Morals,* links national interests and national security with morality and the home. The Victorian ideal of progress, which, as we have seen, is falling prey to cynicism abroad, reverberates in the American connection to scientific progress and invention, to the notion that boxed cereals could save the world.

During the war, reliance on commercially prepared foods—bread, for instance—was cut back and food manufacturers were enlisted in the effort to feed the troops "over there." But the preparation of food in the home had become a matter of scientific study and implementation that required the latest equipment and technique. Cather, on the other hand, retained the notion that cooking was an art; she loved fresh food and its preparation. Speaking to the Fine Arts Society in Omaha on the subject of "Standardization and Art," Cather blasted "overzealous patriots" who tried to force immigrants to adopt new American ways, including the use of prepared foods. "The Americanization committee worker," she proclaimed, "who persuades an old Bohemian housewife that it is better for her to feed her family out of tin cans instead of cooking them a steaming goose for dinner is committing a crime against art."[9] True, this idealistic image factored out the drudgery involved in preparing from scratch every food item, from breads to pickles, the latest equipment notwithstanding, but Cather herself knew how to cook and, according to Woodress, considered herself "no mean cook."[10] While Cather seems to have seen the hazards of relying too much on prepared foods, she did not see the liberating effect such products could have in women's lives, nor, for that matter, did the crusaders who fought to send girls to cooking schools and to make home economics a part of school curricula. What the crusaders sought was compliance, which in many ways they got. Indeed, in *One of Ours*, all that is worst about American culture, its superficiality, repression, and hypocrisy, is represented by materialism—the love of gadgets, including kitchen gadgets—and canned salmon, which Claude Wheeler eats while his wife Enid is out campaigning for the Anti-Saloon League. Like Britain's Purity Crusade, the temperance and domestic science movements sought to institute social control as a way of preventing change. The domestic science movement cloaked itself in the ideal of technological progress, but its goal was to maintain the status quo of male dominance, materialism, and consumption. By looking at Edwardian relationships and Edwardian sexuality, *The Good Soldier* and "The Return" explore the superficiality and repression of the Purity Crusade's moral posturing, and they reveal the peculiar sanity that originates in its hollow pronouncements. By revealing the materialism and superficiality of America's heartland, its virtual enslavement to technological progress, *One of Ours* also uncovers the peculiar sanity lurking there.

"The Little Good for Nothing's Good for Something After All": Cather's *One of Ours*

Published in 1922 and capturing the Pulitzer Prize in 1923, Willa Cather's novel *One of Ours* begins in the summer of 1912 on the Wheeler farm in Frankfort, Nebraska. Modeled on Red Cloud, the small farming community where Cather spent much of her youth, Frankfort is drawn from the same spiritual landscape that produced Sherwood Anderson's *Winesburg, Ohio*.[11] Peopled by frustrated, unrealized men and women, Frankfort, like Branshaw Teleragh, represents the wrong turns a culture can take when its original values of hard work and fair play become tainted by materialism and boredom. Like Ford's good people, the residents of these heartland farms abide by a strict unwritten code of conduct. Cather herself was particularly affected by this code as it related to the conduct of young women. In 1888, Cather created a male persona, William, who, walking the streets of Red Cloud in trousers and a derby hat and with shorn hair, signed himself "William Cather, M.D."[12] Cather wanted to become a doctor and undoubtedly felt her goal was more achievable as a boy. While Sharon O'Brien goes on to consider contemporary questions of gender identity and Freudian psychology, it might seem almost too convenient to read into Cather's behavior anything other than an intellectual rebellion against the conventional role handed to women. And indeed O'Brien does believe that Cather "could reject the female role she found limiting only by continuing to repudiate her sex."[13] Cather dressed as a man because the male persona allowed her to escape the containment of Victorian conventions.

Finally able to leave Red Cloud and attend the University of Nebraska, to pursue goals other than those of marriage and motherhood, Cather eventually resumed female dress. But in her journalistic writings at the university, Cather belittled women's clubs and sororities, what O'Brien calls "culture-hungry clubwomen and female prudes."[14] Cather also strongly identified with her male protagonists. O'Brien calls *My Antonia*'s Jim Burden Cather's "alter ego,"[15] and her relationship with Claude Wheeler was one, in Woodress's words, of "complete possession."[16] When she was writing *One of Ours,* according to Woodress, "she never knew when he would come to her . . . and she got so she had to be alone in case he appeared."[17] Cather's model for Claude Wheeler was her cousin G. P. Cather, who was killed in action in May 1918. She had known him for years and according to Woodress "felt a blood identity . . . a Siegmund and Sieglinde sort of thing" for him.[18] Claude's frustration over never getting off the farm is G. P.'s.

In Claude Wheeler, we see some of Cather's anger toward traditional role expectations. Feminine in his sensibilities, at least in terms of traditional expectations, Claude does not appreciate the grossness of his father and the hired men on the farm. Unlike Cather herself, Claude cannot achieve a new identity by changing his clothes, at least not until the uniform of war becomes available. Claude must give in to Frankfort's demands for conventional behavior, but he is always searching, and never happy.[19]

Certainly Frankfort, Nebraska, is a long way from Branshaw Teleraugh. Here repression reveals itself in anti-intellectualism and bigotry, which after the war begins turns to anti-German sentiment. Violence is acted out against nature and history. Claude's father believes in acquisition for the sake of acquisition, in destruction to make a point. When Claude is a small child, his father cuts down a cherry tree full of fruit because Mrs. Wheeler, who he believes is weak, asks him to help pick the cherries. Claude never completely forgives his father and believes as a child that "God would punish a man who could do that."[20] Mr. Wheeler cannot comprehend the idea that life is to be enjoyed. Even after the war begins in Europe, Nat Wheeler's primary concern is getting his grain to market to take advantage of high prices.[21] On leave in France with his friend David Gerhardt, Claude dreams of farming in Europe once the war is over. Sure that he cannot go back to Nebraska, Claude understands that "[t]here was no chance for the kind of life he wanted at home, where people were always buying and selling, building and pulling down. He had begun to believe that the Americans were a people of shallow emotions" (328). The war has provided Claude with this escape, or he believes it has, but his only escape is in death.

The concept of peculiar sanity is particularly appropriate to *One of Ours*. Materialistic and anti-intellectual, pre–World War I Frankfort becomes a milieu from which Claude struggles to escape, first through his abortive attempt to get an education, and finally through his involvement in the Great War itself. Boredom is prevalent in Frankfort, but Claude is not interested in buying the latest technology, which amuses his father and his brother Ralph when they are bored. Since few residents of Frankfort believe in the essential value of education, Claude is allowed to attend the cheaper and less threatening church-affiliated Temple College in Lincoln instead of the University of Nebraska where he wants to go. Claude is not temperamentally suited for farming, but when his father buys a ranch in Montana, he is forced to take over the family farm. Physically strong enough to perform his tasks easily, Claude is still bored by the intellectual vacuum of his existence.

In addition, Claude must cope with the knowledge that his brother Bayliss and his father believe he is not a good farmer. After Mr. Wheeler leaves Claude in charge of the farm, a massive snowfall caves in the roof of the hog barn, and twelve of the Wheeler's hogs suffocate. Claude is angry and humiliated because he knows he is expected to fail. He believes that his whole family is convinced there is "something wrong with him" (86). Claude's father and brothers treat him as they might treat a flighty female. Claude's intellectual pursuits and enjoyment of the collegiate experience earn derogatory remarks from them all. Bayliss does not want Claude to play football in college, and tells Mr. Wheeler, "If Claude wants exercise, he might put in the fall wheat" (24). Claude conjectures that everyone sees in him the thing most feared or hated. Mr. Wheeler, an anti-intellectual and practical joker, believed Claude was "one of those visionary fellows who make unnecessary difficulties for themselves and other people. Mrs. Wheeler thought the trouble with her son was that he had not yet found his Saviour. Bayliss was convinced that his brother was a moral rebel, that behind his reticence and his guarded manner he concealed the most dangerous opinions. The neighbors liked Claude, but they laughed at him and said it was a good thing his father was well-fixed" (86).

Cather's feminization of Claude, her portrayal of him as a dissatisfied dilettante, and even worse, as the equivalent of the bad housekeeper, capitalizes on portrayals of women before and during the war. We have seen the blame heaped on women who are not good housekeepers, women who don't adopt the new, progressive ways of domestic science, and we have seen the suggestion that women can, by being good girls, good wives, and good mothers, save the world. Popular songs often belittled women, in particular, one called "The Little Good for Nothing's Good for Something After All." Before the war the "girl" in question, Mary Brown, was a "tom boy 'round the town" and "wild," a girl who made the townsfolk "frown." But when the war begins, Mary joins the Red Cross and goes "over there" and "the ones that used to sneer are the first ones now to cheer—the little good for nothing's good for something after all."[22] This depiction parallels that of Claude, down to his role as nurse on the influenza-stricken troop ship. Claude is only verified as a man, as a member of the community, when he joins up. His inability to master the techniques of farming can be forgiven by his patriotic sacrifice.

When America enters the war, Claude is among the first to enlist, with his parents' blessings. Though he may be leaving home, he will be "one of ours," a soldier in the war to end all wars. Ironically, the conventional wisdom that fuels this war fervor finally provides Claude with the existential stimulus he needs to give his life validity. Claude suffers from his cultural ignorance in France, but he is able to experience the joy of freedom. On the troop ship that takes him to Europe, Claude proves to be immune to the deadly influenza virus that kills one of his bunkmates. Functioning as a nurse, Claude realizes that "[he is] enjoying himself all the while and [doesn't] want to be safe anywhere" (251). He understands that only through violence and catastrophe can his life be validated. The irony in Claude's situation is an indictment of middle-class values, and at the same time, a strong antiwar statement. Cather knew well the intellectual stagnation Claude escapes. She also understood how appealing the promise of war can be. Gilbert and Gubar argue in the second volume of *No Man's*

Land that Cather herself felt Claude's exhilaration over going to war, that "her vision of the doomed Claude's good fortune is surely a way of dreaming her own release from the deadening decorum of the provincial prairie town where she herself had always longed to be a sturdy 'Willie' rather than a submissive Willa."[23] Claude's friend David Gerhardt tells him that war is "a costly way of providing adventure for the young" (339). But for Claude, Bayliss and the German war machine are too much alike. Claude is fighting the "careful planners" who want to "put [the world] into a straitjacket" (339), and if he must die to vanquish them, then so be it.

Lovely Creek: Another Prison Full of Screaming Hysterics

Cather's portrait of prewar America rivals Sherwood Anderson's vision of the hell created by small-town repression. From the very beginning of the novel, in the small pleasure of going to the circus with his Bohemian-born friend, Ernest Havel, Claude feels the pinch of restriction, of "things a Wheeler does not do." Forced to share Ernest's picnic lunch and forbidden beer under trees beside the creek, Claude wishes he could treat his friend to dinner at the hotel in Frankfort. Claude has more than enough money but does not go to the hotel because "[i]f his father or Bayliss heard he had been there—and Bayliss heard everything—they would say he was putting on airs, and would get back at him" (11). This refusal to spend money on anything pleasurable becomes a motif throughout the novel. Instead, money itself becomes, if not a source of pleasure, at least a relief from intellectual boredom, from the spiritual impoverishment that breeds peculiar sanity. And money allows the Wheelers to keep pace with scientific developments, not all of which are practical. Claude's brothers, Ralph and Bayliss, both revel in the idea of technological progress, with "the bristling march of invention" (18). The Wheeler basement is littered with photographic equipment and other mechanical objects Ralph has bought, but cannot or does not use—enough, Claude muses, to have "put a boy through college" (19). Here anti-intellectualism fosters waste, and in a sense, becomes self-perpetuating by keeping Claude out of the university.

Ralph's purchases are clearly products of the new domestic science. Mrs. Wheeler and old Mahailey, the Wheeler's cook, are forced to use the new stove Ralph has bought, but it does not draw as well as the old one. And Ralph tries to force them to use a mechanical cream separator that takes more time to scald between uses than skimming by hand. Mrs. Wheeler complains about the machine because she doesn't process enough milk to make it practical. Ralph's response invokes domestic science and belittles his mother for lagging behind. "[Y]ou're prejudiced," he tells her. "Nobody ever thinks of skimming milk now-a-days. Every up-to-date farmer uses a separator" (17). In both cases, what should be a laborsaving device becomes a Rube Goldberg machine, a tribute to technology. Claude understands the sense of spiritual poverty which moves Ralph to buy these gadgets for the fun of it. Thinking of his intellectual friends the Erlichs whom he has met in Lincoln, Claude contrasts their way of spending money on "almost everything he had been taught to shun" (38). The Erlichs are never bored; they are not afraid of having extended conversations that Claude has been taught to believe conceited. "Since you never said anything," Claude explains to himself, "you didn't form the habit of thinking. If you got too much bored, you went to town and bought something new" (39). Early in the novel, in an act of rebellion against the things a Wheeler does not do, Claude sends Mrs. Erlich a box of red roses before he leaves Lincoln for the Christmas holidays.

Bayliss, who sells machinery, is even worse than Ralph. Acquisitive and controlling, Bayliss is a destroyer both of happiness and property. He embodies all that is wrong with Frankfort, and by extension, much that is wrong with small-town America. A Prohibitionist, Bayliss reveals the kind of religious intolerance and hypocrisy that ultimately turns Claude against religion. Claude's mother, who is genuinely spiritual if in a limited way, falls victim to Bayliss's religious fervor at Christmas dinner. Sadly shocked because she pours herself a second cup of coffee, Bayliss chastises her for using a "stimulant." Claude, also enjoying a second cup before going to the barn for his afterdinner cigar, analyzes Bayliss's condemnation. "What worse could it be, his tone implied! When you said anything was a 'stimulant,' you had sufficiently condemned it; there was no more noxious word" (76). But Bayliss's ability to kill hope and joy sadly reaches beyond the dinner table. As Claude courts his school friend Enid, Bayliss pursues Gladys Farmer, also Claude's good friend. In an act that aligns him with the enemy machine, Bayliss buys an old mansion on the edge of town, one Gladys has a romantic attachment to as a town landmark. But Bayliss only wants the house because it is there and tells Gladys that "if I decide to live there, I'll pull down that old trap and put up something modern" (93). In another example of missed opportunity, Claude himself should marry Gladys, not the cold Enid who would turn Claude into a man like Enid's father, "a big machine with the springs broken inside" (129), an eventuality only prevented by the war. Gladys, who is a schoolteacher, and understands the evil of men like Bayliss, understands that "all things which might make the world beautiful—love and kindness, leisure and art—were shut up in prison, and that successful men like Bayliss Wheeler held the keys" (129).

Enid Royce, the woman Claude marries, embodies the worst qualities of Bayliss and Ralph. She is also everything that Claude isn't—she is very much the new woman who drives her own car, consults domestic science books on everything from decorating and housekeeping to raising poultry, and she engages in the politics of religious conversion and temperance. A vegetarian, Enid accompanies her mother every year to a "vegetarian sanatorium in Michigan, where [they] learned to live on nuts and toasted cereals" (103). Enid's sister Carrie is a missionary in China, and Enid's own missionary fervor finds fault with Claude's friend Ernest Havel because he is a freethinker and "people say you and he read that kind of books together" (106). But Claude persists in his desire to marry Enid even when her father warns him not to do it. "We'll always be better friends than is common between father and son-in-law," Mr. Royce tells Claude. "You'll find out that pretty nearly everything you believe about life—about marriage, especially—is lies. I don't know why people prefer to live in that kind of world, but they do" (125). Blinded by his fondness for Enid, Claude ignores Mr. Royce. For one thing, Claude foolishly believes he can cure Enid of her missionary zeal. But all of Frankfort knows Claude is misguided.

Enid's kitchen is a masterpiece of domestic science, and her dinners are planned according to the new concept of calories, an idea neighbor Leonard Dawson's wife Susie finds puzzling. Susie is the kind of housewife Thetta Quay Franks condemns. She does not rely on prepared foods and cooks three meals a day from scratch. Leonard is furious over Enid's newfangled ideas about raising poultry. Fertile eggs, she has learned, spoil faster than the unfertile ones, and so her hen yard is without roosters. When Leonard drops in on Claude to ask about using the Wheeler's thrasher, he finds Claude alone eating his dinner of canned salmon and hardboiled eggs. Piqued about Claude's predicament and the war news he has heard that day, Leonard steps out into the yard among Enid's hens. "Where are all your roosters?" he asks Claude. Claude replies that they have only one, and he is cooped. Leonard explodes, "I raise chickens on a natural basis, or I don't raise 'em at all" (167). Susie later alludes to Enid's poultry books, but Leonard remains adamant that Enid will not do "any missionary work among [his] chickens" (168). Here the conflict between science and tradition becomes one of sexual morality. For Leonard, Enid's virgin hens are as insidious as her temperance propaganda, which she has tacked up all over town. Claude suffers from Enid's lack of warmth and from her similarities to his brother Bayliss, who occasionally joins them for Enid's "vegetarian dinners" and Prohibition business (173). Claude, of course, shuns what he understands to be the hypocrisy of Prohibition. Bayliss, Claude believes, "hated [alcohol] less for the harm it did than for the pleasure it gave" (173). Beginning to sense the truth of what Mr. Royce told him about Enid, Claude "suffer[s] . . . in his ideals, in his vague sense of what was beautiful. Enid could make his life hideous to him without even knowing it. At such times, he hated himself for accepting all her grudging hospitality" (173).

Enid's missionary zeal finally takes her away from Lovely Creek to China to nurse her sister who has become ill. Unable to convince her to stay, Claude becomes bitter and speaks his mind about the flaws of her kind of evangelism. Enid and Bayliss represent for Cather the stultifying false morality, cloaked in the idea of progress, that keeps peculiar sanity alive and well in Frankfort, the false morality that keeps Claude from a university education and Gladys Farmer from going to the opera in Omaha. Gladys is a constant victim of gossip that later in the war will become atrocity stories and ultimately propaganda. Gladys is single, teaching in the local school for a living. Gladys's mother is a widow and constantly in arrears on her property taxes. But Gladys dresses well, and the old women in town talk about her expensive, stylish clothes. Gladys also loves music and has gone to Omaha to the opera, but does not do so the year Claude marries Enid because Gladys is due a raise from the school board, and she is afraid the raise will be canceled if she seems to be putting on airs. Enid also dresses well, but her clothes are an extension of her public morality—she wears white dresses, shoes, and stockings as she works in her pristine kitchen. Enid's homemaking methods, learned from books such as Franks's, are another extension of her calculated and superficial faith that seeks to control rather than to comfort, to indoctrinate rather than to enlighten, to restrict rather than to grant freedom.

Without the freedom of personal expression, Claude cannot survive in Frankfort. Fortunately for him, the war provides that freedom. But Claude's sense of frustration is so great, his idealism about the war so strong, that he believes that "[n]o battlefield or shattered country he had seen was as ugly as this world would be if men like his brother Bayliss controlled it altogether" (339). Burdened by no sense of medieval honor or responsibility (unlike Teddy Ashburnham) and no sense of historical idealism, Bayliss completely lacks restraint. Much like *Mrs. Dalloway*'s Sir William Bradshaw, whom we will discuss later, Bayliss is intent on the idea of conversion, of forcing his own bloodless ways on everyone else. As Clarissa and Septimus Warren Smith are correct to fear Sir William, so Claude is correct to fear his brother. Suspicious, small-minded, and materialistic, Bayliss is an early version of Joe McCarthy, a man capable of ruining lives. Before he marries Susie Gray, Leonard Dawson blacks Bayliss's eye because Bayliss criticizes her. Susie talks back to the advance man for the circus, and Bayliss thinks she is too fresh (14). He makes the mistake of criticizing her in front of Leonard, and Leonard defends Susie. If allowed to spread, this kind of gossip can destroy a young woman in a place like Frankfort, and Bayliss does not care.

Claude's tragedy is that he cannot prevail against the strength of social pressure in Frankfort. The question of rebellion never arises, and thus Claude's life remains one of missed opportunities. Shocked at the anti-German sentiments that threaten some of his old friends in Frankfort, Claude is still among the first to enlist when America enters the war. In France, Claude is repulsed by a "Boche" baby, a child of rape, which he refers to sarcastically as "Kamerad" and carries awkwardly at arms' length with "loathing" (293). This innocent victim of war becomes for Claude an object of peculiar sanity. Willing to defend the old German woman who owns a restaurant on the train line between Frankfort and Lincoln, Claude depersonalizes and vilifies the baby, attributing to it "enemy" characteristics. We are told that "he hated it for its square, tow-thatched head and bloodless ears" (292). Ironically, enlisting offers Claude the power of choice previously denied to him. For the first time he is able to leave the deadening safety of the farm with his family's blessing. The money, he believes, that buys that safety, that security, is the source of all that is wrong in Frankfort. Security is "what [is] the matter with everybody; . . . only perfect safety [is] required to kill all the best qualities in people and develop the mean ones" (86). Certainly that Victorian essence, so profound in Bayliss and in Enid, is what Claude struggles against, what excludes him. While he fights and dies, becoming an American hero, Claude is never one of ours without his uniform.

The Good Soldier, "The Return," and *One of Ours* all analyze the paralyzing effects of conventionality, of its superficiality and hypocrisy. Society, in all three works, deploys the lie to maintain the status quo. In *The Good Soldier* and "The Return," deception maintains the discrepancy between the public and the private self; in *One of Ours,* the lie denies individuality and shifts the focus of human values from intellectual or spiritual to the material. The reliance on principles, especially outmoded ones, rather than on individual choice and responsibility, reinforces superficiality and hypocrisy. The lie, then, is even more necessary in maintaining appearances. Of course, the unfortunate side-effect of living the lie is neurosis; it flourishes in the gap between reality and appearance; it becomes in this case the peculiar sanity of transition, which under the stress of war develops into war mania, and the lie takes on national significance when it sustains propaganda. But between the stress of transition and the stress of war lies the peculiar sanity of colonialism, which, as it is expressed in Conrad's *Heart of Darkness,* serves as an apt metaphor for the peculiar sanity of war.

Hollow Men: Conrad's *Heart of Darkness*

Very much a part of the Victorian idea of progress, and therefore tied to Victorian and Edwardian morality, colonialism provided a rallying point for righteous Britains (and Americans, for that matter) who believed, as did John Dowell, that the Tory life "is the most desirable type of life in the world. . . ."[24] Most of Great Britain was bent on spreading Tory values to the ends of the earth and did not take kindly to resistance abroad any more than it took kindly to resistance at home. In the Congo, Belgium, which in 1914 would be overrun by Germany, was largely the aggressor. But the result is the same no matter which flag flies at the top of the flag pole. The colonial experience casts colonized peoples in the same role in which war experience casts the enemy—that is, as a group of inferior humans whose actual humanity is at times questioned. In Allied propaganda from World War I, Germans are depicted as barbarians who have no notion of civilized life, at least not the kind of civilized life the Allies lived. An Australian propaganda poster with a question mark as its title ("?") depicts a fanged, bloodstained, blue-eyed ape in a Prussian helmet on the verge of grasping a bloody earth. As a metaphor for the dehumanization of both a war enemy and colonized populations, this poster offers several details. First, Australia was a colony of the British empire and thus served a double function as a subdued population and as part of the British war machine. While many Australians fighting in the Great War were colonizers themselves, regiments of colonial populations, among them Indians, Burmese, and Africans, did exist. Christopher Tietjens, protagonist of Ford's *Parade's End,* captains a regiment of colonials, many of whom are Canadian. But the figure in the poster, the aggressive ape, is a figure also used to characterize colonized populations as subhuman creatures who need to be guided, uplifted, and civilized. If such civilizing motions produced resistance, there was little surprise—barbarians are by nature resistant to the forces of civilization. Barbarians don't realize what is in their own best interests and if force is necessary to enlighten them, then so be it. When Conrad's Kurtz scrawls "'Exterminate all the brutes'" across his report to the International Society for the Suppression of Savage Customs, he is both dehumanizing the "enemy" and justifying violence as a means of achieving colonial ends—he is declaring war. Marlow calls the words "the exposition of a method."[25] Kurtz, in the report, suggests that to the savages, colonizers "must appear . . . in the nature of supernatural beings—we approach them with the might as of a deity" (118). Marlow understands that Kurtz has in fact made himself a god to the natives and declares the passage "ominous." But Kurtz continues in an even more ominous fashion to suggest that the natives can thus be forced into whatever the "gods" see fit, although Kurtz believes that "we can exert a power for good practically unbounded" (118). Good, of course, means civilization, but especially European civilization.

But the pretense of doing good quickly becomes overshadowed by the realities of greed and evil once the wilderness removes all social restraint. Escape is complete and, as Hannah Arendt examining "the scramble for Africa" in *The Origins of Totalitarianism* explains, Kurtz and men like him are "thrown back upon themselves and still [have] nothing to fall back upon except, here and there, a streak of talent which [makes] them . . . dangerous."[26] Indeed, Arendt sees Africa as a place where "[t]he perfect gentleman and the perfect scoundrel came to know each other well."[27] Combining the elements of race (as a substitute for nationality) and bureaucracy, these men performed crimes with "civilized coldness" and "create[d] a vicious, refined atmosphere around [their] crimes."[28] Superfluous men who serve society only in the sense of contributing to an economic system that does not need their contributions, Kurtz and his real-life counterparts focus on the commission of their crimes. As Arendt maintains,

> [o]utside all social restraint and hypocrisy, against the backdrop of native life, the gentleman and the criminal felt not only the closeness of men who share the same color of skin, but the impact of a world of infinite possibilities for crimes committed in the spirit of play, for the combination of horror and laughter, that is for the full realization of their own phantom-like existence.[29]

That existence is, of course, most phantom-like at home. Kurtz has escaped a home where, like Claude Wheeler, he was, in Arendt's words "superfluous." But in the case of Kurtz, it is capitalism itself which has "spat [him] out."[30] And so the world of colonialism, of war, presents the potential for self-realization through crimes and horrors. This world of horrors functions best in an environment where racial divisions allow natives to be dehumanized, othered, where war is declared against those others whose humanity is questionable. "The world of native savages," Arendt argues, "was a perfect setting for men who had escaped the reality of civiliza-tion."[31] Not only has Kurtz escaped, but he also seems to combine the qualities of the gentleman and the criminal. Kurtz is the quintessential hollow man. In comparing him to his real-life counterparts, Arendt seems to agree.[32]

Sven Lindqvist, in his narrative on the British colonization of Africa, *Exterminate All the Brutes,* also examines the unspeakable violence of expeditions into Africa, including Stanley's march through Ituri, the "forest of death," in search of the British ally Emin Pasha, a provincial Sudanese governor who was still holding out after the defeat of the British at Khartoum. According to Lindqvist, Stanley murdered and pillaged his way to Lake Albert where he found Emin Pasha, who was not at all in need of Stanley's assistance. But because of Stanley's violent march, Pasha was again attacked and later forced to leave. Having dragged Emin back to England against his will, Stanley was given a hero's welcome.[33] Lindqvist believes that genocide was indeed the intent of African colonization. *Heart of Darkness,* written during the aftermath of Stanley's triumph, tells a similar story.[34]

Writing in the introduction to *Youth,* the volume containing *Heart of Darkness,* Conrad speaks of his own experiences in colonial Africa. "It is well known," he explains, "that curious men go prying into all sorts of places (where they have no business) and come out of them with all kinds of spoil. This story, [*Heart of Darkness*] and one other, not in this volume are all the spoil I brought out from the center of Africa where, really, I had no sort of business" (x–xi). The concept of noblesse oblige that appeals so strongly to Teddy Ashburnham leads men like Kurtz into Africa (where they have no business) on the pretext of spreading civilization, but in the absence of that proverbial policeman on the corner, peculiar sanity appears and spoil—war profit—becomes the colonizer's goal. While Conrad's spoil is limited to two books, the amount of booty removed from Africa and India is legendary, and Conrad knew it well. As a child, Conrad vowed before his schoolmates to visit the dark continent, and was derided by the boys who watched him point a sure finger at a map. Recalling the incident as he lies awake on a steamboat under the African sky, Conrad feels very much alone in his memory and in his knowledge of the reality of African exploration. "[N]o great haunting memory" visits him, "only the unholy recollection of a prosaic newspaper stunt and the distasteful knowledge of the vilest scramble for loot that ever disfigured the history of human

conscience and geographical exploration. What an end to the idealized realities of a boy's daydreams!"[35] In *Heart of Darkness,* ivory is the loot and to
get it, Kurtz, like the Belgians, enlists, or compels, the support of the natives. Kurtz's hubris, in Africa, becomes caught up in his idea of possession—"'My Intended, my ivory, my station, my river, my—' everything
belonged to him," Marlow observes, and then goes on to worry about the
consequences of such arrogance. "It made me hold my breath in expecta-
tion of hearing the wilderness burst into a prodigious peal of laughter that
would shake the fixed stars in their places" (116). For many, the Great War
did shake the stars.

Kurtz's hubris, developing into megalomania under the spell of the wilderness, reflects many of the evils of colonial Europe, evils that, once per-
petrated, make the thought of a world war more plausible. In Africa to
pilfer ivory, the company employing Kurtz and Marlow sees nothing
wrong with the fact that Kurtz has amassed much of the ivory belonging to
the African tribes. The manager is largely concerned with Kurtz's methods.
Kurtz has made no effort to suppress savage customs, no effort to civilize
the African tribes as he robs them. Instead, Kurtz has "taken a high seat
amongst the devils of the land" (116), as Marlow explains, "literally."
Kurtz has taken literally his assertion that he, by virtue of his origins, approaches the natives with the might of a god. In effect, his megalomania
has been fed by his mixed European origins. He had been "educated partly
in England . . . His mother was half-English, his father was half-French. All
Europe contributed to the making of Kurtz" (117). Faced with the appeal
of becoming a god, Kurtz cannot resist temptation. Marlow, as he explains
Kurtz's fall to his companions on the deck of the Nellie, chides the men for
the relative safety of their lives, which he attributes to the force of convention. "You can't understand," he tells his listeners,

> How could you?—with solid pavement under your feet, surrounded by kind
> neighbors ready to cheer you or to fall on you, stepping delicately between the
> butcher and the policeman, in the holy terror of scandal and gallows and lunatic
> asylums—how can you imagine what particular region of the first ages a man's
> untrammeled feet may take him into by the way of solitude—utter solitude
> without a policeman—utter silence, where no warning voice of a kind neighbor
> can be heard whispering of public opinion? (116)

Like Claude Wheeler, Marlow sees the danger in such safety, but he also
fears the force of solitude because men like Kurtz lack innate, or inner
strength, that is, they lack the will to resist the forces of anarchy, or the
forces of solitude. European civilization, in its insistence on the importance of public opinion and the kind neighbor who may fall on you as soon

as cheer you, does not foster inner strength. Instead, in its reliance on external restraint, European civilization produces men like Kurtz who are "hollow at the core" (131). Marlow, who is cut from the same cloth as Kurtz, saves himself through work, through duty, and through a restraint that Kurtz completely lacks. But Marlow is still close enough to Kurtz to sense his own complicity in Kurtz's madness, although he waffles at moments on the question. When Marlow goes to fetch Kurtz after his escape from the boat, he tries to reason with him to avoid having to "throttle" him. "I wasn't arguing with a lunatic either," Marlow insists. "Believe me or not, his intelligence was perfectly clear" (144). Kurtz, whose education and ability to articulate ideas have not left him, still talks a good game even if his words betray "his own exalted and incredible degradation" (144). And yet, Marlow continues, Kurtz's soul which "knew no restraint, no faith, and no fear," is mad (145). Herein lies the paradox of peculiar sanity. Kurtz's madness is only recognizable in the wilderness where he adopts native ways and sets himself up as a god, that is, his "method is unsound" (137). Colonialism sets the colonizer up as a god, but only on the colonizer's own terms, that is, as a harbinger of Christianity and an enforcer of stern European justice. The manager believes Kurtz has harmed the ivory trade because he "did not see the time was not ripe for vigorous action" (137). The manager does not care that Kurtz has plundered the country. In fact, he seizes the ivory for the Company. Kurtz's error is, as Marlow points out, that his "nerves, went wrong, and caused him to preside at certain midnight dances ending with unspeakable rites, which . . . were offered up to him" (117–8).

Kurtz's unsound methods are only a slight exaggeration (or perhaps no exaggeration at all) of the methods used in general by colonials in Africa. Conrad biographer Zdzisław Najder details some of Conrad's days in the Belgian Congo. Najder believes Conrad went into the Congo with a knowledge of Leopold II's 1884 manifesto "promoting the civilization and commerce of Africa and . . . other humane and benevolent purposes."[36] But Conrad saw immediately the hypocrisy of these words, which call to mind the euphemisms and evasions of the Vietnam era in which the peculiar sanity of war and the peculiar sanity of colonialism converged. As Najder explains, Conrad

> saw for himself what those "humane and benevolent purposes" meant in practice; how under the guise of "maintaining order" bloody pacifications and hunting for laborers took place; how crops were being destroyed and villages burnt in order to force the natives to work; how minor offences were punished by flog-

ging men or cutting off their hands; and how in every case the main motive of action was the desire for a quick gain.[37]

Clearly Conrad sees this madness in the colonial venture and uses examples of that madness to prepare us for the eventuality of Kurtz. Three images particularly capture the absurd and violent nature of colonialism. The first of these occurs on the ship before Marlow gets to the Congo. As they sail along what Marlow describes as an unchanging coastline, passing trading posts with names "that seemed to belong to some sordid farce acted in front of a sinister back-cloth"(61), they encounter a French ship which is, as Marlow puts it, "shelling the bush" (61). No village, no trading post, not even a "shed" occupies the site. "There she was," Marlow observes, "incomprehensible, firing into a continent" (62). But the insanity, Marlow's word here, of the shelling is lost on the other men aboard Marlow's ship, one of whom assures Marlow that "there was a camp of natives—he called them enemies!—hidden out of sight somewhere"(62). This passage clearly illustrates the warlike nature of colonialism—wherein the colonized are referred to as the enemy—and illustrates the complete lack of reason demonstrated by colonial forces. Like Kurtz, all Europe contributed to colonialism.

The second image Conrad creates demonstrates not only the absurdity of colonialism, but its barbarity and cruelty as well. And perhaps to remind us of his intentions, Conrad refers to the first incident as he describes the second. When Marlow finally reaches the Company's first station, he discovers more irrational destruction. A work crew is building a railroad and in the process blasting, with little effect, a rock cliff that does not need to be moved in order to build the railroad. Marlow thinks, as he hears repeated blasts, of the similar ineffectual shelling of "a continent." But the natives involved here are prisoners who "could by no stretch of imagination be called enemies" (64). Instead, these men are being punished for crimes which they are unaware of having committed, as Marlow suggests, "the outraged law, like the bursting shells, had come to them, an insoluble mystery from the sea" (64). This forced labor is gradually killing these men, as Marlow quickly observes. Marlow also implicates himself in this madness as he sees a black overseer who salutes him and with "a glance at his charge, seemed to take me into partnership in his exalted trust. After all, I also was a part of the great cause of these high and just proceedings" (65).[38] Marlow also knows that he has participated in violence "without counting the exact cost, according to the demands of such sort of life as I had blundered into" (65). But Marlow, who is able to recognize the humanity of the chained men, is still shocked at what he sees here, and later. The moment becomes one of foreshadowing as he looks on this scene of torture, what Najder calls a scene of "confusion, stupidity, and cruelty" (127).

> [A]s I stood on this hillside, I foresaw that in the blinding sunshine of that land I would become acquainted with a flabby, pretending, weak-eyed devil of a rapacious and pitiless folly. How insidious he could be, too, I was only to find out several months later and a thousand miles farther. For a moment I stood appalled, as though by a warning. (65)

What Marlow finds when he descends the hill is a glade peopled by dying natives, one, a young boy, too weak to eat the biscuit Marlow offers him. The hellish nature of this scene foreshadows the inner station where Marlow mistakes heads impaled on poles for wooden fence posts. Because these deaths in the glade are extracted in the name of progress, in service of what Marlow calls "the merry dance of death and trade" (62), they pass unnoticed by anyone except Marlow.

After the glade of death, Conrad immediately offers up the third image in sharp contrast to the second. Marlow approaches the Company station and meets there the chief accountant "in such an unexpected elegance of get-up that in the first moment, [Marlow] took him for a sort of vision" (67). Marlow learns that the accountant has taught, much to her distaste, a native woman how to iron. This is the impeccably dressed bureaucrat, not unlike Alvan Hervey. The inappropriateness of this dress in the jungle where men, both black and white, are dying from the work and from the climate reveals both the superficiality of the bureaucrat/colonialist and the extent to which that superficiality has become his substance,[39] and once again calls to mind Arendt's "vicious, refined atmosphere" which surrounded the crimes of colonialism.

These three images reflect the irrationality of colonialism, its cruelty, and the superficiality of European bureaucrats, of whom Kurtz is one. Socially sanctioned, socially applauded, colonialism's "logical" product is Kurtz. While the accountant at the outer station may have his clothes pressed by natives, he is still too close to civilization, to the policeman on the corner, to become Kurtz (although we have seen the effectiveness of Edward Ashburnham as the policeman on the corner). But once the colonial effort becomes far enough removed from its origins, a man like Kurtz arises; Kurtz is inherent in the nature of colonialism.[40] In the same way, peculiar sanity is a logical outgrowth of superficiality and repression once they are placed in the context of war; that is, they are removed from their normal context and placed within one which seems to condone lawless behavior. In *Heart of Darkness* Conrad examines the insane logic of colonialism and links that insanity to the world of bourgeois Europe when Marlow visits the Intended at the end of the story. As Marlow enters her house, he sees Kurtz and the wilderness, a vision he calls a "moment of triumph for the wilderness" (156). As he waits before the mahogany door he hears Kurtz's last words, "The horror! The horror!" (156). The room in which he meets the Intended grows dark as their interview progresses and finally as she asks Marlow to repeat the last words, Marlow tells us that he was "on the point of crying at her, 'Don't you hear them?'" Marlow then goes on to say that "[t]he dusk was repeating them in a persistent whisper all around us, in a whisper that seemed to swell menacingly like the first whisper of a rising wind" (161). Marlow's decision to tell the Lie, however benevolent his intentions, inadvertently maintains the status quo, a truth we must assume Marlow understands—hence his telling of the story. Marlow's lie supports the lie that colonialism is good for the colonized nations by perpetuating a romantic image of colonialists, an image that allows the continued dehumanization of natives and theft of natural resources. But even more important, Marlow's lie conceals all he knows about the truth of colonialism and Kurtz. The lie hides the horror from the bourgeois who support colonialism and allows its interest in possessions to remain hidden. Marlow, like Conrad, assumes responsibility for what he saw in Africa when he tells the truth—the story—of colonialism's peculiar sanity. Frederick Karl suggests that by the time Conrad wrote *Heart of Darkness*, "he was interested in a Congo of the mind, and his version seems a greater truth than the actual Congo he had experienced almost ten years earlier."[41] (473). Unfortunately, that truth remained hidden to the Bayliss Wheelers of the world, and by 1914, the peculiar sanity of war has enveloped Europe.

Chapter 3
THE EVE OF APOCALYPSE

The Endless Summer

Well into the summer of 1914, many people believed war could still be avoided. Even the assassination of Archduke Ferdinand failed to convince the worst skeptics, those who believed the leaders of Europe would never allow such a conflagration to occur. As late as July fifth, Kaiser Wilhelm declared that he "did not believe that there was any prospect of great war-like developments," and that "there was no need to make special disposi-tions."[1] It is not surprising then that many intellectuals saw no need to anticipate a European war. H. G. Wells, who in 1914 had written of atomic bombs and a "Central European" invasion of France through Bel-gium in the novel *The World Set Free,* did not anticipate the war. Biogra-pher Michael Coren writes of Wells's surprise at the onset of war. "I saw long ahead how it would happen," Wells explains, "and wove fantastic sto-ries about it. I let my imagination play about it, but at the bottom of my heart I could not feel and believe it would really be let happen."[2]

Joseph Conrad found himself vacationing in Poland on August 4, 1914, and wrote about the moment and those that led up to it in "Poland Revisited" and "First News." Explaining in "Poland Revisited" why he would embark on such a journey during the third week of July 1914, Conrad concludes that "there was no room in my consciousness for the apprehension of a European war. I don't mean to say that I ignored the possibility; I simply did not think of it."[3] Once mobilization occurred, Conrad, as did Henry James, expressed fears that civilization as he then knew it was at an end. In a Cracow hotel with what he refers to as "a few men of mark," Conrad concludes that "[a]ll the past was gone, and there was no future, whatever happened; no road which did not seem to lead to moral annihilation."[4]

This fear of breaking with the Edwardian past also anticipates the break with sanity heralded by the onset of war, the "moral annihilation" that pitched the world into the second decade of the century devoid of even the pretensions that motivate John Dowell and Teddy Ashburnham. As we have seen, the Edwardian understanding of morality was hypocritical. And there is a sense of betrayal in the words of James, an acknowledgment that the past was not after all what he thought it had been. In a letter to Rhoda Broughton on August 10, 1914, James expresses his despair over the onset of war:

> Black and hideous to me is the tragedy that gathers, and I'm sick beyond cure to have lived on to see it. You and I, the ornaments of our generation should have been spared this wreck of our belief that through the long years we had seen civilization grow and the worst become impossible. The tide that bore us along was then all the while moving to *this* as its grand Niagara—yet what a blessing we didn't know it. It seems to me to *undo* everything, everything that was ours in the most horrible retroactive way. . . .[5]

Edith Wharton, a close friend of James, felt the war killed him. "He struggled," she writes in *A Backward Glance,* "through two years of it, then veiled his eyes from the endless perspective of destruction. It was the gesture of Agamemnon, covering his face with his cloak before the unbearable."[6] Before he died, James renounced his American citizenship to become a British subject because the U.S. did not respond as he thought it should to the sinking of the Lusitania. Wharton thought the act "rather puerile, and altogether unlike him," and as a result did not write to him on the occasion.[7] But James's renunciation serves as an example of the way the war's peculiar sanity could and did affect intellectuals.

Samuel Hynes in *A War Imagined: The First World War and English Culture* believes that for men such as Henry James, the onset of war was a "contradiction of the values that they had *thought* made Europe one civilization."[8] The emptiness of Victorian and Edwardian conventions, which were not only unable to prevent the outbreak of violence but seemed in their inflexibility to make it inevitable, left those who had depended on them without ethical moorings. The horror of Conrad's wilderness where principles have flown off at the first good shake invades civilization on the home front. Now that the bonds of convention have been dissolved, peculiar sanity thrives, even in the least likely places—in the hearts of the artists and writers who shape and reflect public opinion. Two novels, H. G. Wells's *Mr. Britling Sees It Through* and Edith Wharton's *A Son at the Front,* reflect the subtle personality changes war produces in writers and artists. Both protagonists are artists and fathers of sons who are, or become, eligible for front line duty. Concerned for the lives of their sons, each still in his own way succumbs to war mania and willingly sends his son to slaughter. While propaganda in England and America depicted rabid mothers eager to sacrifice the lives of their sons to the cause, these two novels shift the responsibility to men who allow their hatred of German militarism and German "atrocities" to obscure their logical thinking. Britling, like his creator Wells, is a normally cynical man, but faced with the death of his son at the end of the novel, he can only think of God whom he calls the "Captain of Mankind."[9] His use of military metaphor here illustrates the extent to which even the most intellectual among us give in to war mania and to the force of cliché. Both novels make clear the truth that no one is immune to hatred, to suspicion, to the desire to kill—no one is immune to peculiar sanity, not even those whose heads we expect to remain cool.

Reasoned Rhetoric

At the end of *Fighting France,* Edith Wharton describes what she calls "reasoned courage," the ability of the French, when attacked, to fight for their own independence.[10] The French are not, she claims, militaristic. They have never "enjoyed the savage forms of sport which stimulate the blood of more apathetic or more brutal races. Neither prizefighting nor bullfighting is of the soil in France, and Frenchmen do not settle their private differences impromptu with their fists: they do it, logically and with deliberation, on the duelling-ground."[11] Wharton includes her own countrymen, we must assume, among the "more brutal races," yet she, as did James, also felt shame that America delayed for so long its entry into the war. In both *The Marne* and *A Son at the Front,* Wharton ridicules Americans who saw France as a place to vacation, Americans who thought their money could buy them out of France in the early days of the war. In *The Marne,* the Belknaps, after war breaks out, book passage on a steamer sailing from England "for a sum that would have fitted up an ambulance."[12] Back in New York, Troy Belknap decries the young women who were "doing up parcels, planning war-tableaux and charity dances, rushing to 'propaganda' lectures given by handsome French officers, and keeping up a kind of continuous picnic on the ruins of civilization."[13]

Wharton's distinction here between French resistance and American war fervor merits comment for several reasons. First, on the obvious level, the French are in fact responding to an invasion by a hostile army—they have little choice but to fight; this is what Wharton calls "reasoned recognition of their peril."[14] Wharton, and many other Americans as well, respected this tenacity in the face of what may have seemed an impending doom, and Wharton, unlike other Americans who fled at the first shot, felt a need to contribute to the war effort of a country where she had lived off and on for many years. At the other end of this spectrum, Wharton criticizes the "peculiar sanity" of Americans who had no idea what was going on in Europe but answered the call of propaganda anyway. Wharton does not delve into the gray area that lies somewhere between propaganda and fact, between jingoism and "reasoned" rhetoric, of which there was a great deal, including Wharton's own. The countless hours Wharton spent on behalf of refugees, artists, and working women displaced by the war resulted in a heart attack, according to Shari Benstock in her introduction to *Son*.[15] Wharton herself describes in *A Backward Glance* organizing a work room where ninety out-of-work women made lingerie to order.[16] She also saw, on trips to hospitals at or near the front, the destruction and horror of battle. Clearly Wharton contributed to the war effort to the extent a woman of her social class could. But in her novels and nonfiction, she at times uses, it would seem without shame, those words which, according to Hemingway, "you could not stand to hear."[17] On the supply mission that takes *The Marne*'s Troy Belknap and his mother near the setting of the battle of the Marne, a name which will later become his nickname, "Marny," Troy listens to the tales of their guide "till he forgot the horror of war, and thought only of its splendours." Belknap believes that "[t]o save France . . . was the clear duty of the world, as he saw it."[18]

While the irony and reticence of a Jake Barnes is lacking in Wharton's prose, Wharton's personal actions are little different from the male authors who signed up to fight or drive ambulances. Ford and Wells, after all, wrote copious propaganda during the war and Ford signed up at the age of forty, largely to prove his loyalty to England in spite of his German father. Wharton's rhetoric, however patriotic, attempts to make a distinction between defensive action and posturing or warmongering. Informing Wharton's views about the war, however, is the idea that France is the undisputed cradle of civilization and deserving of American intervention. This idea, this construction, FRANCE, implies civilization and sanity, while the construction GERMANY implies barbarism and insanity. In a letter to Sara Norton on September 2, 1914, Wharton writes of the German advance on Paris and tells her, "The 'atrocities' one hears of *are true*. I know of many, alas, too well authenticated. Spread it abroad as much as you can. It should be known that it is to America's interest to help stem this hideous flood of savagery by opinion if it may not be by action. No civilized race can remain neutral in feeling now."[19] In *The Marne*, Troy Belknap, remembering his French tutor whose grave he has stumbled upon near the Marne battlefield, envies the French's long connection to the past and to history. The young Belknap thinks that "[e]very stone that France had carved, every song she had sung, every new idea she had struck out, every beauty she had created in her thousand fruitful years, was a tie between her and her children. These things were more glorious than her battles, for it was because of them that all civilization was bound up in her, and that nothing that concerned her could concern her only."[20]

Nearly twenty years later with war building again in Europe, Wharton in *A Backward Glance* calls the war "the terrible and interminable epic of France's long defense."[21] Arguments for or against American isolationism notwithstanding, Troy Belknap's words reflect a kind of cultural idealism, an intellectual romanticism. These are the clichés that, coupled with atrocity stories and appropriately toned down, ultimately garnered American support for the war. Wharton did not necessarily see herself as a pacifist. Once more in *A Backward Glance,* she recalls an expedition in August 1915 to the camp of the Chasseurs Alpins in the Vosges. Remembering the moment vividly, Wharton tells us "I saw myself, an eager grotesque figure, bestriding a mule in the long tight skirts of 1915, and suddenly appearing, a prosaic Walkyrie laden with cigarettes."[22] Here Wharton not only chronicles her emotional involvement in the war, but sees herself as this most ardent of German war goddesses, although astride a mule, not a mythological charger. She makes no apology for her rhetoric, but in her depictions of blatant propaganda and cliché, shows us the extreme to which "unreasoning" use of these tools can take us. Wharton's objective observations of herself also tie her to her character *A Son at the Front*'s John Campton by their shared obsession with the war in spite of a certain degree of intellectual distance from it. Shortly, we shall see the formation of cliché and the inflammatory uses to which it is often put when we examine the work of H. G. Wells.

The Prosaic Walkyrie: Wharton's *A Son at the Front*

Like Conrad, Edith Wharton was traveling in the summer of 1914. On July 30, she was on the road between Poitiers and Paris. In *Fighting France* she describes the beauty of the French countryside as she and her companions motor past. "The air," she explains, "seemed full of the long murmur of human effort, the rhythm of oft repeated tasks; the serenity of the scene smiled away the war rumours which had hung on us since morning."[23] Back in Paris on the morning of August 1, Wharton tells us that "the air was thundery with rumours" which no one believed.[24] She had planned to go to England to spend the last days of summer in a house she had leased from Mrs. Humphrey Ward, but the declaration of war left her, as it had many others, stuck in Paris with no money and no way out. This account of her adjustment in the early days of the war, in *Fighting France* and *A Backward Glance,* first to mobilization then to living under martial law, parallels the account of John Campton's experiences in *A Son at the Front.* Begun early in 1918 while the war dragged on, *A Son at the Front* was not published until 1922 and then was not well received. In her introduction to the novel, Shari Benstock addresses the question of *Son*'s lukewarm reception. The already growing threat of another war cast into doubt, Benstock argues, all war fiction that did not view war as a lesson in futility. Compared to the war fictions of Hemingway, Dos Passos, and e. e. cummings, Wharton's novel must have seemed "maudlin and full of hackneyed and false patriotic sentiments," a reference no doubt to Wharton's above-described admiration of French courage as reflected in her fiction.[25] Not as shamelessly patriotic or pro-French as *The Marne* that appeared in 1918, perhaps *A Son at the Front* did not give Wharton's readership what it might have expected of her, while at the same time it failed to interest those readers who yearned for a more cynical voice, as Hemingway's would later become. In an essay on Wharton's short fiction from the war, Julie Olin-Ammentorp suggests that the war fiction reflects a "mixture of emotions" that in *Fighting France* emerge as a "tension . . . between the unremittingly realistic and horrible and the reassuringly romantic vision of war."[26] Clearly Wharton's sharp eye for the foibles of her class sees the pretension and superficiality of much war talk and war work, as we have seen. But as we have also seen in *Fighting France,* she "believes" in the war, as did the cynical Hemingway who went to Italy to drive an ambulance. Ultimately, we seem to be dealing with a similar ambivalence couched in a different kind of language.

But Wharton does not attempt to recreate the soldier's frontline experience in *A Son at the Front.* While she had firsthand knowledge of the front from numerous excursions that she chronicles in *Fighting France,* Wharton's purpose in *A Son at the Front* is to detail the tensions, the deprivations, the waiting, and the loss felt by those left at home, as she explains in *A Backward Glance,* "that strange war-world of the rear, with its unnatural sharpness of outline and over-heightening of colour," its peculiar sanity.[27] Indeed, part of that peculiar sanity is the reliance on clichés and stereotypes that follow the intense propaganda campaigns of the Great War.

Because *A Son at the Front*'s John Campton is not French, he does not share in the French sense of "reason" that gives them their quiet determination. Like Wharton herself, Campton has travel plans for the beginning of

August 1914. When the novel opens on July 30, he awaits the arrival of his son George, who is to travel with him to southern Italy and perhaps Spain. Divorced from George's mother, Campton feels cheated of the experience of his son's childhood and looks forward to the trip that the war ultimately thwarts. Two preoccupations prevent Campton from acknowledging the probability of war. First, he is unwilling to postpone the trip with George, but more important, he is aware that if George is in France at the time of mobilization, he will have to join up. By a quirk of fate, George was born in Paris, and even though he has American citizenship, he is subject to French conscription. Campton, who has lived in Paris for years, is not eager for battle as is his French friend Paul Dastrey who tells Campton that there will be war within three days. Naively, Campton believes that Dastrey is "breathing fire and fury on an enemy one knew to be engaged, at that very moment, in meeting England and France more than half-way in the effort to smooth over diplomatic difficulties."[28] Both Dastrey and Campton's old concierge Mme. Lebel are prepared for the worst. With the understanding that if war breaks out she will have four sons involved, Mme. Lebel tells Campton that "*this sort of thing has got to stop*" (12, italics Wharton's), one of the first of many war clichés that will hound and then convert Campton.

At the outset, many Americans—Wharton and her creation Campton among them—found themselves in Paris with little money and no transportation. Wharton did manage to get out for a few weeks in the fall, but went back to Paris at the first opportunity to resume work with the war charities she had already begun to organize. Wharton had little sympathy for Americans who found the war, in the words of John Campton, "an unwarrantable interference with his private plans" (11). While Campton understands the selfishness of his feelings, many Americans did not. In *The Marne,* Wharton blasts her fellow countrymen for such feelings. One of Mrs. Belknap's acquaintances, allowing for the possibility of a German invasion of Paris, asks of another American woman, "If they do come, what do you plan to do about your pearls?"[29] While Wharton herself was concerned with whether or not her servants, who had gone ahead to England to staff the Ward residence, had money to pay local tradesmen for groceries, the scene suggests she was aware of the idiocy of a concern for jewelry in the face of an invasion.[30]

John Campton's concern for his son's future is complicated by the presence in Paris of George's mother and stepfather, Julia and Anderson Brant, who both also want to keep George out of the fray. Brant is a wealthy banker whom Campton despises on general principles, but when Campton is summoned by Julia, he agrees that if George is called in spite of a recent bout with tuberculosis, Brant is to use his influence to keep George at a desk somewhere. The alliance with Julia and Anderson Brant galls Campton's Bohemian sensibilities as well as his possessiveness toward George, but his concern for his son's safety wins out. The thought that he might owe France some sort of sacrifice occurs to Campton, but he is unwilling to let that sacrifice be his only son. George's inclinations are not part of the consideration, and Campton agrees with the Brants, not only to keep George away from the front, but also not to let him know they have acted.

Campton's transformation is a gradual one and it involves coming to terms with George's feelings. When George arrives in Paris on the eve of war, he expresses the same doubt that war can ever occur again. Speaking for his own generation which he calls "international," George tells his father that

> [t]hey don't believe the world will ever stand for another war. It's too stupidly uneconomic, to begin with. . . . Then life's worth too much, and nowadays too many millions of people know it. That's the way we all feel. Think of everything that counts—art and science and poetry, and all the rest—going to smash at the nod of some doddering diplomatist. . . . they're not going off to die in a ditch to oblige anybody. (21)

But die in ditches they will. The conversion of George's rhetoric from prewar cliché to war cliché is quick and dramatic. When Germany invades Belgium a day later, George echoes old Mme. Lebel's words. "This kind of thing has got to stop," he tells his father. "We shall go straight back to cannibalism if it doesn't" (51). Implied in George's exclamation is the notion that Germans are cannibals, an idea later hinted at in rumors that became part of Allied propaganda of a so-called corpse factory where bodies of soldiers supposedly emerged as glycerine for weapons and food for hogs and poultry. Both Fussell and Ponsonby believe the problem arose over the mistranslation—Ponsonby suggests deliberate—of the German word *Kadaver,* a word most often used to refer to the corpses of horses, which both sides ate and which were rendered for fat and byproducts in German rendering plants. In spite of German protests that the word was never used to refer to human remains, *The Times,* citing dictionaries to show that it was, continued to publish articles on the subject and the British government allowed the rumors to be spread, especially in India where they were found to be particularly offensive.[31] Arthur Ponsonby reports that in an article in the April 20, 1917, issue of *The Times,* a British sergeant claimed that a German prisoner had told him about the factories. The British soldier stated that "[t]his fellow told me that Fritz calls his margarine 'corpse fat' because they suspect that's what it comes from."[32] Once put forth, an accusation of this kind was hard to disprove.[33]

When Germany marched through Belgium, rumors of atrocities abounded; one of the worst among them was that Germans were mutilating babies.[34] Robert Graves, an officer in the Royal Welsh Fusiliers, writes about such atrocities in *Good-Bye to All That*. Graves actually saw babies without hands and feet, but believed the injuries were "merely the result of shell fire" and not deliberate mutilations.[35] He goes so far as to accuse the Belgians of lying about atrocities, "knowing the Belgians now at first-hand" he explains.[36] Nevertheless, the image of mutilated babies later appeared on war posters in England and in the United States, where it served as a tool for generating enthusiasm for America's entry into the war. Already before August 4, rumors of these atrocities had placed Germany in the position of "savage"enemy, much like the natives in *Heart of Darkness*. George Campton goes on to tell his father, when the elder Campton tries "to think up Pacifist arguments" (51), that Belgium has identified Germans as villains who are "not fit to live with white people, and" he continues, "the sooner they're shown it the better" (51). This statement goes beyond "reasoned recognition of . . . peril." George's rhetoric removes him from the position of quiet defender of home and places him in the realm of peculiar sanity. However, George's father thinks only of their time together and does all that he can to keep George from the front. After George is mobilized, John Campton is accosted by his American cousin Benny Upsher, who shares George's hasty hatred for the enemy and his inclination to see the Germans as savages. Inarticulate except for cliché, Upsher tells Campton that he wants to join George's regiment, because he "want[s] to be *in* this" (58, italics Wharton's). When Campton points out that George is only "in this" because he had the bad luck to be born in France, Upsher once again villainizes Germany as a "hulking bully" (58). In response to Campton's question, "You're mad—this is not our war. Do you really want to go out and butcher people?" (58) Upsher replies "Yes—this kind of people" (59). We are reminded here of Kurtz's scrawl at the bottom of his report to the Commission on the Suppression of Savage Customs, "Exterminate all the brutes."

Gradually, John Campton abandons his pacifist position. Three months into the war his own thoughts echo the clichés of earlier scenes; Campton believes in "the monstrous facts of the first few weeks . . . [Germany's] savagery in the field, her premeditated and systematized terrorizing of the civil populations" (64). And yet, Campton rests more easily because he believes George is not at the front. At moments, he wonders how George is able to remain objective in the face of frontline horrors, but he never once suspects the truth, which is that George has abandoned his desk job and without his family's knowledge had himself sent to the front. Campton wonders at a letter from George which reports having seen "a fellow who'd seen Benny Upsher" (87) on his way to the front, but will not admit the likelihood that George himself has seen Benny there.

Campton's real awakening to the ravages of war comes when he learns of the deaths of people he knew, especially when he learns that the physician who treated George for tuberculosis and to whom he had gone earlier to obtain George's medical release has lost his son. Campton remembers his visit with embarrassment and goes to Fortin-Lescluze to offer his sympathy. Campton is shocked when he hears that the physician himself amputated his son's legs, although too late to prevent his death from infection. Two deaths particularly touch Campton. The first is that of Mme. Lebel's granddaughter, who, caught with her mother in occupied territory, is thrown to the ground by a German soldier and dies of a head wound.[37] When her father, too old for the front and so doing civilian guard duty, learns of the death, he enlists and dies himself. But even more important in terms of Campton's conversion to the war effort, is the death of René Davril, a young painter who reminds Campton of George. Davril's death occurs on the heels of the reappearance of Harvey Mayhew, Benny Upsher's uncle and Campton's distant relative. Mayhew has been on a peace mission to the Hague, but unfortunately has arrived in Luxembourg the same day Germany invaded the city. Jailed for one night and then placed under house arrest at his hotel for eight days before being shipped back to the United States, Mayhew believes the Germans have committed an atrocity against him. He tells Campton that his goal is to "show up these people, to proclaim to the world what they really are, to rouse public opinion in America against a nation of savages who ought to be hunted off the face of the globe like vermin—like the vermin in their own prison cells! . . . I come to bring not Peace but a Sword!" (78). Mayhew, who becomes a true villain before the novel's end, utters the kinds of clichés we saw in *The Marne* and the same clichés we heard on the lips of Benny Upsher and George Campton. Wharton contrasts Mayhew's self-proclaimed martyrdom against the death of Davril, a talented young artist who because of his poverty has been unable to pursue his art, or to avoid military action.

Campton goes to Davril at the request of George's "friend" Madge Talkett, a wealthy New York matron who is nursing in Paris so she can remain near George. Hallucinating from the effects of a high fever, Davril believes that his paintings are in the room where Campton can seen them. Misunderstanding Davril's needs, Campton gives him a sketch of George. Until that moment, Campton resisted giving away his work to war charities because he didn't want to undermine the value of his paintings for George's sake. When Davril dies and his family refuses to sell the sketch, Campton does so himself and donates the proceeds to The Friends of French Art that will support the Davril family. Davril's sacrifice and the sacrifices of his family clearly come under the definition of reasoned action, while the rhetoric of Harvey Mayhew becomes the epitome of peculiar sanity. John Campton, at first at least, does not question Mayhew's claim, but ushers him around Paris and into the drawing rooms of other wealthy Americans who use his speeches to fund their own projects. René Davril's death draws Campton into the world of relief work that he has hitherto avoided. But the force of these deaths combined with the death of Ladislas Isador, a man of nearly forty who had been kept from the front by the efforts of his wealthy French mistress, converts Campton to the war effort. Isador is rooted out of his desk job and killed his first day in the trenches. Campton realizes that his influence and the Brant money can no longer justify keeping George out of the fray. Incredulous at his change of heart, Julia Brant demands to know "What has changed you?" (99). Campton himself is not sure, but the stunning truth remains that he no longer places his son's safety above the war effort. Remembering George's words that no one of his generation would die in a ditch for a diplomat, Campton is now touched by what he refers to as "the clear-eyed sacrifice of the few who knew why they were dying. Jean Fortin, René Davril, and such lads as young Louis Dastrey, with his reasoned horror of butchery and waste in general, and his instant grasp of the necessity of this particular sacrifice: it was they who had first shed light on the dark problem" (99). The line between reasoned recognition of peril and peculiar sanity is fine here. Fortin, Davril, and Dastrey are all French, but Campton concludes that his own response to their peril, to George's peril, would have been the same whether the country in question was his own or not. Once a professor of pacifist views, Campton now believes in the war. In a key passage he explains these new beliefs in words that echo the propaganda of the day:

> Campton had never before, at least consciously, thought of himself and the few beings he cared for as part of a greater whole, component elements of the immense amazing spectacle. But the last four months had shown him man as a defenseless animal suddenly torn from his shell, stripped of all the interwoven tendrils of association, habit, background, daily ways and words, daily sights and sounds, and flung out of the human habitable world into naked ether, where nothing breathes or lives. *That was what war did: that was why those who*

best understood it in all its farthest-reaching abomination willingly gave their lives to put an end to it. (99, italics mine)

Glancing back for a moment at Conrad's "Autocracy and War," we may remember the graphic and cynical passage that describes that Dantesque battlefield we viewed earlier where "from the frozen ground . . . a chorus of groans call[s] for vengeance from Heaven; [where men] kill and retreat, or kill and advance, without intermission or rest for twenty hours, for fifty hours, for whole weeks of fatigue, hunger, cold, and murder—till their ghastly labour, . . . passing through the stages of courage, of fury, of hopelessness, sinks into the night of crazy despair."[38] The resulting "moral and physical misery" that produces peculiar sanity parallels the naked ether Wharton describes, the human stripped of all the interwoven tendrils of daily life. But Campton speaks from an observation of war dead, of the idealism with which they enter battle before that "night of crazy despair" sets in. For Campton, idealism seems a reality, not the grim battlefield Conrad describes. Campton, the artist, the intellectual, embraces the clichés, the propaganda, the notion that fighting a war can end war, the idea that the death of a soldier could become "suffering transmuted into poetry" (104). Even though he believes George is still at a desk job, Campton "no longer [thinks] that any civilized man could afford to stand aside from such a conflict" (102), an echo of Wharton's letter to Sara Norton.

All the while Campton struggles with his views of the war, Wharton continues to remind us of the peculiar sanity displayed by many of his compatriots. When Campton, dispatched by Anderson Brant, goes to tell Harvey Mayhew that their relative Benny Upsher is missing and presumed dead, Mayhew is rehearsing his speech about atrocities to be delivered at a fund raiser hosted by George's mother, Julia Brant. Campton hears Mayhew's empty words echoing through the Brant's ballroom, which has been stripped of its priceless antiques for the event. "All that I have to give," Mayhew declares from his platform, "yes, all that is most precious to me, I am ready to surrender, to offer up, to lay down in the Great Struggle which is to save the world from barbarism. I, who was one of the first Victims of that barbarism . . . of that hideous barbarism" (109). Ironically, Mayhew's nephew has, in fact, laid down his life, making the supreme sacrifice, on the initial basis, as we saw earlier, of idealism. We do not know if he carried his idealism with him to the grave, or if, before his sacrifice, he has "butchered" any Germans. Once again Wharton juxtaposes jingoism and hypocrisy with the stark reality of war. Mayhew's self-aggrandizement may be well intentioned, but it is not innocent. Clearly he sees his imprisonment in a hotel room for a week as one of those "unwarrantable interference[s] with his private plans" (11), a major inconvenience and personal insult for which he means to seek revenge on the Germans. Like the American ladies who are concerned with their pearls, Mayhew reveals a complete lack of reason, a peculiar sanity. While Campton still sees the posturing in Mayhew's words, his thoughts reflect their own confused jingoism. Visiting his old friend Adele Anthony with a new and puzzling letter from George, Campton wonders if George has had himself transferred to the front but won't admit it. We learn later that this is indeed the case, but Campton continues to cling to the hope that George is safe. At the same time, Campton now feels that George should be at the front. His reaction to George's letter is one of "shame;" he is "ashamed of George, as well as of himself" (115). When Miss Anthony asks if Campton is "satisfied" with George's letter, he is unable to tell her what he feels because his thoughts are so contradictory. Campton asks himself,

> How could he say: 'I'm satisfied, but I wish to God that George were not'? . . . And how could he define, or even be sure that he was actually experiencing, a feeling so contradictory that it seemed to be made up of anxiety for his son's safety, shame at that anxiety, shame at George's own complacent acceptance of his lot, and terror of a possible change in that lot? (115)

Campton's ambivalence toward George's participation in the war was shared by many parents of fighting-age men. Even at the front, men expressed a similar emotion, the desire to be elsewhere, along with the desire to defeat the Germans. This ambivalence appeared frequently in popular songs. In one episode of the documentary series made for public television, *The American Experience,* "The Great War, 1918," a journalist who covered the war relates an incident having to do with the then popular song, "I Didn't Raise My Boy to Be a Soldier." Early in the day the journalist reports hearing the song in one area of the trenches and by day's end the song has traveled from one end of the battlefield to the other. The refrain, sung from the point of view of a boy's mother, expresses a reluctance to send the son into battle.

> I didn't raise my boy to be a soldier,
> I brought him up to be my pride and joy,
> Who dares to place a musket on his shoulder,
> To shoot some other mother's darling boy?
> Let nations arbitrate their future troubles,
> It's time to lay the sword and gun away,
> There'd be no war today,
> If mothers all would say,
> "I didn't raise my boy to be a soldier."

Finding the incident telling, the journalist wrote an article that was not only killed by the censors but also deemed "treasonous."[39] The sheet music of this song from 1915, however, expresses an even more interesting ambivalence. Above the title, the song is billed as "A Mother's Plea for Peace," but the drawing implies a kind of cowardice in that plea. The mother, in her armchair, clings to her son, who is on his knees. Both wear expressions of extreme fear. Above the hearth scene, a cloud containing battle images floats.[40] The boy clinging to his mother's skirts is certainly an image no boy "worth his salt" would want to convey. And the idea that women are weak is one of the great misogynistic clichés, something that is expected of women but must be contradicted by men. While it is true that the song was published before America entered the war, at a time when noninvolvement was very popular, the implied cowardice remains.[41] John Campton, a father, feels the same softness toward his son, but also the "appropriate" shame at the implied cowardice.

Campton's fears have also separated him from his art for the first year of the war. Drawn into the world of other wealthy Americans "who've resolutely, unanimously, unshakeably decided, for a certain number of hours each day, to forget the war" (125), Campton resumes painting. Campton is never quite comfortable with his ex-wife's associates, but continues to visit the salon of Madge Talkett, a rich married American with whom, unbeknownst to Campton, George is in love. Campton paints his fellow Americans to the chagrin of Dastrey who will not join him there. Quarreling with Dastrey, Campton tells him, "You think we're all a lot of shirks, of drones, of international loafers—I don't know what you call us. But I'm one of them" (125). But Campton does not stay one of them for long. One result of his decision to forget is relief from the thought that George may actually be at the front. Campton's relief, however, is short-lived when he learns that George has in fact been wounded. Driven to the field hospital in one of Anderson Brant's autos, Campton gets a hasty lesson in the grim reality of war. A nurse leads Campton into a fly-infested room where, on a rough pallet, he beholds a "middle-aged bearded man, heavily bandaged about the chest and left arm: he was snoring, his mouth open, his gaunt cheeks drawn in with the fight for breath. Campton said to himself that if his own boy lived he should like some day to do something for this poor devil who was his roommate" (149). Campton recoils when he realizes that this "poor devil" is George. What Campton sees in his face, apart from the pain of a life-threatening wound, is the "difference" the experience of war produces; Campton understands that "the son he had known [is] lost to him forever" (149).

Away from the rhetoric and cliché of upper-middle-class life in Paris, Campton's feelings about the war change again. Campton finds a sort of peace in the white hospital staffed by nuns who read daily battlefield communiqués and in that way draw him back into the war. Their proximity to the front, to the wounded and dying, and especially George's condition, should completely awaken Campton to the horrors of war, but it does not. He believes, we are told later, "in the regenerative power of war—the salutary shock of great moral and social upheavals . . . and never more intensely than at George's bedside at Doullens, in that air so cleansed by passion and pain that mere living seemed a meaningless gesture compared to the chosen surrender of life" (176).[42]

Once he returns to Paris, Campton sees more clearly the superficiality of the wealthy Americans with whom he had "forgotten the war," but he also quickly abandons that idealism of Doullens. His former "friends" now sicken him, especially "[p]oor fatuous Mayhew" (176) who is staging a coup at the Friends of French Art, in Campton's words, "an ugly little allegory of Germany's manoeuvring the world into war" (196). Echoing the words of Troy Belknap in *The Marne*, Campton is "sick to the point of wanting to chuck it all—to chuck everything connected with this hideous world that was dancing and flirting and money-making on the great red mounds of dead" (176). Even in this accusation against the poseurs of the war, Wharton uses the rhetoric of the prosaic Walkyrie. The great red mounds of dead, while a stunning reality, was also a romantic idealization of death. Back on a more even keel, Campton does continue to paint; this time, however, it is the war-worn face of old Madame Lebel, who sacrifices four sons in the defense of France, that occupies his easel. After his old friend Dastrey loses his nephew Louis, Campton asks him, "If we're giving all we care for so that those little worms can reopen their dance-halls on the ruins, what in God's name is left?" (193). But when it is time for George to return to the front, he does so with Campton's blessing. When George departs for the second time, he tells his father, "We chaps haven't any futures to dispose of till this job we're in is finished" (201–2), and Campton, "in his heart of hearts . . . knew he was glad" of George's departure (200). Campton, of course, will make the supreme sacrifice himself by the novel's end. Wounded a second time and back in Paris, George succumbs, in one of the few strokes of irony in the novel, the day America enters the war.

Edith Wharton believed in the war as the defense of civilization against German barbarism. She had no use for Americans who did not do what she perceived to be their duty. According to biographer R. W. B. Lewis, Wharton counted Campton among them (457). But in this portrait of a father who tries to hold on to his son at whatever cost, Wharton places more faith than in the false war gods and goddesses who danced on the ruins of civilization. A war goddess herself in the true sense, at least according to her own sensibilities, Wharton understood the nature of peculiar sanity and tried to establish the fine line between it and reasoned recognition of peril.

The War That Will End War

Perhaps the greatest cliché of the Great War was first used by H. G. Wells. A published collection of newspaper pieces, *The War That Will End War* appeared late in 1914, but Wells also wrote almost daily letters to *The Times* and *The Nation*. Wells's letters and the pieces that appear in *War* argue for what he calls "a war against militarism."[43] In the article, "Why Britain Went to War," Wells fills his pages with oxymorons designed to promote the war against Germany. "[T]his is now a war for peace," he insists. "It aims straight at disarmament. It aims at a settlement that shall stop this sort of thing for ever. Every soldier who fights against Germany now is a crusader against war. This, the greatest of all wars, is not just another war—it is the last war!"[44] This rhetoric very obviously foreshadows phrases which would be used in a more dangerous way to obfuscate inexplicable actions in later wars. In his classic essay "Politics and the English Language," George Orwell refers, by way of example, to the term "pacification," a euphemism used to gloss over the destruction of towns and villages in wartime.[45] During the Vietnam war, the catchphrase was, "We had to destroy the village to save it." Of course Wells is not condoning the murder of civilians or the indiscriminate bombing of cities and towns with his rhetoric. His writings, fiction and nonfiction alike, deplore such action. Nor would there seem to be in Orwell's words a "gap between [his] real and [his] declared aims."[46] Wells believes his words are true, accurate. And yet the illogic of word choice here fosters the coinage of cliché and the spread of jingoism just as readily as deliberate obfuscation; it promotes peculiar sanity. Wells blames the war—and the German militarism that started it, which he calls "organized scoundrelism"—not on the German people but on the Kaiser and on Krupps, the German manufacturer of arms; but this does not cool his war fervor.[47] The idealism expressed in these phrases might not have been expected of a writer who had predicted such a conflagration in his previous writings. Michael Foot, in his biography of Wells, argues that "the paradox [of Wells's predictions] was that, when the catastrophe came, he himself seemed to be swept along by the same fevers."[48]

In 1918, two years after the publication of *Mr. Britling,* Wells was appointed to a committee to serve the Director of Propaganda in Enemy Countries, Viscount Northcliffe, a sort of British William Randolph Hurst whose newspapers thrived on Yellow journalism. Wells became First Director of German Section. *Secrets of Crewe House* chronicles the efforts of the Propaganda Committee to undermine the solidarity of the enemy abroad. In the preface to a memorandum on German susceptibility to propaganda, Wells declares that "German minds are particularly susceptible to systematic statements,"[49] an observation that stereotypes German thinking. But even in this preface, Wells continues to argue that "to establish a world peace that shall preclude the resumption of war" is the aim of the Allies in fighting the war.[50] Wells gathered information about economic conditions in Germany and wrote a memorandum on constructing a propaganda campaign there. While biographer Michael Coren argues that in 1914 Wells "evinced an almost pathological hatred of Germany and all things German,"[51] in "Why Britain Went to War," Wells staunchly maintains that "we are fighting without any hatred of the German people."[52] Lord Northcliffe, on the other hand, continued in his newspapers, according to Wells, to engage in "a campaign of indiscriminate and irrational denunciation of all things German,"[53] a pursuit that caused Wells in July of 1918 to resign his position as Director of German Section. Wells maintained that he had been trying to reassure "all republican, pacific, and liberal minded Germans" and that Northcliffe's hate campaign, his Yellow journalism, was undermining those efforts.[54] Here we see a fine distinction between Northcliffe's hate rhetoric and Wells's "rational" propaganda. True, Wells eschewed the kind of anti-Germanism that stones German dogs in the streets.[55] Yet he relied on war clichés, many of which he created, and his fictional counterpart, Mr. Britling, gives in, for a time, to his own anti-German sentiments. And both Wells and his character Britling believed without hesitation, as did Edith Wharton, commonly reported atrocity stories, stories Northcliffe published that dehumanized and vilified the ordinary German soldier. Atrocity stories often originated in "official" sources such as the Bryce Report,[56] which contains hundreds of eyewitness testimonials from refugees and soldiers chronicling German brutality. Public distribution of official documents such as the Bryce Report gives credence to rumors that are then mythologized in Northcliffe's newspapers and in propaganda art, pamphlets and posters, further inflaming already angry citizens against "the enemy"; these images pick up where Wells's propaganda "phrases" leave off.

These atrocity stories, true or not, backed by nationalistic idealism, find their way into propaganda art. Already we have seen in Australian posters the presentation of the German soldier as an apelike figure. British and American posters do the same. An American Liberty Bond poster with the title "Beat Back the Hun" by F. Strothmann (fig. 3.1) depicts the head and shoulders of an apelike soldier in a pickelhaube pulling the horizon toward him as if to devour it. Another Liberty Bond poster called "Hun or Home" by Raleigh (fig. 3.2) shows a grossly featured soldier, once again in a pickelhaube, threatening a young girl and a baby over the corpse of their mother, an image repeated in testimonials from the Bryce report.[57] Posters such as "Hunger," which was put out by the U.S. Food Administration, also relied on images of starving Belgian women and children. (fig. 3.3) Men such as the fictional Mayhew in *Son* and the not-so-fictional Northcliffe relied on the mythologization of atrocity stories to further their own ends. For those citizens immersed in the fear and horror of war, resisting the appeal of such images would have been difficult, especially when contemporary wisdom so soundly repeated their appeal. A pervasive atmosphere of peculiar sanity is thus created. In *Mr. Britling Sees it Through*, Wells chronicles that creation, and in so doing, aids it.

Hockey and War at the Dower House: Wells's *Mr. Britling Sees It Through*

Like John Campton, Mr. Britling at first believes there will be no war. Early in the novel, Britling tells us that he doesn't believe "human weakness and folly [will] ever let the mine actually explode."[58] He has seen France and Germany bickering before and is sure that "at bottom Germany [is] sane and her militarism a bluff" (125). When Germany invades Belgium, Britling senses the insanity of the proceedings, but falls immediately into his own sort of clichéd hostility. Admitting that he was wrong to believe war would disappear, Britling goes on to declare that "the world is altogether mad. And so there is nothing else for us to do but win . . ." (171). Britling's militarism has been apparent from the beginning of the novel; curiously, it is presented from the perspective of the American, Mr. Direck, who has come to England to invite Mr. Britling to lecture to a group back home. Direck is assaulted almost immediately on his arrival with talk of the field hockey game played every Sunday afternoon at Matchings Easy, Mr. Britling's home. Direck decides he will sit out the game, but everyone he tells of his plans advises him on how to play the

Fig. 3.1. World War I poster "Beat Back the Hun" by Fred Strothmann

Fig. 3.2. World War I poster "Hun or Home" by Henry Patrick Raleigh

Fig. 3.3. World War I poster "Hunger" by Henry Patrick Raleigh

game which becomes a metaphor for militarism, down to the insistence that everyone join in. When the actual war starts, of course, Direck cannot join in because of American neutrality, a subject causing arguments between Direck and Cecily Corner. But hockey does not permit neutrality and Direck must "join up." When one of the Britlings' female guests emerges from the house dressed in a short skirt and shin guards, Direck thinks she looks like a "short stout dismounted Valkyr" (79). Direck finds himself on the opposite side of the field from Cecily, a young woman who has sparked his interest; Direck tells himself chivalrously that he will "be very gentle with Cecily, and see that she didn't get hurt" (80). Of course, Direck quickly learns that Cecily is among the best on the field. In the description of the first goal, we are told that "the struggle . . . ceased to be a game and became something between a fight and a social gathering" (83). Dialogue is punctuated by emphatic "whacks" until Direck's team scores. At half time, all the combatants are hot but happy and "in everybody's eyes [shines] the light of battle" (84). Monday morning after Direck's first game, the news of the assassination of the Austrian archduke hits the papers.

Wells is not the first, or indeed the last, to link sports and war. In a poem called "Disabled," Wilfred Owen describes a multiple amputee sitting in the park in a wheelchair. Remembering the wound that took his legs, the soldier thinks

> One time he liked a blood-smear down his leg,
> After the matches, carried shoulder-high.
> It was after football, when he'd drunk a peg,
> He thought he'd better join.—He wonders why.[59]

Paul Fussell writes of "the sporting spirit," an emotion embedded in British culture long before the Great War. Sir Henry Newbolt, a longtime friend of the beleaguered commander of British forces Douglas Haig, creates, in his poem "Vitaï Lampada," the image of the perfect British schoolboy/soldier who treats all life's challenges as a cricket game. As the soldier faces death at the hand of "natives," he remembers the cry, "Play up!"[60] Lord Northcliffe also uses sports metaphors to describe the bravery of British tank corps, young men who "enter upon their task in a sporting spirit with the same cheery enthusiasm as they would show for football."[61] Fussell goes on to tell the story of Captain W. P. Nevill, a company commander who gave a football to each of his four platoons and offered a prize to the platoon that kicked the football to the German lines. Nevill, of course, was killed in the charge.[62]

Wells's focus on the long hockey games in *Mr. Britling* serves a multiple purpose. First, the games underscore the innocence and ignorance of the summer of 1914. But the games also reveal an enjoyment of combat, a pleasure in the defense of territory. In a letter home from the front, Mr. Britling's son Hugh describes the war as "absolutely the best game in the world" (321). Refuting his father's pamphlets that emphasize war's malignity, Hugh goes on to say that war is "such a big game. Instead of being fenced in to a field and tied down to one set of tools as you are in almost every other game, you have all the world to play with, and you may use whatever you can use" (321). This remark explains Britling's willingness to shift gears once the war starts. In thinly veiled autobiography, Britling writes a treatise called "And Now War Ends" in which he repeats all the "phrases that had to be said now" (180). Like John Campton, Mr. Britling may vacillate in his war fervor. When a neighbor drives by in her automobile laden with stores of food she plans to hoard, Britling is scandalized. But days later, when he journeys to London to volunteer to the war office for civilian duty, he is rebuffed by a war machine set in its ways and highly exclusive. Britling is angry and believes "Business as Usual" and "Leave things to Kitchener" have become the "truest form of patriotism" (209).

Britling's naïveté, placed in the context of anti-German sentiment, moves closer to peculiar sanity as the war begins to affect his household. Teddy, Britling's secretary, secures a commission for which Britling helps pay, and Mr. Britling's underage son Hugh joins the Territorials (243). Hugh, without Mr. Britling's knowledge, has lied about his age and soon finds himself at the front. Explaining why he has joined the Territorials, Hugh echoes Wharton's George Campton when he tells Mr. Britling, "this job has to be done by someone" (245). Then he reflects on his father's propaganda to which he points as justification. "Haven't you been saying as much all day? . . . It's like turning out to chase a burglar or suppress a mad dog. It's like necessary sanitation . . ." (245). Although he does not acknowledge it, Britling's rhetoric comes back to haunt him.

The Britlings also take in a Belgian refugee, Mr. Van der Pant, who has seen the killing firsthand on his retreat from the war zone. After listening to stories of dismembered civilians, of "pools of blood, and the torn-off arms and shoulder-blades of women" (252), Britling interprets Mr. Van der Pant's feelings as endorsing genocide of the German people. The Belgian "regarded [Germans] as people to be killed," Britling tells us. "They were just an evil accident that had happened to Belgium and mankind. They had to be destroyed" (252). Britling reports these inclinations without comment on their implications. Ironically, because Mr. Van der Pant left his possessions behind in Belgium, the Britlings give him the house slippers that belonged to the children's German tutor Herr Heinrich, who has gone off to fight for his country. The slippers fit perfectly. Fated to die in a Russian prison, Herr Heinrich becomes a symbol for Mr. Britling, the only thing that keeps Britling from believing that "Germany and the whole German race was essentially wicked, essentially a canting robber nation" (274).

But Britling's charity is tested when Aunt Wilshire, his cousin, is mortally wounded in a Zeppelin attack. Britling learns of Aunt Wilshire's injuries after a lengthy passage in which he tries, unsuccessfully, to exonerate "ordinary" Germans of war crimes. Mr. Britling "[fights] against the persuasion that the whole mass of a great civilised nation could be inspired by a genuine and sustained hatred" (268). And yet the question of hatred is inescapable. Britling first confronts the idea of German "malignity" (the title of this section of the novel), when he sees a collection of German caricatures, largely of the English, that display a "bellowing [German] patriotism and a limitless desire to hurt and humiliate" (271). While Wells does not specifically state this, he insinuates that the caricatures involve emasculation of British men. They are, he admits, "the sort of thing that might come out of a lunatic asylum" (271). Here Mr. Britling relies on his memories of Herr Heinrich to keep himself from believing, as many British were then coming to believe, that Germans were intrinsically evil. This is the moment in British history when naturalized German citizens were attacked in their shops and homes (274–5). But not even Mr. Britling can resist atrocity stories. His memories of Herr Heinrich and of happy visits to Germany before the war vanish. He is "flooded with self-righteous indignation, a self-righteous indignation that was indeed entirely Teutonic in its quality, that for a time drowned out his former friendship and every kindly disposition towards Germany, that inspired him with destructive impulses, and obsessed him with a desire to hear of death and more death in every German town and home" (277). Assigning the quality of self-righteousness itself to stereotypical German arrogance, Britling almost sees the connection between his own behavior and that of the "enemy," but still his hatred grows. He admits that "every day some new detail of evil beat into his mind" (278). His example is an atrocity story of a German soldier who admits to killing a woman and her baby at the orders of his superior officer (278). Once again he almost makes the connection with atrocities committed by British colonialists, but his hatred of Germans is not abated. But the concept of atrocity touches the Dower House directly when Mr. Britling arrives at Filmington-on-Sea to visit his Aunt Wilshire. Critically injured in a Zeppelin attack, she barely recognizes him; out of her head, she believes that spies have sought her because of earlier remarks she has made about the Kaiser. Her death soon after he arrives at the hospital throws Britling further into his ruminations on the matter of evil and hatred. In response to the question, "Is the whole scheme of nature evil?" (294), Britling considers various kinds of cruelty including that committed by children. Once more he is led to self-righteousness and moral indignation, and once more stereotypes German behavior. "These Germans were an unsubtle people," he tells us, "they were prone to moral indignation; and moral indignation is the mother of most of the cruelty in the world" (295).

All the while, of course, Britling feeds off his own moral indignation. Harking back to the early days of the war when his writing gloried in the opportunity to put an end to war with war, Britling considers the possibility that hate ultimately becomes a "corrective" to living a stale life, that there may be "a creative and corrective impulse behind all hate" (296). Before he left the Dower House, Britling had been working on an essay, "The Anatomy of Hate." Wandering under the night sky after he has bid Aunt Wilshire farewell, Britling's own hatred escalates, and he considers his attempts to begin the essay. Returning to the idea that hate is a source of creativity, Britling asks himself, "Is not this malignity indeed only the apelike precursor of the great disciplines of a creative state?" (296). Whether he means political state or state of mind is not clear, but he continues to be concerned with what he perceives to be English indolence. It is, he thinks, one of the qualities of the British that enrages German efficiency (295). Perched on a rock by the sea, Britling finally calms himself by thinking of Christ's words on the cross, *"Father, forgive them, for they know not what they do"* (298, italics Wells's). Heretofore an agnostic, Britling falls back on religion when he cannot address the scope of humans' capacity for violence, their capacity for cruelty and evil, although he dismisses the idea that hate may be evil.

Britling turns to religion again at the end of the novel when, after the deaths of Hugh and Herr Heinrich, he attempts to write to Herr Heinrich's parents in Germany. Unable to find words that can justify such losses, Britling thinks of God, to whom he refers as the "Captain of Mankind," (428), an obviously military metaphor, and concludes that the two slain sons have shown him God (432). The subtle changes Britling has undergone during the first two years of the war illustrate the extent to which even the most intellectual among us fall prey to peculiar sanity. Highly articulate at the beginning of the war, now two years later Britling is stricken mute by the force of socially sanctioned violence, violence he has with his own words promoted. We may see his descent into peculiar sanity as similar to shell shock, an emotional response to conditions so horrendous that they remain outside the pale of human comprehension, even though they are conditions wrought by human action. His war fervor at the beginning of the novel, his use of oxymorons, is not rational, but because there is a national movement afloat, he does not sense his illogic. When this man of ideas resorts to Bible verses to explain the irrational death of the harmless Aunt Wilshire, he has come full circle in his peculiar sanity. In a letter home from the front, Hugh Britling comments on the conscripts used in the German army. These men "aren't really soldiers at all. . . They have to see the war as something romantic and melodramatic, or as something moral, or as tragic fate. They have got to bellow songs about 'Deutschland,' or drag in 'Gott'" (322). With a few references changed, this passage could refer to Mr. Britling himself.

Seen as the war to end wars, the Great War is certainly both romantic and melodramatic. H. G. Wells believed that defeating German militarism meant an end to war. Hindsight has revealed to us the romanticism, indeed the folly, of this belief. But at the time, Wells's words carried with them the weight of his literary reputation. Published in 1916, *Mr. Britling Sees It Through* sold well in England and in the United States, revitalizing Wells's career after the critical failure of *Ann Veronica*. Not yet ready for the cynicism of Hemingway, dos Passos, and cummings, readers identified with his moral outrage and his struggle for understanding. He coined all the "phrases that had to be said now" (180) because the "moral misery" of the war left others bereft of the ability to speak, as it ultimately leaves Mr. Britling.

In *A Son at the Front* and *Mr. Britling Sees It Through*, we have seen how peculiar sanity allows propaganda—through the proliferation of cliché, and the dissemination of atrocity stories, and the circulation of rumors originating from official sources—to fan already smouldering fires of hatred. But beyond maintaining the malignity of which Mr. Britling speaks, peculiar sanity, by proliferating atrocity stories, forces normally rational people into irrational behavior.

Chapter 4
SPIES AND LIES

The Hun Next Door

"Spies and Lies," an advertisement placed by the U.S. Committee on Public Information, appears in the July 1918 issue of *Pictorial Review* cautioning Americans to beware of eavesdropping German spies. The ad features a photograph of two women discussing what appears to be a letter from the front while a well-dressed gentleman, pretending to read a newspaper in a nearby chair, obviously listens to their conversation (fig. 4.1). But beyond promoting paranoia, the ad copy goes on to preach against seditious gossip and to ask citizens to "[s]end the names of such persons [who gossip] . . . to the Department of Justice, Washington. Give all the details you can, with names of witnesses if possible. . . ."[1] In detailing the kind of gossip the Committee deems inappropriate, the ad itself hints at impropriety. "Do not," the ad admonishes,

> become a tool of the Hun by passing on the malicious, disheartening rumors which he so eagerly sows. Remember he asks no better service than to have you spread his lies of disasters to our soldiers and sailors, gross scandals in the Red Cross, cruelties, neglect and wholesale executions in our camps, drunkenness and vice in the Expeditionary Force, and other tales certain to disturb American patriots and to bring anxiety and grief to American parents.[2]

Americans who had not heard gossip about the Red Cross might have well asked questions here. The ad does not warn against gossiping about the enemy, and we have indeed seen the extent to which atrocity stories, true or not, become part of the mythology of war, and thereby part of its peculiar sanity. Once mythologized, atrocity stories serve the war machine as readily as official propaganda, drawing even the most intellectual citizens into the war effort. Without the aid of rumor, atrocity stories would perish. Their persistence depends on neighbor telling neighbor, friend telling friend; they depend on the emergence of peculiar sanity. We may recall Edith Wharton's letter to Sara Norton asking her to "spread . . . Abroad" the stories of German atrocities.[3] The effect of gossip and rumor on civilian

Fig. 4.1. "Spies and Lies," an advertisement placed by the Committee on Public Information, in the July 1918 issue of *Pictorial Review,* a ladies' fashion magazine

life in the story of my mother and her perm comes to mind. But other kinds of rumors and gossip affect both the lives of ordinary citizens and national interests. The Committee on Public Information expects citizens to inform on one another, to root out sedition; and, as the McCarthy hearings have since proven, informing often becomes more important than the truth, and personal vendettas gain a role in the implementation of public policy. In such an atmosphere, the force of rumor becomes so strong, in fact, that it itself generates peculiar sanity. Any kind of aberrant behavior can be deemed treason, as can any offhand remark. We have seen the force of convention at work in prewar culture in both Britain and America; we have noted the strength of gossip and the fear of exposure. In *The Good Soldier,* the Ashburnhams live down the scandal of the Kilsyte case, carefully keeping the ugly truth of their relationship secret. When his wife elopes, Alvan Hervey's main concern is the threat of scandal, not his fear of losing her. As we remember from *Heart of Darkness,* the fear of scandal rivals the fear of the gallows.[4] But within the domain of war, the potential for damage, not only to the enemy's reputation and to the reputation of Allied troops but also to the individual, increases exponentially. When everyone, even the writers who are often society's most astute critics, speaks the language of jingoism, no one is safe from the danger of "exposure." Peculiar sanity makes itself felt on the home front, and rumor is its most reliable medium.

Trudi Tate, in *Modernism, History, and the First World War,* focuses on how the pleasure of gossip becomes something prurient when it is used to spread atrocity stories. In a chapter devoted to Ford Madox Ford's *Parade's End,* Tate emphasizes the depth to which gossip goes, especially in wartime; she argues that "the stories people produce—rumours, lies, statistics —are integral to the war, and can affect the lives and deaths of large numbers of people."[5] Used as a recruiting tool, atrocity stories certainly do affect the lives of the men who enlist and the families who relinquish them to military service. "Belgium, the Lusitania, and Edith Cavell," the reasons Leonarad Dawson gives for enlisting in *One of Ours,* all involve well publicized atrocity stories. But in *Parade's End,* personal rumors affect the life of protagonist Christopher Tietjens, as rumors also touched the life of Ford himself. Tate rightly argues that "[g]ossip is fundamental to social organization. . . ."[6] But her assertion that "it is an important source of pleasure as well as a mechanism for policing people" glosses over the deadly seriousness of the policing element and overlooks the crucial way in which truth, lies, and social control interact, with social control overshadowing the distinction between truth and lies.[7] Social control must be achieved at whatever cost. In the atmosphere of war's peculiar sanity, rumor serves the forces of social control. It becomes a way of weeding out nonconformity and promoting jingoism and thereby an atmosphere of peculiar sanity.

The sinister nature of this force becomes fully manifest in the McCarthy hearings during the early fifties. But during the Great War, witch hunts also flourished in America. In *Over Here,* a study of American society during World War I, David M. Kennedy examines the wartime actions of, among others, Postmaster General Albert Sidney Burleson and Attorney General Thomas W. Gregory, men who "were less interested in propagandizing the people, and more disposed to direct methods of extinguishing dissent, by fair means or foul."[8] Burleson and Gregory used the Espionage Act of 1917 and the later amendment to that act, which became known as the Sedition Act, effectively to silence published opposition to the Great War. Burleson withdrew mailing privileges from a number of Socialist publications after promising not to do so unless the publications contained "treasonable or seditious matter."[9] Unfortunately, according to Kennedy, Burleson believed Socialist papers did largely contain treasonable and seditious matter.[10] Burleson even used the Trading with the Enemy Act to censor foreign-language newspapers. Gregory, in a more chilling act, obtained funding for a vigilante organization, the American Protective League. The APL, which Kennedy calls a "band of amateur sleuths and loyalty enforcers," went beyond the call of the "Spies and Lies" ad; they were "a rambunctious, unruly *posse comitatus*" that "bugged, burglarized, slandered, and illegally arrested other Americans."[11] This group of reactionaries would not normally have had mainstream support; their rise to power illustrates how fear and nationalism give way to peculiar sanity during war, how gossip and rumor achieve the power of legal indictment. As Kennedy correctly argues, "That an organization such as the APL was allowed to exist at all testifies to the unusual state of American society in World War I, when fear corrupted usually sober minds. . . ."[12]

The IWW, the socialist Industrial Workers of the World, was particularly subject to scrutiny and arrest. Ralph Chaplin, poet and IWW member, was sentenced to twenty years in prison. According to Scott Nearing's introduction to Chaplin's collection *Bars and Shadows,* Chaplin was jailed for "the expression of his opinions."[13] Nearing's description of the accusations against Chaplin and his associates echoes the "Spies and Lies" ad, or a list of the APL's aims. According to Nearing, "[t]he government did not produce a single witness to show that the war had been obstructed by their activities; but it was argued that the agitation which they had carried on by means of speeches, articles, pamphlets, meetings and organizing campaigns would quite naturally hamper the country in its war work."[14] In a poem called the "I.W.W. Prison Song," Chaplin describes the kind of vigilantism of which the APL was guilty.

> At us the blood-hounds are let loose,
> The lynch-mobs with the knotted noose;
> In legal sanctioned mask and gown
> The New Black Hundreds hunt us down.[15]

Meant to be sung, Chaplin's poem may reflect more union solidarity than poetic strength, but the sentiment is no exaggeration. Kennedy does speak of lynchings, specifically that of Robert Prager, a German-born American who was brutally lynched near St. Louis in April of 1918, not for his politics but for his place of birth. His attackers were caught and tried, but were found not guilty.[16]

In Great Britain, the Defense of the Realm Act, or DORA, supported uniformity of thought and provided the force of law to silence dissension. Samuel Hynes in *A War Imagined: The First World War and English Culture* examines the effects of DORA on society and, more specifically, on the arts.

According to Hynes, DORA gave the British government almost complete control over the lives of British citizens, including "the censoring of wartime English thought and expression."[17] The most obvious difference between the British and American laws during this period is that the British law were enforced without the aid of vigilantes, although gossip and informing remain important elements. In its inception, DORA seemed to lack teeth. It gave the British government the power to prevent communication with the enemy and to secure its docks and railways, but not necessarily to control individuals. But like the American Espionage Act DORA was amended to include prevention of "the spread of reports likely to cause disaffection or alarm," an addition which in its vagueness allowed the government the authority to censor whatever it deemed inflammatory.[18] DORA saw a number of English pacifists jailed, including Bertrand Russell. And socialists were targeted in Britain as well as in the U.S. Hynes cites the case of Fenner Brockway, a socialist whose satirical play about a war between England and Germany, *The Devil's Business,* was actually written in February 1914 but not published until after the start of the war. Brockway, not totally insensitive to wartime protocol, changed some of the play's more inflammatory references and removed the names of specific countries. Still, he was eventually imprisoned.[19]

Like the Espionage Act and the Sedition Act, DORA made the expression of dissent a punishable offense, whether in art or in other kinds of printed material, and discouraged the spread of rumors having to do with Allied activities. But as we have seen repeatedly on both sides of the Atlantic, newspapers and pamphlets based their patriotic appeals on undocumented enemy actions, stories that were often apocryphal, arising out of rumors spread by refugees as they fled German occupation and by vacationing internationals as they fled inconvenience. Lies became part of official dogma and the force of rumor placed in jeopardy anyone with German heritage as well as anyone who was not a flag-waving patriot. In the U.S. heartland where Robert Prager was lynched, anti-German furor was rampant. Kennedy reports that the governor of Iowa forbade any public use of the German language, and words such as hamburger and sauerkraut, by then part of the American vocabulary, were replaced by the jingoistic euphemisms "liberty sandwich" and "liberty cabbage."[20] Posters also promoted anti-German feelings. A 1917 Liberty Bonds poster by J. Allen St. John, "Blot It Out," features a bloody handprint with the caption, "The Hun—His Mark." (fig. 4.2) Willa Cather depicts similar anti-Germanism, as we have seen, in *One of Ours.* But many British and American citizens had German relatives. Robert Graves's mother, although born in England,

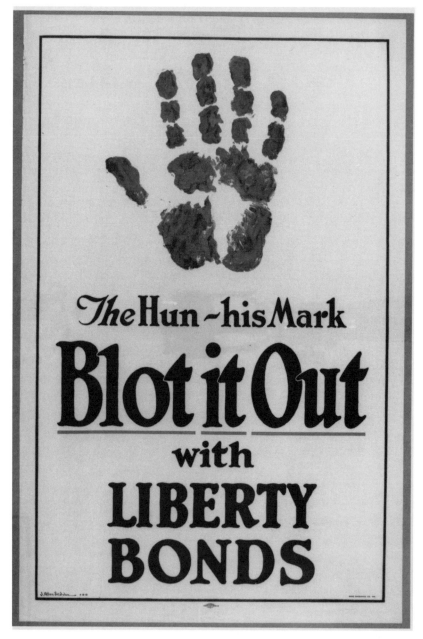

Fig. 4.2. World War I poster "The Hun—His Mark" by J. Allen St. John

was of German ancestry. Graves describes discovering other British officers who had enlisted, as he did, to prove their loyalty to England. Four out of five officers in his company mess had German relatives. Graves quotes one of the men who believed his enlistment had prevented him being accused of spying. "If I'd put it off for a month or two," the officer explains, "they'd have accused me of being a German spy. As it is, I have an uncle interned in Alexandra Palace, and my father's only been allowed to retain the membership of his golf club because he has two sons in the trenches."[21]

Through rumor and gossip, the government kept track of those who had German associations. According to Max Saunders, Ford Madox Ford's father, Francis Hueffer, emigrated from Germany to England in 1869 and, although he anglicized the family name Hüffer, Ford later abandoned it altogether.[22] In July 1915, Ford enlisted at the age of forty-one, and, like Graves, obtained a commission in a Welsh regiment. After enlisting, Ford had his middle name changed from Hermann to Madox after his maternal grandfather, Ford Madox Brown, in what Saunders calls "an official gesture of allegiance to his British grandfather."[23] Even though during the first year of the war Ford wrote two propaganda pieces, *When Blood Is Their Argument* and *Between St. Dennis and St. George,* Saunders maintains he knew he was still thought by some to be pro-German and so believed enlistment would silence his detractors.[24] All the same, when Ford (who was then still Hueffer) changed his middle name, he also had his British nationality confirmed.[25] Because of the weight of gossip and suspicion, of accusation and fingerpointing, Ford had little choice but to proclaim his patriotism as loudly as possible, and enlisting was the most convincing way to do so. Still, there were some who attacked Ford after his enlistment. In one of the most inexplicable personal attacks of the day, what Saunders calls a "squalid affair,"[26] Ford was pilloried in the *New Witness* in a review of *Zeppelin Nights,* the book he cowrote with Violet Hunt. The review was written by J. K. Prothero, pseudonym of Ada Elizabeth Jones, who not long after married the editor of the journal, Cecil Chesterton, G. K. Chesterton's brother. In this review, Jones "accuses" Ford of being Jewish and a coward because the book describes the fear involved in experiencing a Zeppelin attack. J. M. Barrie, in Ford's defense, wrote to point out that Ford was then in uniform and Catholic, not Jewish, and that "the real case against Lieutenant Hueffer . . . is that he considers Ezra Pound a good poet."[27] Not amused by Barrie's joke, Jones fired back that "these facts hardly being of European importance I am content to be labelled 'ignorant' concerning them, as I am of the 'fact' that because a man adopts the Catholic religion he ceases to be a Jew. One might as reasonably say that if a black-a-moor adopts Calvanism [*sic*] he immediately turns white."[28] The importance of this racist and anti-Semitic diatribe against Ford lies in its focus on irrelevant details and on its complete and public dismissal of facts—all attributes of gossip in peace and in war. This malicious assertion fortunately carried no political weight and most likely lost the *New Witness* subscribers, among them Wells, who wrote to G. K. Chesterton to complain of his brother's publication of the review. Calling Prothero "a disgusting little greaser," Wells goes on to say about Cecil Chesterton, "instead of pleading his age and his fat and taking refuge from service in a greasy obesity as your brother has done, [Ford] is serving his country."[29] But had Ford not then been in the service, the persecution could well have continued beyond the pages of the *New Witness.*

An even more telling illustraion of the way rumor develops into action concerns the incident involving Ford, D. H. Lawrence, and his wife Frieda. Frieda was a cousin of the legendary German pilot, Manfred von Richthofen, the Red Baron. No agreement exists as to what happened or what the effects of the incident were; that is, the quality of rumor still surrounds the incident. Saunders reports the incident from several perspectives—Frieda's, Violet Hunt's, and Catherine Wells's. Jeffrey Meyers, in his biography of Lawrence, reports the incident to explain why he believes Lawrence's *The Rainbow* was suppressed in 1915 and the Lawrences ejected from Cornwall in 1917. The Lawrences were, in 1915, living in Sussex and in March of that year, Ford, Violet Hunt, and Catherine Wells, H. G. Wells's wife, went to see them. According to Ford, C. F. G. Masterman asked him to visit in order to ascertain how badly the persecution was affecting Lawrence. Most likely, Lawrence was not there, but visiting Bertrand Russell (a problem in itself because of Russell's pacifism). An argument appears to have ensued between Frieda and Violet Hunt, although accounts have Frieda also arguing with Catherine Wells to the point where she and Ford left the house. Hunt later reported that Frieda had said, "Dirty Belgians! Who cares for them!" which Frieda denied.[30] More important than this squabble, however, is the accusation that Ford went to see Lawrence to spy on him for Masterman, and that the negative report Ford turned in got *The Rainbow* suppressed and the Lawrences kicked out of Cornwall. Jeffrey Meyers's account of the incident reads like a Hollywood gossip column; much of the information is thirdhand, that is, it is true gossip. "In 1957 [David] Garnett told Edward Nehls that Ford was desperate to prove that he was not German and that in another anti-German propaganda book, *When Blood Is Their Argument* (1915), he spoke of his quite imaginary Russian ancestors,"[31] a charge quickly disputed by the preface to the book, which we shall soon see. Nevertheless, the "Garnett told Nehls that Ford" construction maintains the gossipy quality of the story. Meyers continues, "Three years later, Harry Moore told [Richard] Aldington that Garnett 'believes that Ford warned the government in 1915 that the Lawrences were pro-German, and that all their troubles during the rest of the war stemmed from Ford's report.'" On the basis of this remark and Aldington's reply, Meyers concludes that Ford betrayed the Lawrences.[32] Saunders points out that although Frieda, in her account of the incident, lambasts Ford's behavior, she never connects it to their wartime troubles, nor did Lawrence. However, H. D., in her autobiographical novel, *Bid Me To Live* touches on the Lawrence's expulsion from Cornwall—Rico and Elsa appear at Julia's door carrying what possessions they have been able to escape with and later at dinner, Rico shouts at Elsa, "It's you, your fault, you damn Prussian."[33]

While none of these details proves Ford's innocence, Saunders cannot substantiate the charges against him and does not believe them, nor do I. Given the anti-German sentiment during the war, and Frieda's high profile cousin, it should come as no surprise that they, like Ford and Robert Graves's fellow officers, should be suspected of sedition. The surprise would be that they were not suspected. But the spiral of rumor here illustrates once more the way retribution can be achieved by the merest of suggestions. David Garnett apparently spread other rumors about Ford. As Saunders puts it, he was "very liberal with unsubstantiated malicious gossip about Ford."[34] These rumors, along with the gossip about Ford's relationship with Violet Hunt, provide a real-life source for the fictional rumors that plague Christopher Tietjens, if not in substance, then certainly in persistence. And as rumors often are, the ones about Ford were contradictory.

Ford was in fact attacked himself in the early days of the war when he was living in Selsey with Violet Hunt. Both Judd and Saunders report that in the winter of 1914–15 he was threatened with expulsion from the county. Ford connected the threat with Violet's friend and landlord Edward Heron Allen who was extremely anti-German and, according to Saunders, in love with Hunt.[35] At dinner one evening when Ford was present, Allen suggested the possibility of a German submarine invasion in West Sussex and frightened most of the diners except Ford. Judd records that the next morning Ford wrote a story called "The Scaremonger" in which he caricatured Allen as "old Blue Funk," a local squire who "spends every night on the beach in a rough-rider's uniform with three revolvers."[36] The story was published in *The Bystander* as propaganda, but Allen was incensed, and shortly thereafter the Chief Constable demanded Ford leave the county. Only C. F. G. Masterman's intervention allowed Ford to stay. Allen later wrote to Hunt calling Ford a "German Journalist."[37]

Peculiar sanity in the form of the witchhunt thrives on gossip and hatred, and campaigns such as "Spies and Lies" survive only by the grace of gossip and hatred. The unorthodox Ford became the focus of such attacks because they served to differentiate between "us" and "them." If Ford was not "one of us," then he must be one of "them."

Blood and Kultur

Ford bore the brunt of anti-German gossip and propaganda, but, like Wells, he also wrote anti-German propaganda before he enlisted. His close friend C. F. G. Masterman was head of a secret department formed to combat German propaganda in America. Masterman used his position as head of the National Health Insurance Commission in Wellington House as a cover for the propaganda mission. He recruited many of the well-known writers of the period including Hardy and Wells at a meeting at Wellington House in September of 1914. Ford, not present at this meeting, accepted a commission from Masterman and began the first of two books, *When Blood Is Their Argument*. Saunders maintains that in the two books "Ford's arguments are unusually charitable, for propaganda," and could be applied to all "warring nations."[38] True, the books are not the jingoistic propaganda of Wells, the kind of writing that produces memorable phrases as calls to battle. In fact, both of Ford's books seem inaccessible to all but the most educated and sophisticated readers, and therefore prove virtually worthless as propaganda. And in deference to his father's "South German Catholic origin" Ford differentiates between south Germans whom he regards as "ordinary human beings," and Prussians who are monomaniacal and materialistic.[39] At a time when most of England would have found such an intellectual distinction moot, it is not surprising that many thought Ford pro-German.

Whatever the public's perception and however effective the books, both in some ways seem more insidious than other propaganda because they directly and rationally attack German culture, education, and language, not just stereotypes of German culture.[40] And Ford was, of course, not alone in his debunking of all things Teutonic. Kipling's hatred of the Germans is legendary even before his son John's death, and Conrad, at the end of "Autocracy and War," speaks ill of Germany's materialism and imperialism.

Looking toward the future from the vantage point of 1905, Conrad fears the weakening of his old oppressor Russia, which he believes "has given a foreboding of unwonted freedom to the *Welt-politik.*" In a paraphrase of the French patriot Léon Gambetta, Conrad issues "a warning that, so far as a future of liberty, concord, and justice is concerned: '*Le Prussianisme—voilà l'ennemi!*'"[41] Wells squelches his anti-German sentiments only long enough in *Mr. Britling Sees It Through* for Britling to express sympathy for Herr Heinreich and his old parents and to forgive the German aggression that kills Aunt Wilshire. Ford is not so generous. In *When Blood Is Their Argument,* he begins the section entitled "Kultur" with a description of early morning thoughts on the death of Tibullus that are interrupted by the sound of an airplane flying overhead. Ford sees the plane and declares, "*[a]gainst the sky and the clouds it was as clear in outline and in illuminated beauty as is the Victory of Samothrace.*"[42] Immediately on the heels of this romantic image, Ford continues, "And suddenly I heard myself saying to myself: 'Well, thank God, there's an end of the German language.'" This vision is only slightly tempered by his reluctance to imagine "every inhabitant of the German Empire with his throat cut, or her brains blown out."[43] *Between St. Dennis and St. George* is even more vitriolic. Written after *When Blood Is Their Argument,* the book was intended to silence pacifist arguments, among them, those of George Bernard Shaw who, according to Ford, believed "it would be a good thing for England if she were governed by Prussia."[44] By way of answer, Ford asserts, "I hope we are nearing the end of Germany, and I bitterly regret that our minds were ever burdened by the existence of that miserable Power. For our minds, for a generation past, have been burdened by the grossness, the imbecilities, and the materialisms of German minds to an extent that few of us realise."[45] In this hardly "charitable" passage, Ford uses Prussian and German interchangeably. But Ford's verbal violence, his German-bashing, did not stop with these two exercises in propaganda. Explaining Ford's reasons for enlisting at forty-one, Saunders includes Ford's reaction at learning of the combat death of Vorticist sculptor, Henri Gaudier-Brzeska. Long after the war, Ford dramatizes his response in *No Enemy* through the persona of Gringoire, "the writer's friend" who "went to the war."[46] Gringoire recalls reading the notice of Gaudier's death, and remembers his vision of Gaudier, an Emperor in a "low tea-house," a possessor of "Youth, Beauty, Erudition, Fortune, Genius." Gaudier's death is as inexplicable as his life had been and Gringoire suddenly resents those who have kept themselves out of the fray: "I began to want to kill certain people. I still do—for the sake of Gaudier and those few who are like him."[47] Like Claude Wheeler,

Ford/Gringoire compares what is negative about his own culture, in this case London intellectuals, to the German war machine, villainizing both at once. Ford writes of Gaudier, "because of the crowd one hadn't seen him—the crowd of blackmailers, sneak-thieves, suborners, pimps, reviewers, and the commonplace and the indifferent—the Huns of London. Well, it became—and it still more remains! one's duty to try to kill them."[48] Here London intelligentsia receives much of the force of Ford/Gringoire's anger; these are the "literati and the aesthetes [who] were sweating, harder than they ever, ever did after *le mot juste* or the Line of Beauty, to find excuses that should keep them from the trenches . . . "[49] This accusation could surely extend to "J. K. Prothero," the "little greaser" Wells lambasts in the *New Witness.*[50]

Ford was conscious of the conflict that would arise for him by responding to gossip, by asserting his English patriotism and maligning his paternal heritage. Saunders calls our attention to a letter Ford wrote to John Lane asking for the balance of the money Lane owed him for the publication of *The Good Soldier;* in the letter Ford jokes about the conflict, but clearly, it is on his mind. "These are, I know," Ford writes,

> hard up times but I guess I am harder up than you as I have had to give up literature and offer myself for service to George Five; so shortly you may expect to see me pantingly popping cartridges into garrison guns directed against my uncles, cousins and aunts, advancing in pickelhaubes. And presumably if the said uncles cousins and aunts penetrate behind said garrison guns they will suspend me on high. Whereas, though I would daresay you deserve it quite as much, I do not believe they would hang you. So you will perceive the equity of my request.[51]

In fact, Judd and Saunders agree that whatever other motives Ford may have had for joining up, he was patriotic and believed he had a duty to serve his country. Both cite a letter to his mother in which Ford explains, "I cannot imagine taking any other course. If one has enjoyed the privileges of the ruling class of a country all one's life, there seems to be no alternative to fighting for that country if necessary."[52] The "reasoned recognition of peril" expressed here contradicts the peculiar sanity of Ford's propaganda and of *No Enemy.* Ford possessed a complex character, and that complexity allows him to indulge in peculiar sanity while at the same time becoming a victim of it.

Some Do: Ford's *Parade's End*

Parade's End examines peculiar sanity in the form of gossip and rumor from the points of view of Christopher Tietjens, the object of the rumors and, among others, his wife Sylvia, who perpetrates many of them. Most of the rumors serve some personal vendetta although cloaked in patriotism and conformity, just as they did in Ford's life. In *Parade's End,* characters assert their own patriotism by maligning the patriotism of someone else, and Tietjens always seems to be handy. Like John Dowell in *The Good Soldier,* Tietjens refuses to demand the affection of his wife and is thus considered suspect, an outsider in a world of manly men. *Some Do Not,* the first of the four novels, immerses us very quickly into Tietjens's marital troubles and his doomed friendship with Vincent Macmaster, a Scot, author of monographs, and fellow "employee" in the Imperial Department of Statistics. Both relationships flounder, in one way or another, because of rumor. The Tietjenses' marriage is tainted from the start because of Sylvia's fling with Drake, who may or may not be the father of Sylvia's child, the heir to Groby, the ancient Tietjens estate. Sylvia Tietjens is a femme fatale who flirts a great deal and delights in "pulling the strings of shower baths," creating mayhem for the fun of it. Sylvia's flirtations often form the basis of Christopher's troubles. Brownie, the nephew and employee of Tietjens's banker, Lord Port Scatho, hates Tietjens and is in love with Sylvia. Brownie, in an attempt to discredit Tietjens, ignores a letter from Sylvia ordering the bank to deposit a thousand pounds of her money into Christopher's bank account. As a result, Tietjens bounces a check to his club and must resign. In one of the major scenes in *Some Do Not,* Lord Port Scatho, Mark Tietjens, Sylvia, and Christopher hash out the intricate details of Christopher's money that the bounced check propelled into the domain of scandal; they also delve into the question of impropriety in the Macmaster household across the street, which also reflects on Tietjens because he has been seen comforting Edith Ethel Duchemin, Macmaster's wife-in-secret, on a train. The accusations and counter-accusations in the novel are outrageous to the point of being surreal. Sylvia, who has had at least two adulterous affairs, writes to Lord Port Scatho to complain about Edith Ethel "creeping in every Friday under a heavy veil and creeping out every Saturday at four in the morning," because she doesn't "like that sort of thing going on under [her] windows."[53] She believes Edith Ethel is the mistress of both Christopher and Macmaster and declares "it would be like you to have a mistress in common" (157).

At this point, Christopher does not have and has not had a mistress, but because everyone around him is corrupt, he is believed to be as well. Gossip serves to alienate Christopher from most of his acquaintances and, in the beginning, from his brother Mark. The rumors, relayed at the behest of Mark Tietjens to their father, also result in the elder Tietjens's suicide. Sylvia knows how the old man came to find out about the rumors that Christopher has had a child by Valentine Wannop, and tells him before Lord Port Scatho and Mark arrive to discuss Christopher's money. Contrite, it would seem, about her role in this affair, Sylvia screams at Tietjens, "Your father died of a broken heart . . . because your brother's best friend Ruggles told him you were a squit who lived on women's money and had got the daughter of his oldest friend with child" (178). Ruggles accomplishes this feat by working the rumor mill to its fullest capacity.

Ruggles's connection to Mark Tietjens begins when the two occupy the same floor of an apartment house and share a toilet. Because Ruggles has never asked to borrow money from Mark and because he belongs to the same club, Mark "consider[s] him an entirely honorable man" (205). He isn't. As the two shave, Ruggles fills Mark in on all the latest gossip, and when Mark wants to get the latest on Christopher, he enlists Ruggles's help. In a passage outlining fully the characteristics of gossip, Ford describes Ruggles's glee as he sets out on his task, basically to ruin Tietjens.

> Armed then with this commission Mr. Ruggles appears to have displayed extraordinary activity in preparing a Christopher Tietjens dossier. It is not often that an inveterate gossip gets a chance at a man whilst being at the same time practically shielded against the law of libel. And Ruggles disliked Christopher Tietjens with the inveterate dislike of the man who revels in gossip for the man who never gossips. And Christopher Tietjens had displayed more than his usual insolence to Ruggles. So Ruggles' coat-tails flashed round an unusual number of doors and his top-hat gleamed before an unusual number of tall portals during the next week. (206)

Tietjens, back in England from the trenches because of shell shock, is not helped by the common knowledge that Sylvia visits Austrian officers in prison camp, or by negative intelligence reports prepared by Drake, the man who is thought to be the father of Sylvia's child. Once Ruggles is done accumulating his ammunition, Mark Tietjens, who never doubts the truth of the information, sends Ruggles to his father because he doesn't know if he "'could keep all these particulars accurately in [his] head'" (209). Ruggles tells the elder Tietjens that Sylvia was pregnant when she married Christopher, that Sylvia has eloped with Perowne and Christopher has not done anything about it, and that he was suspected of being a French agent, all to get money for the Wannops and his illegitimate child by Valentine, and for Macmaster and Mrs. Duchemin, who was also Christopher's mistress. The only truth Ruggles tells is that Sylvia has run off with Perowne. Christopher has calculated the birth of their son and knows that he cannot be Drake's, and he has calculated Valentine Wannop's birth to ascertain that she is not his half sister, as Mark later suggests. Sylvia attempts an explanation for the vindictiveness of Christopher's enemies when she tells him, speaking of Brownie, "'of course he hates you for being in the army. All the men who aren't hate all the men who are. And, of course, when there's a woman between them the men who aren't do all they can to do the others in'" (161). But her explanation cannot touch the source of Tietjens's family's willingness to believe the gossip. We must look to the peculiar sanity associated with blind obedience to social convention, or at least to the appearance of social convention.

The Book: Ford's *Parade's End*

When *The Good Soldier*'s John Dowell describes his life as one of the "good people," he lists a number of assumptions concerning their behavior. The underdone beef, the brandy, the cold baths, and membership in the Anglican Church are all part of an unwritten code, a set of rules to which everyone agrees, but no one can document. In *Some Do Not*, Ford addresses the question of unwritten codes and the book which contains the names of those who violate them. As Ruggles begins his quest to destroy Tietjens, the narrator describes the book and those who believe in it. "There is said to be a book," he begins,

> kept in a holy of holies, in which bad marks are set down against men of family and position in England. In this book Mark Tietjens and his father—in common with a great number of hard-headed Englishmen of county rank—implicitly believed. Christopher Tietjens didn't; . . . Mark and his father looked abroad upon English society and saw fellows, apparently with every qualification for successful careers in one service or the other; and these fellows got no advancements, orders, titles or preferments of any kind. Just, rather mysteriously, they didn't make their marks. This they put down to the workings of the book. (206)

When Ruggles goes to the Tietjens men about the failings of Christopher, the narrator alludes to their belief in "the great book" (209). Christopher has not "got on" and his father is only too willing to assume that it is because he has bucked convention. The elder Tietjens has also considered marrying Valentine Wannop himself and feels "a slight tinge of jealousy" toward his son (210). But the elder Tietjens's unquestioning belief in the book and the system supporting it allows him to believe the worst of his son. Even his religion convinces him that Christopher is guilty. In a piece of convoluted logic, Mr. Tietjens deduces that he must suffer before his death in order to be able, as a rich man, to enter heaven (211). Without attempting to test the veracity of Ruggles's accusations, the old man crawls under a fence with his shotgun under his chin, a method of suicide used by "[h]undreds of men, mostly farmers" every year (211).

This black comedy of errors continues after the scene with Sylvia, Mark, and Port Scatho when Mark actually asks Tietjens about the rumors and finally, after a lengthy conversation, accepts Christopher's denial. Christopher offers to show Mark his bank records for the past ten years and Mark tells his brother, "Why the devil shouldn't I believe you? It's either believing you're a gentleman or Ruggles a liar. It's only commonsense to believe Ruggles a liar, in that case. I didn't before because I had no grounds to" (214). Christopher's response explains again the force of gossip. "I doubt if liar is the right word. He picked up things that were said against me. No doubt he reported them faithfully enough. Things *are* said against me. I don't know why" (214, italics Ford's). But Christopher will not forgive Mark nor his father for setting Ruggles on him and refuses to accept his inheritance, except that of Groby, the estate, for his son.

This refusal leads to another rumor that arises in *No More Parades,* one Sylvia Tietjens starts to discredit Tietjens after he is back at the front in France. Sylvia has shown up in France near Tietjens's unit, with no papers and Perowne, who is now the General's adjutant there, in tow. In a moment of deliberate vindictiveness, she tells General Campion, Christopher's godfather, that Christopher is a socialist. Campion's response is so strong that Sylvia immediately wishes she had not made the remark, but the damage is done. Campion attributes all the lies about Christopher, which he still believes, to this newly discovered fact. He also, in a lengthy diatribe, suggests that if Christopher had been more selective and more careful, his indiscretions would not have been so serious. That is, Christopher could do wrong as long as he did it according to the rules, a truth Edward Ashburnham learns too late. Campion, grieved beyond belief, babbles to Sylvia, "'You tell me he seduced the little Wannop girl. . . . The last person in the world he should have seduced. . . . Ain't there millions of other women? . . . . Along with keeping a girl in a tobacco-shop'" (410). Nothing Campion believes here is true. But the irony is intensified and linked to larger political issues when Campion blames it all on Socialism.

"You can forgive a man for doing wrong with women," the general continues,

> We all do. . . . We've all set up girls in tobacco-shops in our time. . . . But, damn it all, if the fellow's a Socialist it puts a different complexion. . . . I could forgive him even for the little Wannop girl, if he wasn't. . . . But . . . Good God, isn't it just the thing that a dirty-minded Socialist would do? . . . To seduce the daughter of his father's oldest friend, next to me. (410)

The general's hatred of Socialists quickly moves to questions of treason when he proclaims that "these fellows aim at sapping the heart of the army. . . . They say they distribute thousands of pamphlets recommending the rank and file to shoot their officers and go over to the Germans" (411). The general's use of the phrase "they say" suggests gossip and rumor; he doesn't even know for sure what the Socialists' role in the war is, but he believes it must be treason because socialism contradicts the British system of ownership. Christopher is able later to convince the general of his loyalty by telling him that he is an anachronism, a Tory of the same ilk as Edward Ashburnham. "Ruggles told my father what he did," Christopher explains

> because it is not a good thing to belong to the seventeenth or eighteenth centuries in the twentieth. Or really, because it is not good to have taken one's public school's ethical system seriously. I am really, sir, the English public schoolboy. What with the love of truth that—God help me!—they rammed into me at Clifton and the belief Arnold forced upon Rugby that the vilest of sins—the vilest of sins—is to peach to the head master! That's me, sir. Other men get over their schooling. I never have. (490)

Of course, Christopher's love of truth does not exclude the white lie upon which the entire social structure is built. The general points this out and observes that if the white lie were excluded, "'your servants could not say you were not at home'" (495). Lies are, in fact, even for the general, a way of adhering to convention, but the lies have to be constructed according to the rules. The general, as he finally accepts Christopher's innocence, remembers a conversation with Tietjens before the war when Tietjens had let him believe lies about him in order to shield Sylvia, who was then off with Perowne, and to shield Macmaster, whose mistress Tietjens had dumped for him.

Trudi Tate also cites this passage from *Some Do Not* in which General Campion questions Tietjens for the first time about his alleged affair with Valentine Wannop. Tate focuses on the importance of Campion's words implying that Tietjens tells the wrong kind of lies.[54] And indeed Tietjens does. But the complexity of this scene also illustrates the complex role of rumor throughout the novel. In the scene, the general angrily accuses

Tietjens of having an affair with Valentine Wannop. The irony of the gossip at this point is that Tietjens has only met the girl the day before this conversation. The "girl" Tietjens had been seen with earlier in London, the source of the gossip, was the mistress of Macmaster, and Tietjens was trying to get rid of her for his friend. Here the complexity begins and the conversation develops in a way that rivals the convoluted conversations of Joseph Heller's *Catch-22*. Tietjens's schoolboy ethic, of course, rules and he cannot name Macmaster. When Tietjens tells Campion, "I was trying to get that young woman . . . off a friend's back" (72), Campion very nearly chokes. "If . . . my G.S.O. II.—who's the stupidest ass I know—told me such a damn-fool lie as that I'd have him broke tomorrow" (72). Tietjens's truth sounds like a lie even though, according to convention, he is shielding Macmaster. But Campion reminds Tietjens of a perhaps more important convention, that of the "correct" lie. "Damn it all," he continues, "it's the first duty of a soldier—it's the first duty of all Englishmen—to be able to tell a good lie in answer to a charge. But a lie like that . . ." (72). Tietjens is relieved that Campion doubts the story, but when he continues to deny any connection with Valentine Wannop, Campion completely ignores him. "Put her back. Her father was a great friend of your father's . . ." (73), he tells Tietjens, and continues several paragraphs later, "choose a girl that you can set up in a tobacco shop and do your courting in the back parlour" (74). This is the tobacco shop the general remembers as a reality in *No More Parades*. But the general's later assertion that Tietjens must rely on the white lie is substantiated.

Before her departure with Perowne, Sylvia has "let drop" to the general's sister, Claudine Sandbach, that Tietjen's "views are immoral" (74) and this has infuriated Claudine's husband, the "gossip" who saw Tietjens with Macmaster's mistress in London. Campion continues to insist that he needs a plausible lie to tell Claudine, or an "obvious lie as long as it shows you're not flying in the face of society—as walking up the Haymarket with the little Wannop when your wife's left you because of her would be" (74). We must remember that the girl in the Haymarket is Macmaster's mistress, a bookmaker's clerk, and Sylvia has left him to elope with another man, but clearly here the truth is irrelevant. Tietjens's eighteenth-century schoolboy morality fails him in the face of Sylvia's twentieth-century immorality. Only the appearance of morality, the acceptance of social conventions, is wanted, and oddly enough, Sylvia passes muster because Christopher shields her. Tietjens's punishment for the Wannop gossip, the general confesses, will be his exclusion from Claudine's visiting list; it happens when Tietjens sues the general over an accident involving Valentine and an injured horse. The results of the later scene in France, however, are more dire than social exclusion. Sylvia's exploits, which include leading Perowne to believe she wants him to come to her room when she knows Christopher will be there, get Tietjens sent up the line even though his health is bad and he has not completely recovered from the earlier shell shock. Though the general finally believes Christopher, he cannot allow such rows to go on near the battle zone. And the general still blames Christopher for Sylvia's misbehavior; according to the general, Christopher should either divorce his wife or bed her (492). Sylvia's actions and the resulting gossip finally do their dirty work.

In the introduction to *Parade's End*, Robie Macauley examines the tetralogy in the context of the older war novels of Tolstoy and Crane who saw war as "the adventure story of a single man lost in the tremendous confusion."[55] Ford's generation, he continues, added a "contempt for illusion"; they saw war as "a savage hideous thing . . . a kind of entity in itself, an unexplained adventure that had little to do with the normal course of the world."[56] But Ford seems to fit the normal course of the world, the gossip and insistence on conformity, into the context of war and once there renders them inseparable, as they are in such legislative acts as the Sedition Act and DORA. The general's first conversation with Tietjens takes place before the war; the second, which sends him up the line, takes place near the front as the war rages. The gossip has not changed but only become more serious as the question not just of "flying in the face of society" but also of treason arises. The role of gossip before and during the war supports Macauley's claim that "Ford's war is seen as something like a violent intensification of all the troubles of a foundering society."[57] The madness, the peculiar sanity, in this case, of gossip and rumor, carry over into the war and become magnified into a dangerous and threatening force. Following his conversation with General Campion in *Some Do Not*, Tietjens considers the nature of humanity and concludes that all humanity is "Cats and monkeys" (79). He wonders

> why it was that humanity that was next to always agreeable in its units was, as a mass, a phenomenon so hideous. You look at a dozen men, each of them not by any means detestable and not uninteresting. . . . you formed them into a Government or a club and at once, with oppressions, inaccuracies, gossip, backbiting, lying, corruptions and vileness, you had the combination of wolf, tiger, weasel and louse-covered ape that was human society. (79)

During war, of course, this kind of proclamation generally applies to the enemy, and Ford himself applies it to the Prussians in his two propaganda books. But in *Parade's End* Ford looks at the world of *The Good Soldier*, the world of the good people, and takes their corruption to its "logical" conclusion in the apocalypse of war. The violence of Leonora Ashburnham toward Nancy Rufford becomes the battle of Verdun. As John Dowell wonders why the good people don't "gouge out each other's eyes with carving knives,"[58] he is foreshadowing the violence of the trenches.

When in *Madness and Civilization* Foucault examines the shifting role madness has played in our definition of society, he invites us always to consider first the nature of the society that defines madness. During the Great War, the madness submerged in Edwardian culture erupts full force into a major conflagration. The role of gossip, always a part of that society, escalates at a pace comparable to the violence and madness, and in fact enhances both. As Macauley points out, madness, "psychological danger," becomes a primary danger, and in Macauley's words, "Tietjens's question: 'Am I going mad?' becomes a universal one and while protagonists of other war novels see villages wrecked, Tietjens sees a civilization going to ruin" (xiii). Peculiar sanity, the strange and often public madness of war, through rumor threatens the personal freedom and safety of any who do not participate in it. Ford, Graves, and Lawrence all struggled to survive it and, to the extent that they lived to tell the tale, they did. But many, such as Robert Prager and others like him, did not. Dogged by rumor and supposition, these men perished. Such is the fate of the Northman of Conrad's story "The Tale," to which we will now turn.

Rumor and Duty: Conrad's "The Tale"

Rumor unfortunately allows for little ambiguity. The us/them dichotomy inherent in rumor tends to place its victims firmly in one camp or the other. The old cliché, "If you are not one of us, you must be one of them," echoed through Ford's life and work, as it echoes through Conrad's story. In Ford's life and in *Parade's End*, specific rumors, based on inappropriate and hasty interpretations of facts and impressions, run rampant. But in "The Tale," another kind of rumor abounds, the kind located in propaganda, the kind on which the Spies and Lies advertisement is based. The implication of that advertisement is that spies are everywhere, only too eager to relay the minutest details of overheard conversations to an enemy who will use those details to our destruction. The paranoia on which this kind of campaign relies grows out of rumor and scaremongering, Ford's intent in writing his story notwithstanding. In the hands of an ordinary citizen, this kind of campaign can ruin lives and destroy friendships. Ford and his fictional creation Tietjens were lucky to have enough friends in high places who could save them from irreparable harm. The German farmers in *One of Ours,* on the other hand, must go to court to prove their innocence against charges of treason. But in a military man, the fear of spies and treachery can mean immediate life or death. Peculiar sanity exhibited by irate mothers is one thing; by a commanding officer it is another.

Reflected in Conrad's only World War I story, "The Tale," peculiar sanity informs the action and places the story's Commanding Officer, also its narrator, in a moral as well as literal fog. In the story's frame, when he is asked by his female companion to tell her a tale, one "not of this world," the narrator, momentarily silenced, slips into his story of "seas and continents and islands" which, although resembling those of earth, certainly are not the familiar landscape of our rational existence.[59] Although it is deceivingly quiet, this "other world" is the war zone. Even the setting of the frame is shrouded in mystery. The great war, from which the narrator and his companion are "on leave," is never directly named. Conrad keeps us in the "darkening room" of the frame's setting, or, in the tale itself, on the deck of a fog-shrouded ship, only hinting at its location and at the source of the moral quagmire into which it is plunged. We accompany the Commanding Officer, "a man made of common tormented clay on a voyage of discovery," (61) a discovery that the narrator, normally a fair-minded, rational man, has been easily drawn into the madness of war and will for the remainder of his life suffer the consequences of his actions—sinking a ship that was most likely neutral. Irrational fear, goaded by rumor and xenophobic rage, has become for him under the stress of war a substitute for reason. Once out of the war zone, the Officer realizes his folly, but the jingoistic climate of the home front prevents anyone from questioning his behavior.

From the outset, one of the most challenging aspects of "The Tale" proves to be the story's frame. Jeremy Hawthorn, Jakob Lothe, and William W. Bonney attempt to establish parallels between the frame and the tale told by the commanding officer by breaking the story up into three or four concentric tales.[60] One point of argument concerns whether or not the "grave murmur" the Commander hears, which is his inner voice, constitutes one of the concentric tales. Though examinations of this kind remain interesting, they may also distract us from larger questions by allowing the moral issues raised by the story to be obliterated in questions of semantics. All three critics provide useful structural analyses of the story without delving into the historical context which in fact creates its "peculiar sanity." Although Jeremy Hawthorn offers an enlightening investigation into shipping agreements in existence early in the war that justify the Northman's destination of an English port, his focus remains other than that of establishing a further historical context. We might note that in his development of parallels between the story's layers, Hawthorn at the end of the story compares the Commanding Officer's companion, lying immobile on her couch, to the neutral ship. Deferring to the habit of referring to ships as *she,* we also might point out that such examples best illustrate the problems created by purely textual examinations.

It would seem, however, that the gravest error is that of Bonney, who locates the source of what both he and Hawthorn refer to as the neurosis of the Commanding Officer. According to Bonney, "manifestations of [the commanding officer's] neurosis are primarily linguistic."[61] A sunken ship is more than a linguistic manifestation. If we limit ourselves to semantic games and lose sight of historical context, we may fail to admit that in war a sunken ship is a palpable object, a location of death that, in the case of "The Tale," becomes the Commander's responsibility.

Hawthorn comes closest to pinpointing the location of the officer's peculiar sanity when he compares the Commanding Officer to Alvan Hervey of "The Return." Totally bound up in social convention, as we have seen, Hervey finds his wife's elopement unthinkable; her departure shakes the foundations of all his beliefs. Hervey's adherence to "the rules" has defined his marriage—he has invested little emotion in the relationship and is thus likely responsible for her defection. His wife's return home and her declaration that she could not finally elope with her lover cannot restore his faith in his marriage or in society. Hervey is not capable of starting over with new rules. Like the Commanding Officer in "The Tale," Hervey detests the "lie" with a pathological vehemence.

In linking these two stories, Hawthorn accurately illustrates that both men are "unwilling to accept incertitude as a condition of living," that is, neither can deal with ambiguity.[62] Both also believe, or sincerely want to believe, that the rules provide the certitude they seek. But as Marlow reminds us in *Heart of Darkness,* "Principles won't do." The rules, like the "acquisitions"—the clothes, the "pretty rags," the superficial trappings Conrad names—"fly off at the first good shake."[63] War and perhaps love gone awry provide that good shake. Hawthorn stops short of making that connection, of looking to the historical contexts of change and war for the source of contradiction and neurosis. "Is it not believable," he asks, "that Conrad was exploring a neurosis in 'The Tale' similar to that considered in 'The Return'? If so, it is quite appropriate that the Northman and his ship should present the commanding officer with evidence which is inconclusive.

It is almost as if Conrad scatters contradictory evidence and clues in front of him."[64] Popular mythology notwithstanding, war is full of contradictions, and there is no wonder that Conrad placed them in the way of his protagonist to test his "principles." Both protagonists suffer a gap between reality and their perception of it; they are deluded. Reality is undoubtedly an elusive construct but, wherever it may lie, it does not necessarily lie in popular social mythology, especially during the Great War. Since both Hervey and the Commanding Officer insist that Truth can be found in contemporary wisdom, we might look there for the neurosis that Conrad explores. When Hervey realizes that the solid foundation he believes underpins his relationship with his wife is shaky, he has nowhere to turn; when he sees himself as "an exiled forlorn figure in a realm of ungovernable, of unrestrained folly," where "[n]othing could be foreseen, foretold—guarded against," he cannot "stand it."[65] This threat to Hervey's way of life underscores the difference between reality and Hervey's perception of it. That difference and the lie that grows out of it offer a parallel between Hervey and the Commanding Officer and their neuroses.

Perhaps no greater gap exists than the one between the popular mythology surrounding war and its reality. The lie, something the Commanding Officer detests, becomes the foundation of morality. In his 1928 study of war hysteria, *Falsehood in War-Time,* Arthur Ponsonby describes the various ways untruth worked in the Great War.[66] He proposes that "[t]here must have been more deliberate lying in the world from 1914 to 1918 than in any other period of the world's history."[67] There was the deliberate official lie; the deliberate lie or concocted story, such as that of nurse Grace Hume, reported by her 'sister' to have died as a result of having both breasts cut off by German soldiers; the mistranslation; the "general obsession, started by rumor and magnified by repetition and elaborated by hysteria"; the concealment of truth; and the faked photograph, among others.[68] "War is fought," Ponsonby continues, "in this fog of falsehood, a great deal of it undiscovered and accepted as truth. The fog arises from fear and is fed by panic. Any attempt to doubt or deny even the most fantastic story has to be condemned at once as unpatriotic, if not traitorous."[69] Ponsonby's words very accurately describe the behavior of the Commanding Officer. Conventional morality of the kind Alvan Hervey and the Commanding Officer believe in condemns the lie and celebrates the truth, yet even in peacetime the white lie, General Campion maintains, serves to hold conventional society together. But in wartime, Ponsonby observes, "failure to lie is negligence, the doubting of a lie a misdemeanor, the declaration of the truth a crime."[70] DORA and the Sedition Act, of course, legitimized mythmaking by promoting propaganda. This ethical "fog," the source of what Hawthorn and Bonney identify as the Commanding Officer's neurosis, is a disease fed by the officer's milieu—and constitutes a national disease.

To return to the function of the frame, then, it might be instructive to look back at the ways in which the home front, the location of the frame, enables and supports the war effort. Even a casual reader of Conrad knows the writer often resorts to the use of frames. *Heart of Darkness* is also a tale within a tale—Marlow's tale of Kurtz framed by the unnamed narrator who hears the story on the deck of the Nellie and later shares it with the reader. Like "The Tale," *Heart of Darkness* begins in twilight and continues as the sky darkens. Marlow's voice becomes gradually disembodied as the listeners on the deck of the Nellie realize they are going to "hear about one of [his] inconclusive experiences."[71] Marlow's first words in the sinking gloom on deck, "And this also has been one of the dark places of the earth," serve to link the place of the telling, London, with the place of the tale, the Congo.[72] In establishing this connection, Conrad draws both the listeners on deck and the reader into Marlow's story and establishes a complicity between those at home and those who physically seek to extend the boundaries of empire. Indeed the very last words of that novel lead us on the Thames "into the heart of an immense darkness."[73] In the same way the frame of *Heart of Darkness* links the civilized world with the "uncivilized," the frame of "The Tale" links the world of the Great War with the home front. Uncharacteristically, Conrad's listener here is a woman. If the frame's most important function is to bring the war, the front line as it were, into the parlor, even into the boudoir, then the female listener is a logical choice.

We have already seen how the home front, both in England and in America, played a significant role in the war effort. And women, in the roles of sister, wife, mother, and nurse, formed a basis for propaganda, both official and unofficial. Samuel Hynes reports in *A War Imagined: The First World War and English Culture* that the suffrage movement was put on hold for the duration of the war. Suffragists, in his words, "shifted their belligerency to a different war."[74] Both propaganda posters and popular songs in England and America enlist the image of the pure and sacrificing female. The Red Cross nurse becomes "The Rose of No Man's Land," the

> one red rose the soldier knows,
> It's the work of the Master's hand;
> 'Mid the war's great curse stands the Red Cross Nurse,
> She's the rose of 'No Man's Land.'[75]

On the cover of this sheet music, the nurse stands, arms extended in a pleading gesture, bathed in celestial light. (fig. 4.3) The image of the sacrificing, but demanding, mother also appears in popular images of the time. A song printed in both America and Great Britain asks, "Are You Half the Man Your Mother Thought You'd Be?"

In this vein, perhaps the most stunning image is that of "the little mother" whose letter Robert Graves reports, with very little comment, in *Good-Bye to All That*. Falsely reported dead to his parents, Graves returns home for treatment of his wounds. In what becomes a sort of rebirth, Graves enters once again into "normal" life and is puzzled by it. "England looked strange to us returned soldiers," he reports. "We could not understand the war madness that ran about everywhere, looking for a pseudo-military outlet. The civilians talked a foreign language; and it was newspaper language."[76] As an illustration of this phenomenon, Graves quotes the letter verbatim. In it, the little mother refers to "we who 'mother the men' who have to uphold the honour and traditions not only of our Empire but of the whole civilized world."[77] Incensed at calls for peace, this woman insists that "[t]here is only one temperature for the women of the British race, and that is white heat. . . . We women pass on the ammunition of 'only sons' . . . so that when the 'common soldier' looks back before going 'over the top' he may see the women of the British race at his heels, reliable, dependent, uncomplaining."[78] This image of motherhood sending its sons to almost certain death is chilling and most soundly illustrates the national neurosis reflected by the Commanding Officer and his companion who, at the end of his tale, offers the absolution he is unable to accept.

In revealing the moral misery the Commanding Officer suffers, the frame, like the tale itself, illustrates the specific nature of war madness. In a civilization priding itself on truth, truth is a crime. Patriotism insists on a world in which issues are clear cut, black or white, but reality reveals only ambiguity, especially on the sea where there is no "final brutality," no "taste of primitive passion" (64). "One envies the soldiers at the end of the day," the officer tells his companion, "wiping the sweat and blood from their faces, counting the dead fallen to their hands" (64). The sea that swallows up friend and foe alike offers no such finality, only "the hypocrisy of an old friend" (64), the possibility of sudden death. The ambiguity of the story, then, should come as no surprise. War is full of contradictions and "The Tale" reflects those uncertainties in the inexplicable behavior of the Commanding Officer and the "extraordinary response" of his companion.[79]

The vagueness of the Officer's mission "to be sent out along certain coasts to see—what he could see" (63), leads him to an acute paranoia

Fig. 4.3. World War I sheet music "The Rose of No Man's Land"

heightened by the real threat of being blown out of the water by a mine or a submarine, by something, the narrator says, "you have not seen" (64). Seeing, or the inability to see, as Lothe and Hawthorn point out, further complicates the officer's muddle. Reliable information remains sketchy. Rumor has it that neutral merchant ships have been dropping supplies to enemy submarines. "This was generally believed," the narrator explains, "if not absolutely known" (66). Here begins the juxtaposition of reality and rumor, the exaggerated truths and outright lies, outlined by Ponsonby and Graves. The tragedy inherent in the proliferation of half-truth, in the insistence that gossip become gospel, is the unfortunate reality that both sides frequently acted on speculation. The cliché "Shoot first and ask questions later" becomes a modus operandi. Ill-timed rumors on both sides could send suspected spies to their deaths.

In his examination of mythmaking in the Great War, Paul Fussell investigates the atmosphere of rumor, which, as he explains, was "especially fertile" during World War I. Resulting from what he calls "inexplicable terror long and inexplicably endured," rumors, superstitions, legends and other "unmodern" phenomena proliferated in the trenches, creating in Fussell's words "an approximation of the popular psychological atmosphere of the Middle Ages."[80] From the story of the Crucified Canadian to myths of German ghosts appearing in the trenches, these stories serve to vilify the enemy, to explain what cannot be explained by logic. Harold Krebs, narrator of Hemingway's story, "Soldier's Home," speaks of lies, of "stating as facts certain apocryphal incidents familiar to all soldiers."[81] Krebs remembers "detailed accounts of German women found chained to machine guns in the Argonne forest."[82] H. G. Wells, in *Mr. Britling Sees it Through,* refers to "[t]ales of torture and mutilation, tales of the kind that arise nowhere and out of nothing, and poison men's minds to the most pitiless retaliations, [which] drifted along the opposing fronts. . . ."[83] But Britling himself understands that the "realities were evil enough without any rumors."[84] Such rumors, disconnected from logical examination, remain unsubstantiated and seem relatively harmless until we remember, as Ponsonby compels us, that "the purpose of most of them is to fan indignation and induce the flower of the country's youth to be ready to make the supreme sacrifice."[85]

Rumors of noncombatants aiding the enemy resulted in lynchings in the U.S. and in executions abroad. According to Fussell, a Belgian farmer was reported shot for allegedly signaling the Germans by particular alignments of his plow horses. Other Belgian farmers allegedly signaled the enemy with laundry, windmills that rotated backwards, white cows, and steeple clocks.[86] D. H. Lawrence, suspected of being pro-German before and after the Ford incident, became the victim of further war rumors in Cornwall. Lawrence biographer, Harry T. Moore, reports that when the Lawrences lived in Cornwall, they were accused of supplying German submarines, and Frieda was accused of taking photographs with what proved to be a loaf of bread. Once frolicking on the beach, Frieda allowed her long white scarf to blow in the wind. Seeing the danger, Lawrence screamed at her, "Stop it, stop it, you fool! Can't you see that they'll think you're signaling to the enemy!"[87] More fortunate than the Belgian farmers, the Lawrences at least were not shot.

Even Conrad himself experienced war paranoia; in a letter to Pinker, he writes of the threat of spies. After going out on a minesweeper as part of a tour of naval bases (background material he used in "The Tale"), Conrad anticipated the cruise in northern waters that had been scheduled and then postponed. In the letter, Conrad speaks as if he may not return from the trip. "[I]ts [*sic*] no use ignoring the fact that the vessel has made three trips already and she may have been spotted. Also there are spies about. The prospect of an expedition of this sort gives a curious force to the idea of spies."[88] As the editors of the letters point out, "The Tale" reflects this unease.

No Absolutes, No Absolutions: Conrad's "The Tale"

Executions based on suspicions of spying were so commonplace that Robert Graves refuses, in *Good-Bye to All That,* to consider them atrocities.[89] Herein lies the vital question the narrator of "The Tale" raises when he attaches an infinity of absolution to the performance of duty. When the narrator tells the woman that he likes the word *duty,* she replies, "It is horrible—sometimes" (61). And so it is when it involves serious moral conflict. But the narrator, knowing he has made a questionable moral choice in the performance of his duties, builds into that performance forgiveness, a forgiveness he is ultimately unable to accept. Indeed, at the beginning of the story, by his construction of another world in which to place the tale, he refuses even to admit to his actions. The Commanding Officer's sense of duty, combined with both profound xenophobia and paranoia, allows the hysteria of rumor to cloud his reason.

From the beginning a lack of facts impairs the judgment of the officer. His information is limited only to the kind that was "about as useful as information trying to convey the locality and intentions of a cloud . . ." (63). Relying on the wisdom of a world that "was not very wise" (62), he believes that certain neutrals must be "watched by acute minds" (62). When the "object" appears one day as the ship patrols a rocky coast, we are told that "twenty pairs of eyes on . . . deck stared in all directions trying to see—what they could see" (65). Since they are traveling in a thick fog, they can see little. The unnamed object, which "may have been nothing more remarkable than, say, a barrel of a certain shape and colour," performs double duty here (65). First, it sets in motion the Commanding Officer's speculations as to its source. Second, the object becomes, in the tale itself, as vague and imprecise as the Officer's orders and the rumors concerning the behavior of certain neutrals; it symbolizes in a way the nature of rumor wrought from the peculiar sanity of war. Referring to the rumors that link neutral merchant ships to enemy submarines, the narrator declares, "[t]he object . . . put it beyond doubt that something of the sort had been done somewhere in the neighborhood" (66). In other words, no one knows what, if anything, had been done, or where, or by whom. The officer and his second in command decide that the object has been dumped in haste and that "[t]he parties are miles away" (66), but the Commanding Officer remains rankled at "the murderous stealthiness of methods and the atrocious callousness of complicities that seemed to taint the very source of men's deep emotions and noblest activities . . ." (67). His indignation is indeed fanned. As fog surrounding the ship thickens, the Officer only considers the possibility that he is in the grips of folly.

Easing the ship into a cove to wait out the fog, the crew discovers another vessel not far off. Questions immediately arise in the captain's already anxious mind. When the boarding party he dispatches returns with the news that the ship is a neutral, the captain begins to build his case against it. Aware that "[s]uch suspicions as the one which had entered his head are not defended easily" (70), the Commanding Officer decides to go aboard the ship anyway. Captained by a Northman, the ship is said to be headed to an English port. Here we find the first of several references to the real world. Drawn into the tension of his tale, and possibly assuming his listener is drawn in as well, the narrator lapses into moments of truth, or confusion as to which "world" he is speaking of. Again the vagueness of his mission emerges in the narrator's descriptions of what he expects to find on the neutral ship. Because all the logs and papers on board are in order, all he can search for is "the atmosphere of gratuitous treachery" (71). The narrator finds it in the drunken paranoia of the Northman. Rightly suspecting himself to be in danger, the Northman is nervous and defensive. Well aware of the force of rumor, he appeals to the Commanding officer's sense of justice. Again we are edged back into the real world when the narrator actually refers to himself as an Englishman. Echoing Marlow in *Heart of Darkness,* he deplores the possibility of a lie, "an enormous lie, solid like a wall, with no way round to get at the truth, whose ugly murderous face he seemed to see peeping over at him with a cynical grin" (76). What the narrator refers to here, we must suppose, assuming a deliberately misplaced modifier, is the liquor-illuminated visage of the Northman, but to call it truth, both ugly and murderous, he must also see something of his own reflection there, as Alvan Hervey sees in the mirrors of his dressing room. The narrator is about to become a probable murderer, and in retelling the tale he understands his own treachery.

The tale becomes more ironic as virtually everything the narrator says of the Northman points to his own irrational behavior. In the chartroom, which the Northman uses as a cabin, we are told "[t]he air . . . was thick with guilt and falsehood braving the discovery, defying simple right, common decency, all humanity of feeling, every scruple of conduct" (78). The Northman then says, "Well, we know that you English are gentlemen" (78). But shrouded in the fog of moral misery, those gentlemanly values the Northman counts on fail him. In fact, his reliance on English values dooms him because the Commanding Officer, as Gaetano D'Elia points out, believes those values are being abused.[90] "They don't feel in danger of their life," the narrator asserts, "[b]ecause they know England and English ways too well" (76). What the narrator learns too late, however, is that the peculiar sanity of war, ratified by rumors and lies, undermines reason by invoking an unreasonable and unreasoning sense of duty to those very values. In the same way the elder Tietjens's values allow him to believe the worst of his son and thus to commit suicide, his values push the Commanding Officer over the edge.

Throughout his questioning, the Northman maintains that he is lost in the fog, an assertion that, if true, probably validates his innocence. Carried away by his fury at "the atmosphere of murderous complicity" (79) he senses on the merchant ship, the narrator devises a curiously cowardly "test" for the Northman. He forces the ship out of the cove and gives him directions which, if the Northman is really lost, will send him to his death. If he is lying and really does know where he is, he will escape. The outcome here becomes the only documented "truth" in "The Tale," that is, the Northman does not know where he is and perishes with his crew on the rocks. Back in "the real world" of the frame, the narrator admits that the certainty he felt in the heat of the moment may have been misguided. "I don't know whether I have done stern retribution," he tells us, "—or murder; whether I have added to the corpses that litter the bed of the unreadable sea the bodies of men completely innocent or basely guilty. I don't know. I shall never know" (80). Because the "unreadable sea" has swallowed any evidence which might have confirmed the Commander's suspicions, he is left in perennial fog.

Conrad biographer Zdzisław Najder reports that Conrad wrote "The Tale" in the fall of 1916 after visiting the Royal Navy shipyards in Scotland where he heard war stories told. R. B. Cunninghame Graham, in his preface to *Tales of Hearsay,* the collection in which "The Tale" appears, compares Conrad's treatment of this story which a sailor had "probably badly told in skeleton" to Shakespeare's elaborations of historical episodes he took from Holinshead. "[S]o," Graham says, "Conrad dealt with this sailor's yarn and left it glorified."[91] Najder compares the story to Graves' *Good-Bye to All That* because, like Graves' memoir, it offers in Najder's words, "a marked contrast to the military stories then common. . . ."[92] Clearly, from his own experience, Conrad understood the force of war mania. With his son Borys at the front, he knew the tension of waiting. After completing his northern cruise in November of 1916, Conrad wrote to J. M. Dent that because "mankind is essentially forgetful" he did not believe the war would change human nature. "It isn't so much the war itself," he writes, "as the course it has taken. . . . I am more emotional, it appears, than I imagined myself to be."[93] Conrad, like Graves, it would appear, was able to recognize the human capacity for folly; "The Tale" does not condone action based on emotion. The Commanding Officer will forever live with the consequences of war hysteria, of acting on the basis of hearsay.

"The Tale" becomes appropriate to the collection's title *Tales of Hearsay* in two ways. The tale itself is one Conrad heard, one of the exaggerated or apocryphal stories of the kind Fussell, Hemingway, and Wells describe. But hearsay also works within this story in the shape of the rumors which inform the Commanding Officer's actions. Reality, truth, innuendo, reason, and folly merge here in the cloaking fog; the ship becomes both literally and symbolically a Ship of Fools. In *Mr. Britling Sees It Through,* Wells specifically uses this term to describe the marauding Zeppelin that has killed Aunt Wilshire. After her death, Britling wails to a cold night sky: "Oh bloodstained fools! . . . Even that vile airship was a ship of fools!"[94] Foucault describes these ships in *Madness and Civilization* as "highly symbolic cargoes of madmen in search of their reason."[95] Historical realities, Ships of Fools ferried wandering madmen from city to city. According to Foucault, the custom served a purpose beyond ridding medieval cities of the insane. In some cases, lunatics were escorted to religious shrines where it was hoped they would be cured. But for others, the passage over water itself also carried the possibility of "purification." In "The Tale," the Commanding Officer's "voyage of discovery" over this purifying element, as Foucault explains of the Ship of Fools,

> delivers [him] to the uncertainty of fate; on water each of us is in the hands of his own destiny; every embarkation is, potentially, the last. It is for *the other world* that the madman sets sail in his fools' boat; it is from *the other world* that he comes when he disembarks. The madman's voyage is at once a rigorous division and an absolute passage.[96]

Conrad's narrator in "The Tale" is compelled by the peculiar sanity of war to abandon reason to the illogic of rumor. Lost in a fog in that other world, he commits what might be deemed a reprehensible act, an act exonerated by the infinity of absolution he believes to be associated with the performance of duty. Only "possibly" aware that he might be guilty of folly when he sails along the coast to see what he can see, the Officer questions his actions once he disembarks into the "real world." Although publicly absolved, once back on land he sees more clearly what war mania has insisted that he forget; he commits the crime of delving into the truth. The Officer tells the tale, perhaps hoping in that way to achieve the private absolution he has not yet felt, but he is not absolved. His companion understands his conflict because she knows "his passion for truth, his horror of deceit, his humanity" (81). Although she tries to offer consolation with words of possession, "Oh, my poor, poor——" (81), she cannot relieve his sense of guilt. The possessive pronoun might seem to cancel the uncertainty of their earlier exchange, but the Officer's acceptance of existential responsibility ignores her offer. "I shall never know," he says as he leaves the room and the sympathy of her love. Although he may never know the true mission of the Northman, he knows he has acted without restraint; the rules have indeed flown off at the first hint of a shake. Like Alvan Hervey, the Commanding Officer now has nowhere to turn; he must also become "an exiled forlorn figure in a realm of ungovernable, of unrestrained folly. . . ."[97] The greatest irony perhaps lies in the realization that the world Hervey describes is one of peace, not war. In either case, we are only left with the uncertainty we know both men fear and despise. All we know "beyond doubt," as the narrator puts it, "[is] that something of the sort had been done somewhere in the neighborhood" (66).

Chapter 5

PSYCHIC STRESS AND PSYCHOBABBLE

Memory and Repression

When Joseph Conrad wrote of the peculiar sanity of war, as we have noted, he was writing of the Russo-Japanese War. Describing the battlefield from the vantage point of 1905, Conrad foreshadows the grim desolation of World War I Europe. The great battles of history, he writes,

> sink into insignificance before the struggles in Manchuria engaging half a million men on fronts of sixty miles, struggles lasting for weeks, flaming up fiercely and dying away from sheer exhaustion, to flame up again in desperate persistence, and end—as we have seen them end more than once—not from the victor obtaining a crushing advantage, but through the mortal weariness of the combatants.[1]

With the reference to Manchuria removed and the numbers adjusted upward, this passage could very well describe the combat of the Great War. But Conrad was also right to note the psychic stress of the earlier war. In his study of military psychiatry, *From Shell Shock to Combat Stress*, Hans Binneveld traces the beginnings of military psychiatry to the Russo-Japanese War. Binneveld, who also notes the foreshadowing of the Great War in the earlier war, traces the origins of frontline psychiatry to the Russian army, which was the first to use what he calls "forward psychiatry." The Russians actually evacuated psychiatric casualties to a different location than the one used for bodily wounds and established a psychiatric hospital behind the lines at Harbin.[2] Binneveld believes that the system failed largely because of "evacuation-syndrome"; that is, once such a service is created, soldiers need it. The hospital was overrun with patients and eventually shut down, leaving the Red Cross to pick up the pieces. Nevertheless, in their attention to the treatment of what came to be known as shell shock, the Russians established an important precedent, setting up hospitals near the front line. Of course, the Russians did not have the luxury of shipping the mentally wounded back to Moscow because distances were too great—the trip back took forty days by train.[3] Out of this necessity, however, developed the concept of proximity, the idea that if a soldier was not evacuated very far from the front, it would not, in Binneveld's words, "be rewarding to display the symptoms of hysteria."[4] Implicit in this concept is the idea that shell shock can be controlled by the soldier, that it is in fact a ploy to get out of fighting.

Until 1917, the British did evacuate its mentally wounded soldiers back to Britain. Siegfried Sassoon and Wilfred Owen were sent to Scotland to Craiglockhart Hospital for treatment of shell shock. But in 1917, when travel across the English Channel became more difficult, the idea of proximity was put into practice. The British, also in an attempt to limit the power of suggestion, forbade the use of the term shell shock. "General Routine Order No. 2384" declares that any soldier "who without any visible wound become[s] non-effective" will not be diagnosed at all but noted "Not Yet Diagnosed, Nervous."[5] Once again, shell shock is classified as a problem of nerves, an avoidable malady.

But in Conrad's assessment of the effects of long periods of battle that seem to the soldier to produce little tangible result lies the key to the reality of shell shock and to the concept of peculiar sanity. The two are not necessarily the same. As we have seen in our examination of home front behavior, propaganda, rumor, and gossip draw noncombatants into a groundswell of war mania; well-meaning citizens seem to take leave of their senses, and the peculiar sanity of war appears. But to the soldier who witnesses firsthand the horrors of combat, and civilians who witness bombing and shelling, peculiar sanity becomes a more elusive construct. Conrad's use of the term proves particularly revealing in light of our observation that war mania at home has little to do with the reality of the front. As Wilfred Owen so clearly illustrates in "Dulce et Decorum Est," political rhetoric would carry less weight if those who resorted to it understood or acknowledged the visceral reality of war. The soldier is in a double sense betrayed, not just because he has been sent to the front where he may be asked to sacrifice his life, but because it is not politic for those at home to acknowledge the truth of his mission. But most disturbing, if the soldier cannot, for whatever reason, tolerate the stress of battle, then he is declared nervous, neurasthenic, in some cases cowardly. The peculiar sanity we have seen on the home front portrays the shell-shocked soldier as mentally incompetent. Back home he will be "treated" in order to return to the trenches, and if he dares venture into the streets without his uniform, he is given the white feather, symbol of cowardice, by a zealous patriot. Noncombatants thus define war stress without ever having experienced it. Their disconnection from home, exacerbated of course by living under the stress of battle conditions, forms the basis for the "moral misery" against which Conrad's struggling soldiers "protest."[6] Once again in "Autocracy and War," Conrad describes those battle conditions with glaring accuracy. A doomed generation of men, he insists, was born to

> fill the ditches and cover the fields of Manchuria with their torn limbs; to send up from the frozen ground of battlefields a chorus of groans calling for vengeance from Heaven; to kill and retreat, or kill and advance, without intermission or rest for twenty hours, for fifty hours, for whole weeks of fatigue, hunger, cold, and murder—till their ghastly labour, worthy of a place amongst the punishments of Dante's Inferno, passing through the stages of courage, of fury, of hopelessness, sinks into the night of crazy despair.

Conrad implies in this passage and that previously quoted, that the "madness" of soldiers is almost an appropriate response to what we have come to see as the peculiar sanity of war. The madness is not to be found in those being treated for it. Inherent in the fact that most treatments for shell shock address the symptoms and not the cause is the implication that the cause of shell shock—the horror of war—shatters human sanity. The definition of madness is indeed subjective—shell shock is called madness by those who are mad with the urgency of war.

It may be helpful at this point to review the origins of peculiar sanity on the home front. Issues of purity, of conformity, linked in British and American minds to patriotism and manhood, created the image of the perfect soldier, the good soldier Teddy Ashburnham as he appears in public. But as we know, the good soldier is a sham. In "The Return," we see that long before Edward's ascension to the throne the old standards had become hollow; yet insistence on the validity of those standards was still strong. Rigid class divisions, especially in Great Britain, exacted a high price from working-class soldiers, but also from field officers who were among the best of the upper middle class—Robert Graves, Siegfried Sassoon, Wilfred Owen, Ford Madox Ford (and from the fictional world, Christopher Tietjens and Chris Baldry). All suffered physical and emotional wounds, and of course, Owen sacrificed his life. In the face of such losses, sanity, normalcy, seems a near affront to human dignity.

The medical community's response to shell shock ranged from the belief that nervous disorders were a form of malingering to the idea that shell shock could be linked to previous breakdowns or a family history of insanity. Edwin Ash in *The Problem of Nervous Breakdown* uses the term "shell-shock" but prefers the Freudian terms "war-neurasthenia" and "war-hysteria," terms that feminized war trauma.[7] Ash also believes in the power of "certain predisposing conditions," including previous break-downs, family predisposition to breakdown, and "acquired nerve weakness—intemperate habits or previous injury to the head."[8]

Shell shock appeared in varying degrees of severity. Ash lists symptoms associated with a number of case studies. One such study depicts a soldier who, after weeks of retreat, was wounded and left on the battlefield with other wounded men for hours. Once retrieved and treated for his physical wounds, the soldier "was for a long time incapacitated by inability to sustain any mental or physical effort, irritability, feelings of apprehension, and involuntary remembrances of his experiences whilst lying wounded."[9] Other symptoms of mild shell shock include "[e]xhaustion, headache, disturbed sleep, and extreme sensitiveness of the whole nervous system."[10] More severe symptoms include loss of hearing and speech, partial paralysis, and loss of memory. Regardless of the symptoms, the goal of the medical community is to get the soldier back on his feet and at the front line. The psychic wounds, products of warfare, in no way suggest to the medical or military communities, as they did to Conrad, that the peculiar sanity lies in the "state of war" itself.[11]

Shell shock is frequently approached with a certain amount of embarrassment, with the sense that the man of war has lost his self-control, or worse, that he is misbehaving as a child might. Treatment in many cases resembles in barbarity the application of leeches as a cure for all maladies. The most barbaric of these treatments involved the use of electric shock applied directly to whatever body part refused to function. This treatment was first put into use in Germany by Dr. Fritz Kaufmann. Binneveld's description of the Kaufmann-Kur reveals the lack of sensitivity for individual psychiatric needs and the more far-reaching implication that the doctor is in total control of the patient. Describing the method, Binneveld explains that "[l]imbs affected by disorders that hampered movement were subjected to a powerful form of electrotherapy. The current was left on for several minutes at a time. Afterwards the patient had to do exercises, and then the electricity was applied once again. During the treatment, the soldier was advised to get well quickly."[12] He then goes on to say, "Kaufmann himself knew that his approach was harsh and merciless."[13] Harsh or not, Kaufmann's method was adopted in England by Lewis Yealland who describes his work in *Hysterical Disorders of Warfare*. Depicted in Pat Barker's *Regeneration* as a kind of nemesis of Captain W. H. R. Rivers, whose theories we will see shortly, Yealland treats his patients with the cold distraction of the torturer. Before applying electricity to the "lower limb" of a soldier suffering from "hysterical monoplegia," Yealland speaks to the man as if he is about to receive punishment. First the soldier is belittled. "You do not understand your disorder because you are not a medical man," Yealland explains. "You have been given electricity for several months, and have improved, . . . but you require persuasion with the electricity. . . . The treatment that I shall adopt will unquestionably fulfil its purpose. But there is one thing which is very important, do not forget it—attention."[14] Yealland then applies electric shock to the foot and continues speaking to the patient in the same tone. After several applications of electricity, the patient is ordered to walk, which he does. His joy is quickly doused, however, when Yealland observes, "You stammer; that must be overcome too."[15] In Yealland's application of the Kaufmann-Kur, the physician makes no attempt to treat the source of the malady. Only the symptoms are attacked, that is, the soldier is made fit to fight again.[16]

Slightly less barbaric, but no more in touch with individual needs, was Weir Mitchell's rest cure. Mitchell, of course, was not alive to practice his theories on shell shock patients from the Great War, but others did. Edwin Ash devotes three chapters in *The Problem of Nervous Breakdown* to Mitchell's rest cure as it applies to neurasthenics in general. Since, Ash explains, neurasthenia "was regarded primarily as an exhaustion of nervous tissues," rest, accompanied by rich food, was presumed to be an effective cure.[17] Ash cautions that, improperly administered, the rest cure is not always effective. Treatment must include "regular visits from the physician whose duty was understood to consist partly of encouraging the *invalid*. . . . suggestion and persuasion were to be used as a matter of routine."[18] Ash's version of the rest cure involves less isolation and high-fat milk, but the principles remain the same. The patient is treated like a child and, in some cases, according to Ash, "electrical applications" may also be part of the "cure."[19] Chronicled first in Charlotte Perkins Gilman's "The Yellow Wallpaper," the rest cure also appears as a treatment for belated shell shock in Virginia Woolf's *Mrs. Dalloway.* Proposed as a treatment for Septimus Warren Smith's psychotic episodes, the rest cure and its proponent Sir William Bradshaw come under heavy scrutiny by Woolf. As Rezia and Septimus approach Sir William's office, Rezia believes that "he would cure Septimus at once."[20] But Rezia's optimism is not shared by the narrator nor by Clarissa. Sir William does not believe in madness—"he called it not having a sense of proportion" (96). Proportion and what the narrator calls her "sister" Conversion are "Goddesses" to Sir William and become powerful tools in his hands. "Worshipping proportion," the narrator divulges, "Sir William not only prospered himself but made England prosper, secluded her lunatics, forbade childbirth, penalised despair, made it impossible for the unfit to propagate their views until they, too, shared his sense of proportion" (99).

Even more sinister is the long narrative paragraph describing proportion's sister, conversion. Linked to colonialism and street evangelism, conversion, which "loves blood better than brick, and feasts most subtly on the human will (100)," turned on Sir William's wife, Lady Bradshaw, when she "had gone under" fifteen years before. Once an avid sportswoman who loved fishing for salmon, Lady Bradshaw, under her husband's influence, "cramped, squeezed, pared, pruned, drew back, peeped through . . ." (101), becomes, in so many words, his minion. A man who "swooped . . . devoured (102)," Sir William frightens Rezia when she meets him and moves Septimus closer to his impending suicide by taking control of his life, by telling him, "we will teach you to rest" (97). Sir William's tone here is very like that of Lewis Yealland and Edwin Ash. Septimus is being a naughty boy by speaking of suicide and having hallucinations and he will be disciplined by being put to bed, not without his supper but with a very high-fat one. Clarissa, when Bradshaw comes to her party bearing news of Septimus's death, correctly assesses the danger of a man like Sir William, who is

> a great doctor yet to her obscurely evil, without sex or lust, extremely polite to women, but capable of some indescribable outrage—forcing your soul, that was it—if this young man had gone to him, and Sir William had impressed him, like that, with his power, might he not then have said (indeed she felt it now), Life is made intolerable; they make life intolerable, men like that? (185)

Echoing the tone of the Purity Crusade, propaganda movements, the Temperance movement, and Bayliss Wheeler, Sir William is a masterful amalgam of war and postwar psychiatry, electricity or no, whose goal is not so much to heal as to control. Its rabid belief in conversion reflects peculiar sanity to a much greater degree than the disconnection from reality experienced by shell-shock victims.

A third method of treating shell shock, that practiced by W. H. R. Rivers, involved a "talking cure," a form of Freudian psychoanalysis. Rivers was stationed at Craiglockhart, where he treated Siegfried Sassoon, who was sent there rather than being courtmartialed for writing an antiwar letter to the papers. Robert Graves gives an account of Sassoon's "breakdown" and his own role in getting Sassoon sent to Craiglockhart. Pat Barker, in her contemporary examination of World War I, also depicts Sassoon's days at Craiglockhart with Rivers and with Wilfred Owen, also hospitalized there the year before his death in 1918. Craiglockhart had been a private hospital devoted to the treatment of alcoholism and other ailments of the upper classes, and after the war began it continued to be used primarily for the treatment of officers, not enlisted men.[21] The least Draconian of shell shock treatments, Rivers's methods still visualize the patient as someone to be managed, someone for whom the power of suggestion is all important. Working against the repression of war memories, Rivers attempted to get the mentally wounded soldier to turn the most horrible impressions into "tolerable, if not even pleasant, companions instead of evil influences. . . ."[22] The naïve tone of this passage notwithstanding, Rivers is working with sound theory. In "The Repression of War Experience" a conference paper published in *The Lancet* in February 1918, Rivers observes that memories so profound as those acquired in battle are not likely to be easily forgotten and therefore any suggestion that they be put aside or repressed is a dangerous one. Among other problems, memories repressed during waking hours tend to emerge during sleep. One exception to Rivers's "pleasant companion" theory is the officer, dramatized in *Regeneration,* who found himself after the explosion of a shell, face down in the decomposed belly of a German corpse. Unable to find any suitable way for the officer to live with this memory, Rivers agreed that a medical discharge that would enable the young man to live in the country, away from war talk, was the best solution.[23] Rivers admits what most psychiatrists and military men will not: war experiences are often so horrendous they permanently damage the man or woman who experiences them, and in addition, this damage occurs more often than anyone likes to admit. In the literature and journals we are about to examine, authors and characters permanently shattered by the Great War try to make sense of their own experiences, their own terrors.

Memory

In *The Problem of Nervous Breakdown,* Ash tells us that a shell shock victim may be "sometimes bereaved of memory."[24] Among the 589 cases of shell shock reported in *Shell-Shock and Other Neuropsychiatric Problems,* many of the victims fail to remember the trauma itself. Case 334 describes a soldier whose best friend was blown to bits when the two took refuge in a cellar. After the body parts were removed, the soldier developed amnesia surrounding the event. He gradually regained his strength and appetite, he "grew calmer"and was "discharged for garrison duty," even though the week before his release he had been pronounced "given to lively imaginings and emotion."[25] Another entry tells of a florist who after two days in the trenches was found unconscious as a result of shelling. Without physical wounds, the soldier still had no memory of the shelling and thought he was still in the flower business. After several weeks of treatment he was better, but he still had a six-day gap in his memory. The soldier was "eventually sent back to garrison duty, cured."[26] Southard, who collected the case studies, comments on the nature of amnesia, which he believes can "extend to a prolonged period prior to the accident. Sometimes," he continues, "the amnesias are selective, producing phenomena of pseudo aphasia."[27] Two factors stand out here. The first is that full memory is not deemed necessary to qualify a soldier for garrison duty. As we noted earlier, the point is to get the soldier back to the front. The second is that amnesia can be selective. Both Christopher Tietjens of *Parade's End* and Chris Baldry of *The Return of the Soldier* lose memories of events and facts acquired prior to the war, and both memory losses are appropriate to the characters' circumstances.

Memory Lost: West's *The Return of the Soldier*

The Return of the Soldier was first published in 1918, that is, before the war was over. Rebecca West was only twenty-four at the time and embroiled in a complicated relationship with H. G. Wells. According to biographer Carl Rollyson, in the fall of 1915 Wells set up West and their year-old son Anthony in a house in Hatch End, a London suburb. West, however, was not the ideal mother, at least not according to Anthony's later writings. She once said, "I hate domesticity."[28] And problems occurred because single mothers in those days were not accepted—Anthony had to be presented as her nephew. Air raids and shellings also followed West from the countryside to London. But West's war writings reveal little of this struggle. Early in the war when she was living in a rented farmhouse in Hertfordshire, West billeted eleven soldiers for ten days and was, according to Rollyson, "energized."[29] Though not involved in the propaganda campaign as Wells was, West wrote articles in support of women's war work, especially munitions work, comparing it to Army duty. West believed munitions workers did not receive enough credit for their efforts and wrote about their jobs in great detail.[30]

The Return of the Soldier belongs to this period of West's life. Rollyson explains that the idea for the novel came from a journal article focusing on the case study, not of a shell-shocked soldier, but of a factory worker who had fallen down a flight of stairs and awakened thinking he was still young and single. With no memory of his wife of many years, the worker went in search of his old girlfriend.[31] In a nutshell, this is what happens to Chris Baldry except that Chris's injury is not physical. When Margaret, his old sweetheart, now a bedraggled working-class housewife, informs Chris's wife Kitty and his cousin Jenny, the novel's narrator, that Chris is "hurt," all Margaret can say about the injury is that "[a] shell burst."[32] Chris has in fact been "blown up," a phrase used by medical practitioners of the day to describe being thrown into the air by the concussion of a shell. When Chris comes to, he believes he is twenty-one, not thirty-six, and he has forgotten the death of his father and, more important, his marriage and the death of his young son, which he does not remember until the end of the novel. Chris's amnesia thus erases much of his adulthood, not just the moments surrounding his "injury."

A close examination of Chris's adult life explains why those years might have been targeted by selective amnesia. Much like the life of Alvan Hervey, Chris's life is one of superficiality, complicated, as is Edward Ashburnham's, by feudal responsibility. Once again, we see the failure of Victorian and Edwardian convention and the connection between that failure and the peculiar sanity of war. In Chris's case, the war becomes the final act of peculiar sanity that leads him, in Jenny's words, to reject the entirety of his participation in their lives. Jenny's narrative provides the perspective of a cynical insider not unlike that of John Dowell. Fully believing in the privileged life of Baldry Court, Jenny gradually accepts the possibility that Chris was not happy there; she accepts his amnesia as "the act of genius I had always expected from him" (134). Jenny admits that "[i]t was our peculiar shame that he had rejected us when he had attained to something saner than sanity. His very loss of memory was a triumph over the limitations of language which prevent the mass of men from making explicit statements about their spiritual relationships" (133). That limitation—repression of feeling and speech—is of course the linchpin of prewar morality, what Samuel Hynes in his analysis of the novel calls "the pastness of the pre-war past."[33] Rather than engage in the hypocrisy of the Ashburnhams and Dowells or the inflexibility of Alvan Hervey, Chris Baldry simply forgets; in Hynes's words, he finds "an Eden of love and peace."[34] But society will not allow itself to be forgotten, or its dictates ignored; Chris's love affair with a woman of a class lower than his own cannot long be tolerated. His psychiatrist tries to stop this embarrassing situation and return Chris to the front as soon as possible. Dr. Gilbert Anderson, a jolly, unprofessional-looking psychiatrist, is one of a long line of medical men who try to coax Chris back to the reality of the present. No Sir William Bradshaw, Anderson is committed to curing Chris and so allows Margaret to remind him of their dead child, an act that immediately "returns" him to his family and to soldiering. Anderson knows the subject of progeny, dead or alive, will halt Chris's flight from reality—the reality of blood lines and social structures for which the war is being fought cannot be denied. Chris's childhood and his affair with Margaret lay the foundation for his amnesia. Remembering him as a childhood playmate, Jenny emphasizes Chris's need to live in his imagination, really to believe he is a "Red Indian . . . with a stronger motion of the imagination than the ordinary child's make-believe" (19). Already as a child Chris had the desire to escape his empty life. But after his father died, Chris had to take over the family business, "a business that was weighted by the needs of a mob of female relatives who were all useless either in the old way with antimacassars or in the new way with golf clubs" (20–1). Jenny, of course, is a Baldry and one of those females.

Once Chris takes over the estate at Harrowweald, he also assumes the responsibility for his tenants as well. The feudal system binds the landowner to the kind of life he has shunned in his childhood games and in his relationship with Margaret. Yet it would seem that the responsibility is not what sends Chris back into the arms of his former sweetheart but rather the numbing superficiality of his life at Baldry Court, the hypocrisy of his wife Kitty, whom Jenny calls "the falsest thing on earth, who was in tune with every kind of falsity" (181). Kitty has seen to the refurbishing of the house, and the estate itself has been done by architects, so that it has become "matter for innumerable photographs in the illustrated papers" (12). The house, as sterile and composed as Alvan Hervey's prison of a house, is full of "brittle beautiful things" chosen by Jenny and Kitty to make Chris's life gracious. Kitty, however, is the most brittle and beautiful of the objects at Baldry Court. Her superficiality, her concern for appearances, reveals itself when Margaret appears to tell them Chris "isn't well." Kitty, knowing from the appearance of her card that Margaret is working-class, rises from drying her hair in her dead child's nursery, and declares, "I'm seeing her because she may need something, and I specially want to be kind to people while Chris is away. One wants to deserve well of Heaven" (23).

But her philanthropic intentions, her sense of noblesse oblige, cannot keep down Kitty's revulsion at Margaret's poverty. Her clothes, the raincoat, the bedraggled "sticky" straw hat, the "deplorable" umbrella, make Margaret a "spreading stain on the fabric of [their] lives" (37), even according to

Jenny. Margaret knows Kitty and Jenny have not heard about Chris's illness because her scullery maid is sister to one of Kitty's servants, a detail that renders Kitty immediately aloof and suspicious. She rudely accuses Margaret of making up the story so as to extort money from Chris's family. But even worse, the idea that Chris is shell-shocked, possibly as a result of cowardice, is too much for Kitty to endure. When Jenny admits that the story must be true, Kitty wails "it means that he's mad, our Chris, our splendid sane Chris all broken and queer, not knowing us . . ." (38). The possibility of his madness intruding also like a stain threatens the surface calm, the brittle beauty of Baldry Court. When Chris left for the war, he kissed his women and drove off into the quiet morning. His return as damaged goods is not a picture for the illustrated papers. Kitty even believes he may be malingering and not wounded at all, saying within his hearing, "This is all a blind" (66). Kitty's way of reminding "her Chris" that she is his possession on his first night home is to appear in all her jewelry, necklaces, and rings that weigh down her hand, and to remind him that he gave her the jewels. She is also dressed in a white embroidered dress much like her wedding gown. Her intention is theatrical—as she sits waiting for Chris to enter the room, she arranges herself under a candle sconce near green curtains so that she "looked cold as moonlight, as virginity" (56). And Kitty is virginal in the sense that she is very nearly a piece of furniture. As Jenny examines Margaret from the top of the stair as she waits in the hall below, Margaret becomes a striking contrast to "one of Kitty's prettiest chintz arm-chairs" (23) upon which she sits. Yet Jenny finds something redeeming about Margaret that Kitty will not see. Margaret is worn, but alive, with eyes "full of tenderness" (25). Like the home of Alvan Hervey, Baldry Court itself, as an extension of Kitty's superficiality, becomes a prison to Chris if only because the dark air-raid blinds that the occasional Zeppelin necessitates. Jenny, hearing Chris complain that the house is different, comprehends that "[i]f the soul has to stay in its coffin till the lead is struck asunder, in its captivity it speaks such a voice" (54). Once again, as we have seen in *The Good Soldier* and "The Return," the dining room becomes the focal point for domestic misery and captivity. On this first night Chris clearly thinks of Margaret whom he has not yet seen, and when she senses his betrayal, Kitty "put[s] up her hands as if to defend her jewels" (58). With that tension in place, the three go in to dinner where Chris tries to identify familiar pieces of furniture, a familiar servant, dead for seven years. In his amnesia, Chris is excluded from the domestic tranquility and Jenny wonders if "Baldry Court [is] so sleek a place that the unhappy felt offenders there? Then," she muses, beginning to understand the nature of their lives, "we had all been living wickedly and he too" (59). And Jenny is correct. The older Chris who adds to his already substantial property and goes off to war to defend his feudal way of life is also implicated in the creation of this house that has become in its aesthetic perfection "his prison bars" (62).

A crucial moment of contrast between Margaret's vitality and the sterility of the house occurs when Jenny returns from the suburbs with Margaret, now Mrs. Gray, beside her in the chauffeured car. Observing the "controlled beauty" of the estate, Jenny feels a moment of arrogant pity for the once beautiful Margaret. "Surely," Jenny believes, "she must see that this was no place for beauty that has been not mellowed but lacerated by time, that no one accustomed to live here could help wincing at such external dinginess as hers . . ." (115). To Jenny's surprise, Margaret expresses concern for Chris because of how hard he "must have worked to keep it up" (115). Although Jenny's observations suggest that she understands the superficial nature of her life, she cannot part with that superficiality. She knows "the angels would of a certainty be on [Margaret's] side," but still finds her "physically offensive to our atmosphere" (116). The central image of this scene, however, is a black bowl of flowers on the hall table. This bowl, a "new acquisition of Kitty's decorative genius" (117), becomes for Jenny not only an emblem of their aesthetic sensibility, it represents in the white nymph gracing its center her ideal of womanhood and, she assumes, that of Chris as well. Pale and colorless, devoid of passion and frozen in time, the nymph has little to do with flesh-and-blood women, and little to do with the woman Margaret was when she was young. But Jenny virtually worships the image the nymph conveys. Once again knowing she is shallow to judge Margaret for her poverty, Jenny continues to do so when she cynically asserts of the bowl:

> it was absurd to pay attention to this indictment of a woman by a potter's toy, but that toy happened to be also a little image of Chris's conception of women. Exquisite we were according to our equipment; unflushed by appetite or passion, even noble passion; our small heads bent intently on the white flowers of luxury floating on the black waters of life; and he had known none other than us. (117–8)

But he has known others beside Kitty and Jenny; he has known Margaret and he has known her passion. When Kitty first learns of Margaret, she feels betrayed because Chris has known a woman like that and she complains to Jenny, "It shows there are bits of him we don't know" (39). And there are. His life with Margaret is full of passions and needs, satisfied by her warmth and openness. Unlike the controlled beauty of the Baldry estate,

Margaret's beauty as a girl is spontaneous and romantic. Keeping an inn on Monkey Island with her father, Margaret is close to nature, almost an earthmother. Wearing white dresses, she entertains Chris in the rowboat that ferries him to the island. Chris tells Jenny, "She's got an accurate mind that would have made her a good engineer, but when she picks up facts she kind of gives them a motherly hug. She's charity and love itself" (74). But Chris himself does not give Margaret the trust and respect he would give a woman of his own class, a flaw Rollyson calls childish.[35] Chris remembers his relationship with Margaret up to the moment he dumps her because he finds her in the boat with another innkeeper's nephew, that is, a boy of her own class. But Chris's memory also fails at that moment because his life of superficiality and responsibility is calling him as well. He must go to Mexico, in an echo of Austen's *Mansfield Park,* to "keep the mines going through the revolution, to keep the firm's head above water and Baldry Court sleek and hospitable, to keep everything bright and splendid save only his youth, which after that was dulled by care" (110). The boy who would have been a red Indian submerges his own aspirations and desires in hypocritical, shallow, and imperialistic society. He salvages the business and marries the perfect wife in Kitty, an act Jenny analyzes in a passage that perhaps reflects West's own socialism.[36] Women like Kitty, she believes, "are obscurely aware that it is their civilizing mission to flash the jewel of their beauty before all men, so that they shall desire it and work to get the wealth to buy it, and thus be seduced by a present appetite to a tilling of the earth that serves the future. There is," she continues sarcastically, "you know, really room for all of us; we each have our peculiar use" (154). Chris's marriage is empty; his son dies, a detail Kitty fails to share with any of Chris's doctors, and when the war demands a second sacrifice of individuality, he forgets everything except Margaret before his childish display of jealousy and class-consciousness. Kitty grudgingly allows the reunion with Margaret in the same way Leonora Ashburnham allows Teddy's affair with Florence Dowell, but she is as resentful as Leonora. She employs psychiatrists to "cure" him, to bring him back to her, and finally Dr. Anderson does.

Anderson offers an interesting contrast to the fictional Sir William Bradshaw and to the reality of Lewis Yealland, although his pragmatism borders on that of W. H. R. Rivers. After speaking with Chris, Anderson meets with Kitty, then Jenny and Margaret join the discussion. All the while, Anderson seems reluctant to draw Chris out of the romantic past that his amnesia has constructed. When Kitty declares, "if [Chris] would make an effort . . ." Anderson retorts indignantly, "The mental life that can be controlled by effort isn't the mental life that matters. You've been stuffed up when you were young with talk about a thing called self-control" (163). Chris has, of course, employed self-control in his past, having engaged in repression of his desires and his will. After his affair with Margaret, Chris has become the epitome of the proper gentleman, a model of restraint and of suppressed emotion. Anderson is enough of a Freudian, as is Rivers, to believe that Chris's amnesia has to do with suppressed wishes and sets about discovering what the suppressed wish is. It is, of course, that his life might have had meaning or substance, a vague but valid longing that Jenny senses when she admits that "[n]othing and everything was wrong" (167). Margaret is the only participant who seems to have Chris's welfare at heart. She tells Anderson that he can't cure Chris, he can only "make him ordinary" (168), the goal, as we have seen, of most wartime psychiatry. But Anderson's response emphasizes the truth of Margaret's assertion and questions the nature of madness itself. "It's my profession," he says, "to bring people from various outlying districts of the mind to the normal. There seems to be a general feeling it's the place where they ought to be. Sometimes I don't see the urgency myself" (168). Anderson acknowledges that sanity is subjective and socially determined. Since, as Hynes points out, there is a war on, the "general feeling" is that Chris's "happiness and peace" must succumb to it (213). Ironically, it is Margaret who calls to Anderson's attention the matter of the dead child and to whose lot it finally falls to share the news with Chris. Margaret herself only learns of the child when she sees his photograph in Jenny's room where she has gone to remove her "awful" coat and hat before the interview with Anderson. That Kitty "didn't think it mattered" (169) reveals once again her coldness. The child is no more to her than the little dog who struggles for attention at the nursery door as Margaret selects objects to take to Chris to remind him of the child. Chilling as it is, the end of the novel reveals a once more soldierly Chris striding toward the house, his memory intact and a predatory Kitty watching from the nursery above. Yes, Chris is "cured," but we know that something has been lost in the exchange. Not only has Chris, the individual, been jolted out of his Eden into his feudal responsibilities, but he will now go back to the war to resume his leadership role, not to perform garrison duty. The real tragedy here is not so much what has happened to Chris himself, but the clear indication that peculiar sanity as we saw it in *The Good Soldier*, "The Return," and across the Atlantic in *One of Ours*, triumphs. It triumphs in Kitty's glee that "He's cured!" and it triumphs in psychiatry that promotes the arts of conversion and proportion to the exclusion of all else.

Memory Regained: Ford's *Parade's End*

Chris Baldry's amnesia wipes out fifteen years of his past, a past which gives him little satisfaction and to which he feels little connection. The passion of his love for Margaret asserts itself against the superficiality and pain of his adult life. Christopher Tietjens's amnesia wipes out facts, the knowledge that he had in the past used as an employee in the Department of Statistics. Tietjens's facility for details is legendary and when he loses it, he gives the Department a reason not to re-employ him. What could have been an opportunity to remain in London at an office job vanishes, but Tietjens would rather go back to the front than sacrifice his integrity to dishonesty. Tietjens's job with the Department has been to manipulate information—against Germany and also England's allies—to "fak[e] statistics against the other fellow—until you were sick and tired of faking and your brain reeled."[37] Explaining his job to Valentine Wannop before he goes out the first time, Tietjens emphasizes his moral objections to dishonesty. As we have seen, Tietjens lives by an eighteenth-century code of honor that does not brook such deception. As he speaks to Valentine, he cannot reveal specific facts without committing treason, another violation of his code, so he begins by asking, "Supposing one's asked to manipulate the figures of millions of pairs of boots in order to force someone else to send some miserable general and his troops to, say, Salonika—when they and you and common sense and everyone and everything else, know it's disastrous? . . . And from that to monkeying with your own forces. . . . Starving particular units for political. . . ." (236). When his musings come too close to reality, Tietjens backs off, but it is clear that it is impossible for him to continue in his job. In a stroke of irony, Tietjens suggests that someone like Macmaster will "do them more dishonestly," and of course he later does, when stealing Tietjens's ideas that have been tossed out over lunch as a joke (238). When Tietjens is blown up, then, he loses possession of all the minutiae that facilitated his skills with numbers, the minutiae that made him a part of the immorality. In the crucial scene we have already examined in *Some Do Not,* Tietjens, now pronounced ready for combat, still struggles with his loss of memory. When Sylvia asks if he remembers a poem called "Somewhere," he tells her "No! I haven't been able to get up my poetry again" (163). He also struggles to answer a question put to him by Mrs. Wannop concerning the "evil genius of the Congress of Vienna" (166). Tietjens is reading the encyclopedia to regain his knowledge and only gotten as far as K—he is able to quote the Koran—so he cannot remember Metternich. Sylvia, who isn't sure he isn't faking, screams, "For God's sake say Metternich . . .

you're driving me mad" (166).[38] When Sylvia sees his face as she says Metternich, she knows his memory is truly gone.

Tietjens's struggle with General Campion, who represents the war machine, and his struggle with the hypocritical, rumor-bound society that rewards men like Port Scatho and Ruggles whom we have seen earlier, informs his loss of detail. He will, he tells Valentine, go into the antique business, a vocation suitable to his eighteenth-century sensibilities. But in spite of himself and his amnesia, Tietjens performs the chicanery the Department of Statistics wants. In a gossip-provoking conversation with Valentine, Tietjens explains that, after telling off his superior in the Department of Stastics, he has, "in the merest spirit of bravado," taken Macmaster and a sheaf of papers to lunch. Tietjens prefaces this story to Valentine by telling her that "a little of my mathematical brain seems to have come to life again. I've worked out two or three silly problems . . ." (251). Here his glee at regaining his memory and his love of facts and mathematics overpower his hatred of the war machine and accomplish the very thing Tietjens wants to prevent—the manipulation of information that will "rub into our allies that their losses by devastation had been nothing to write home about" (253). By ignoring lost harvests and pretending that repairing bomb damage was no more costly than making normal yearly repairs, Tietjens claims that the allies could be persuaded to reinforce their own lines. When Valentine points out that Tietjens is violating his own beliefs with these calculations, he laughs her off. Vinnie, who is too stupid to do this work on his own, would, Tietjens believes, "as soon think of picking my pocket as of picking my brains. The soul of honour!" (253). But this soul of honor does both. Macmaster does not live by the same moral code by which Christopher lives. He has borrowed several thousand pounds from Tietjens which Mrs. Macmaster refuses to repay, and he steals these calculations made in jest—calculations for which he is knighted.

Tietjens receives no treatment for shell shock and returns to the front still wounded. Responsible for marching men off to the front, Tietjens understands the politics of war that keeps the machinery oiled. Suffering from depression, he speaks of "intense dejection, endless muddles, endless follies, endless villainies" (296). Like Ford, for the part of his life we witness, Tietjens suffers from intermittent memory loss and depression. Toward the end of *The Last Post*, Tietjens struggles to remember where he has put some prints acquired at an antique sale—he does become an antique dealer—and Valentine remembers that he has rolled them up and stuck them in a jar which he has bartered away to another dealer. Ironically, his lapse of memory prevents Tietjens from being present at his brother's death because he is biking to the dealer to find the prints.

Like Edward Ashburnham, Christopher Tietjens believes in a world that does not exist, a world of honor, honesty, and duty. His participation in a war which has no honor, only horror, haunts him. And after the war is over, it is Sylvia's crowd which flourishes. Sylvia rents out Groby, the Tietjens estate, to Mrs. De Bray Pape, an extremely wealthy American who has Groby Great Tree cut down. The tree has grown into the house and when it is cut, part of the wing of the house falls. But worse than that, the tree has come to symbolize for Tietjens the essence of the passing world to which the war and its aftermath have delivered the coup de grâce. But Tietjens again becomes an unwitting actor in bringing about the end of the era he so longs for. He refuses to accept Groby himself because he is still angry at his father for committing suicide and at Mark for believing Ruggles's lies about him, and when he learns of the damage to the house, he has himself flown up to Groby to view it. Aware of the peculiar sanity that has whipped the nation into a militaristic frenzy, one that does not abate with the Armistice, Tietjens still idealizes the past that produced the peculiar sanity bringing about its own demise.

After his return to the front, Tietjens's memory is still shaky. Speaking to Macmaster's nephew McKechnie, whose name he cannot get right, Tietjens repeats an anecdote about the preparation for a ceremony to disband one of Kitchener's battalions. In the ceremony, the band is scheduled to play "The Land of Hope and Glory" after which the adjutant would say, "There will be no more parades" (306). Tietjens continues, "Don't you see how symbolical it was—the band playing *The Land of Hope and Glory,* and then the adjutant saying *There will be no more parades?* . . . For there won't. There won't, there damn well won't. . . . No more Hope, no more Glory, no more parades for you and me any more. Nor for the country . . . nor for the world, I dare say . . . None . . . Gone . . . Na poo, finny! No . . . more . . . parades!" (307). The slang expression is appropriate here because it employs the words of common soldiers who are being sacrificed with little concern by men like Campion. The bitter truth and intense irony of this remark is underscored in blood when O Nine Morgan, to whom Tietjens has refused leave, stumbles into the room with half his face blown away and remarks " 'Ere's another bloomin' casualty" (307). O Nine Morgan's death in Tietjens's arms is the kind of event Rivers recommends be incorporated into the positive memories of war experience. But Tietjens can neither repress nor incorporate. O Nine Morgan remains, in all his bloody glory, a source of regret for Tietjens. The facts that fled at the moment of his own

injury gradually return, but Tietjens will never be as he was. He has not literally come down in the belly of a corpse, but the smell of death and putre-
faction must long be in his nostrils. As W. H. R. Rivers concludes, there is
really no way to heal the wounds of war. Peculiar sanity here inheres in
the idea that there is a way, that humans can forget and incorporate and
go about the business of their daily lives, and that they are hysterical if
they can't.

Civilians

In *The Problem of Nervous Breakdown,* Ash argues that civilians are also
susceptible to war stress.[39] Among the factors likely to produce that stress,
Ash lists the shock of bad news, waiting for bad news, the "ups and downs"
of a protracted war, bad diet he partly attributes to the unavailability of fat
products, and bombs and shells, or air raids. The effects of air raids, he explains, are likely to produce effects similar to those of frontline disorders.
But his most revealing observation, in light of this study, is his description
of certain kinds of "mental unbalance" in which "stricken persons became
deluded into the false belief that they were pursued by spies, or suspected
of spying, or being persecuted by the Government in various mysterious
ways."[40] Here Ash describes a great deal of what passed for normal civilian
behavior, and according to many of the sources presented in Chapter Four,
civilians were often suspected or accused of spying. And yet civilians did
suffer from shell shock in various ways.

Vera Brittain, who lost her brother, one of her best friends, and finally
her fiancé to the war, spent much of its duration nursing in hospitals in
London, Malta, and for a time near the front in France. When the war was
over, Brittain engaged in what in *Testament of Youth* she refers to as a "battle against nervous breakdown which I waged for eighteen months."[41]
Brittain experienced shelling in the hospital in France and of course suffered the loss of the three men to whom she had been closest in her life.
Brittain reports that a symptom of her journey to the "borderland of craziness" was that she believed she was growing a beard and turning into a
witch.[42] Refusing to seek medical help perhaps prolonged these symptoms
which she later ascribed to fatigue. Willa Cather suffered what Sharon
O'Brien refers to as neuritis in her right arm after she finished *One of Ours.*
Her connection to Claude Wheeler severed and the negative reviews coming in, Cather was unable to write. O'Brien suggests that Cather's infir-
mity might have related to a childhood fear of mutilation, but also reminds

us that the text itself is full of "images of dismemberment, most often injuries to the hand and arm."[43] We need only to consult any one of a number of documentaries on the war to realize that such mutilations were commonplace, but we must also remember that loss of the use of limbs was also a symptom of shell shock. That Cather was suffering a belated sympathetic injury is likely.

Vera Brittain's long-time friend Winifred Holtby writes of running through the streets in a Zeppelin attack in her novel *The Crowded Street*. But here, the novel's heroine Muriel Hammond, perhaps like Claude Wheeler, experiences exhilaration over the existential moment of "standing on the world's edge, staring into the din of chaos."[44] Muriel, once again like Claude, lives a constrained life and finds the excitement ennobling, prefers death to "fac[ing] Marshington again and the artificial complications that entangled her life there."[45] But civilians were frequently wounded in such raids. We saw in *Mr. Britling Sees It Through* the fictional death of Aunt Wilshire from a Zeppelin attack. Journalist Elizabeth Shepley Sergeant was severely wounded when she was touring a battlefield that had not yet been "cleaned up."[46] One of her companions picked up and dropped a hand grenade, which exploded on impact, killing the curious companion and wounding Sergeant and the French soldier who was acting as their guide. Sergeant kept a diary, which she later published as *Shadow-Shapes: The Journal of a Wounded Woman,* of the months she spent recuperating in war hospitals. Aware that she was a woman taking up bed space needed by soldiers, Sergeant saw repeatedly the horrors of war wounds. When old friend Willa Cather published *One of Ours,* Sergeant panned it as a romantic invention and their relationship never quite regained its original intensity.

Among the civilian writings about war stress, perhaps the most extraordinary is that of Hilda Doolittle, H. D. A poet, H. D. wrote intense, surreal prose which, in addition to chronicling her war experiences, tells of her relationships with Richard Aldington (her husband during the war), and D. H. Lawrence, who along with Frieda, moved in with H. D. after his expulsion from Cornwall. H. D.'s emotional connection to the war began on the day war was declared. On that day, according to biographer Barbara Guest, H. D. found out she was pregnant with a child Guest believes she did not want. The child was stillborn after the sinking of the Lusitania. H. D. maintained the news of the sinking, which she claimed she heard in a shocking way, triggered the miscarriage. Guest argues that H. D.'s guilt and not the war news caused the loss of the child,[47] but the connection between the two events illustrates the potential for devastation such a tragedy posed for civilians. Ash, if we recall, does list shocking news as one of the causes of civilian shell shock.

Surreal City: H. D.'s *Kora and Ka* and *Bid Me to Live*

Two works, *Bid Me to Live,* which was first called *Madrigal* and in her words "phoenixed out of [an earlier autobiographical novel] *Asphodel,*"[48] and *Kora and Ka,* a short piece published privately, deal with H. D.'s experiences of the war. *Kora and Ka,* which Trudi Tate calls "a strange impenetrable piece of writing,"[49] deals with the mental breakdown of a man named John Helforth who lost two brothers in the war. Helforth was to have gone himself, but the war ended before he was old enough. Older now and settled into the rut of a businessman's life, Helforth experiences survivor guilt and rage at his mother for having sent her sons so willingly to their deaths. Helforth has traveled to the country with Kora, a woman/lover who has taken him there and seems to be helping with his psychoanalysis. Helforth's Ka, an Egyptian spirit which lives after the body is dead, narrates much of the novel. In a passage listing most of the atrocity stories of the war including the handless Belgian babies, crucified Canadians, and the corpse factory, Helforth argues of British men, "systematically we were trained to blood-lust and hatred. We were sent out, iron shod to quell an enemy who had made life horrible."[50] Helforth uses the inclusive pronoun we, even though he has never worn the uniform of a British soldier. The atrocities, he says, he has read about in the papers which "fed out belching mothers, who belched out in return, fire and carnage in the name of Rule Britannia."[51] Returning, as we have repeatedly, to the Little Mother whose letter Robert Graves quotes in *Good-Bye to All That,* we see once again the operation of peculiar sanity in propaganda and jingoism. In *Kora and Ka,* however, a kind of belated civilian shell shock grows out of war fervor. The fervor itself drives Helforth mad, if only because he cannot participate in the war. Referring to the propensity we have seen for some practitioners to see shell shock as a means of escaping the necessities of war, Trudi Tate suggests that Helforth's "shell shock" is a way for him to "to enter the war and share its suffering," even though now as a cynical man, he can see its true nature.[52] Tate goes on to suggest that the atrocity stories themselves were "unbearable to imagine" and could in that way have produced war neuroses,[53] a prospect that, if true, further implicates the role of propaganda in destructive war behavior.

In *Bid Me to Live,* however, H. D. tells a fairly straightforward, and fairly obvious, autobiographical story of the war. Set in rooms in Mecklenburgh Square where H. D. had lived with Aldington before he went off to war, the novel reveals the emotional tension of a doomed relationship. For Julia Ashton, H. D.'s autobiographical double, memories of her dead child and the realities of war—an ever more estranged husband, air raids, wounded soldiers at the cinema—all merge into a mixture of personal and universal suffering. Julia's personal struggle with her husband Rafe, her confidante Rico (D. H. Lawrence), and her lover-to-be, Vane (Cecil Gray), distracts her from the war, and yet the war intrudes on every element of these relationships. Early in the novel as Julia is remembering an air raid, she thinks of the child she has lost. Running downstairs, she has stumbled and cut her knee. If she had had the child in her arms, she thinks, but the thought will not form and then she claims, "No. She did not think this."[54] Like Septimus Smith, Julia has difficulty processing emotion, as Rafe reminds her. Once again propaganda also plays a role in emotional disturbance. Julia speaks of the slow progression of the war and her growing insensitivity. "Seasons revolved around horrors," she explains, "until one was numb and the posters that screamed at one at streetcorners had no . . . reality" (37). But other characters also seem numb to the trauma of war. Julia's soon-to-be lover, Vane, comes to take her to dinner during an air raid and Julia is astonished that he seems not to have noticed, that he wants only to finish his pipe before they go into the streets. On the darkened stairs, Julia's emotional distance turns her into a child. She suddenly feels she is playing a game of hide-and-seek. Repeatedly she refers to the game as they slip out of the darkened house, past the landlady who would be scandalized to see her leave the safety of home. Avoiding the other occupants, Julia and Vane "crept past the door like children playing a game; her hand was on the front door knob. 'Slide after me'" she tells Vane, "'and if Miss Ames pops out, we'll run'" (109). But once into the street, Julia calls it a "city of dreadful night." Fires burn in the distance, an ambulance screams past, and another bomb falls close by; still Julia thinks about "dining out" (110).

The madness of living in a city torn by war, the pain of losing a child, a husband, press in upon Julia with the force of an invading army. Her torpor, reflected in what Tate calls "remarkably callous moments,"[55] reminds us that shell shock takes many forms. Julia does not hallucinate, as do Helforth and Septimus Smith. And yet what finally emerges is a kind of repression similar to that found often in shell shock. The novel ends with Julia and Vane in Cornwall near the house the Fredericks/Lawrences were driven out of. In a disjointed narrative which is epistolary in nature, Julia addresses Rico/Lawrence. Her memories and observations do not touch directly on the war, but its echoes are there, as they might be in dreams—Rafe's mistress in their flat in London, an opaque reference to a child. Out of London, the war then is obliterated except for these repressed memories.

A Freudian herself, H. D. went to Vienna when she was forty-seven, according to Guest, to study with Freud and enter into analysis with him. Ironically, she was there as signs of the Second World War were appearing in Europe. Guest believes that H. D. gained confidence in herself as a writer, but that she was not "'healed as a person.'"[56] In 1946, she had a mental breakdown. Although its sources were not obvious, Guest connects it to H. D. "overextending" herself, and to her obsession with spiritualism and seances, what Guest calls "a frantic search into the unknown, the invisible—flights from a visible reality whose strains must have pressed upon her consciousness," that is, the strain of experiencing another war.[57]

Medical data, fictional accounts, and biographies all suggest that shell shock, whether it developed as a result of active military service, support service such as nursing, or civilian exposure to shelling and bombs, never fully leaves its victims. Because the war experience is so disturbing to human sensibility, any other name seems inappropriate; to call such a response a neurosis reflects the subjective nature of sanity or madness. If we see the soldier whom Rivers describes in "The Repression of War Experience" as a metaphor for war experience, if war means falling head first into a rotten corpse, then we may wonder how anyone comes away unscathed. In light of post-Vietnam stress disorders, we may conclude no one does. Certainly Ford, West, Brittain, Holtby, Sergeant, H. D. and a host of others[58] lived with the war and wrote about it for the rest of their lives. In *Bid Me to Live,* Julia thinks of the lost child, of her memory of it. "It was shut in her as other things were shut in her because 'the war will be over.' (The war will never be over.)" (12). For those who saw it, it never was.

Pestis Teutonicus: Kipling's "Mary Postgate" and "A Madonna of the Trenches"

Probably the last place we should expect to find references to shell shock, civilian or military, is in the works of Rudyard Kipling. But among Kipling's extensive World War I writings, two stories, "Mary Postgate" and "A Madonna of the Trenches," deal either openly or obliquely with the subject. The war did not spare Kipling—his only son John was killed at the

Battle of Loos in September 1915, but the Kiplings held out hope for months that since his body was not recovered he might turn up wounded in a German prison. He did not. Kipling had long hated Germany. In January 1916, he wrote to Herbert Baillie,

> wherever the German—man or woman—gets a suitable culture to thrive in, he or she means death and loss to civilized people, precisely as germs of any disease suffered to multiply mean death or loss to mankind. There is no question of hate or anger or excitement in the matter, any more than there is in flushing out sinks or putting oil on water to prevent mosquitos hatching eggs. As far as we are concerned, the German is typhoid or plague—Pestis teutonicus, if you like.[59]

By this date, Kipling had for the most part accepted that John, missing since September 27, 1915, was dead.[60] But Kipling's hatred of Germany did not arise out of John's death. Examining the sources of Kipling's militaristic rhetoric, A. Michael Matin points to an entry in the OED tracing the pejorative use of the word Hun; as one of two examples, the dictionary cites a 1902 poem "The Rowers" in which Kipling uses the phrase "the shameless Hun."[61] And as J. I. M. Stewart reminds us, much of Kipling's writing was constructed on the English schoolboy image of sacrifice. The young officers who "died by thousands and tens of thousands while leading and encouraging their men in the mud of Flanders were ruled by a code, fortified . . . by a myth, which Kipling had done as much to create as all the public schools of England put together."[62]

Building on that hatred, Kipling believed the war was a time to "do as much killing as possible."[63] The Germans were responsible for the war and in perpetrating it were guilty of countless atrocities. Much of Kipling's short fiction written during and about the war accepts reports of German atrocities as factual. His letters from the early days of the war admonish Americans to accept the truth of Germany's brutality in Belgium.[64] "Swept and Garnished" and "Mary Postgate" were both written in 1915 before Jack's death and as waves of refugees still poured into England. "Swept and Garnished," the story which precedes "Mary Postgate" in *A Diversity of Creatures,* deals with German brutality through the hallucinations of Frau Ebermann, a compulsively neat middle-class German hausfrau. In her bedroom as she lies ill with flu, Frau Ebermann sees Belgian children who have been murdered by German shellings of civilian neighborhoods. The children wait there for their murdered parents to retrieve them. Frau Ebermann repeats the German propaganda that they must have run into the streets to see the soldiers and been accidentally killed, but the children know better. In a stroke of Kiplingesque sentimentality, the children explain, "There isn't anything left" of their homes including the ducks and the cows.[65] Norman Page and Peter Firchow both link "Swept and Garnished" and "Mary Postgate" because the stories describe what appear to be hallucinations, the Belgian children in "Swept and Garnished" and the German airman in "Mary Postgate."[66] But more striking is the reliance on atrocity stories, not only to establish plot but also to explain aberrant behavior. Also striking is the lack of irony in those explanations. Wharton's Troy Balknap and George Campton repeat anti-German clichés, but the narration maintains an ironic tone, balancing their fervor with Harvey Mayhew's patriotic posturing. Kipling seems to suggest here that the German savages and their war have wrought a kind of psychosis which pervades civilian and military life alike, what Bodelsen refers to as "the spiritual harm that Germany has done to the English."[67] Shell shock, war trauma, is a disease wrought by *Pestis teutonicus*.

Genteel Sadism: Kipling's "Mary Postgate"

Mary Postgate at forty-four is a gentlewoman's companion, one of those women who must, as Mary Wollstonecraft pointed out one hundred years before, support herself in one of three ways available to middle-class women: as a governess, a teacher, or in Mary's case, a companion. Miss Fowler is crippled, and Mary serves as a kind of nurse/servant to her and to her orphaned nephew Wynn. Wynn is full of life and appropriately disrespectful of "the old girls," and when the war arrives, Mary knits him a cardigan and packs him off to join the Flying Corps. From the outset, Miss Fowler's attitude is glib at best. When Wynn asks his aunt for a larger allowance, Miss Fowler tells Mary that he should have the money because "[t]he chances are he won't live long to draw it."[68] And indeed he doesn't, a detail which is revealed early in the story when the war is first invoked. We are told that this war, "unlike all wars that Mary could remember, did not stay decently outside England and in the newspapers, but intruded on the lives of people whom she knew" (423).

After Wynn's plane crashes during a training exercise, Mary and Miss Fowler act with almost indecent haste in putting Wynn away. Shedding no tears, wearing no mourning, the women lament the detail that Wynn has died training rather than fighting. When Mary shows her the death notice, Miss Fowler says cynically, "I never expected anything else, . . . but," she goes on, "I'm sorry it happened before he had done anything." Mary, for whom the room swirls, agrees: "Yes, . . . [i]t's a great pity he didn't die in action after he had killed somebody" (427). Both women demonstrate a vicious fervor here which foreshadows part if not all of the resolution. The women's indecency continues when immediately after Wynn's funeral, they "have a general tidy" (429), that is, they give away Wynn's clothes and burn his remaining possessions. At every step, Miss Fowler reiterates "that disposes of that" (430–1).

Because Miss Fowler is crippled, the actual job of incineration falls to Mary, and in the performance of that duty, Mary's shell shock finally becomes manifest. On her way to the village to buy paraffin for the fire, Mary witnesses the death of a child. Critics make much of this incident and question whether little Edna Gerritt is actually the victim of German atrocity or just poor property maintenance. Mary has stopped to chat with Nurse Eden when the explosion occurs. Nurse Eden does not think of the Germans, but Mary declares without doubt that the destruction was the result of "a bomb" dropped from a German plane (434). Just minutes before, she thought she heard a plane, but believed it was "one of ours" (434). The plane, Mary assumes, must instead have been German and the death a result of bombing. Nurse Eden calls the Germans "filthy pigs," and Mary repeats one of Wynn's phrases, "they are bloody pagans"(434–5). Dr. Hennis, a special constable, decides that the shed in which Edna was playing has fallen because it was old and rotten and tells Mary not to spread the word that a bomb fell. This is the way atrocity stories originate, and Mary is admonished to remain silent. But because this war is not decent, Mary herself believes the indecent, that German bombs shred the bodies of children. Suffering from the stress of Wynn's death, Mary undergoes further trauma when she actually sees Edna Gerritt's mangled body. Already disposed to violence, Mary is now out for blood.

Historically, bombs were dropped from airplanes on both sides as early as October of 1914. Martin Gilbert reports that on October 10, during a German attack of the French city of Lille, a boy and a horse were killed by a bomb dropped from a German airplane. By November 21, the British were also bombing from planes in what he calls "the first long-distance bombing raid of the war." Three planes carrying four bombs apiece flew from Belfort to Friedrichshafen with the mission of bombing the German Zeppelin sheds there. A Zeppelin was hit and damaged in the raid, but part of the incident also closely parallels the climax of "Mary Postgate." One of the planes was forced to land and the pilot was attacked and beaten by German civilians until German soldiers saved him.[69]

Recent critics who have looked at "Mary Postgate" tend to see the final scene as a figment of Mary's imagination, a hallucination.[70] Frau Ebermann's hallucination in "Swept and Garnished" does establish a precedent for such a belief. But Frau Ebermann sees mutilated children in her hallucination; Mary Postgate sees the mutilated body of Edna Gerritt in the flesh and tracks her very real blood into Miss Fowler's house. The murdered children punish Frau Ebermann for her kinsmen's atrocities by showing her their true nature; Mary punishes a specific German for a similar atrocity. After Edna's death, Mary is home burning Wynn's effects at the back of the garden when she sees a downed German pilot who begs her to find a doctor. She believes he is the "pagan" who has murdered Edna Gerritt with a bomb and tells him in German that she will not help him because she has seen the dead child. Mary is aware, as she stokes the fire, of propaganda stories she has read in the papers, but here the war has strayed "indecently" into her life. "It was no question of reading horrors out of newspapers to Miss Fowler," she believes. "[She] had seen it with her own eyes on the 'Royal Oak' kitchen table" (440). "It" is the heap of "vividly coloured strips and strings" that was once Edna Gerritt. That Edna's remains trigger Mary's hatred of all things German, not pity for the dead child, must depend on her knowledge of those horrors in the newspaper. Propaganda and war stress together motivate Mary's behavior. The idea that Mary would not behave the way she does if such an incident were real and not imagined serves only to soften for critics the violence of the resolution. Trained not to dwell on the unpleasant, Mary nonetheless allows her war fervor to trigger perverse sexual urges repressed by that training and herein lies the story's scandal. Mary hums and flushes, she believes from the fire's heat, as she waits for the German to die. Once he obliges, she "dr[aws] her short breath between her teeth and shiver[s] from head to foot" (442). Mary's response is sadistic and certainly not "appropriate" behavior for a gentlewoman's companion. She is infected with the disease *Pestis teutonicus* as Frau Ebermann is infected with flu virus. But to lay the blame for this transgression solely at the feet of Germany ignores the complexities of war and war trauma and further extends the reach of atrocity stories and propaganda.

The Demon of Mons: Kipling's "A Madonna of the Trenches"

Even more puzzling in many ways is "A Madonna of the Trenches." The shell-shock victim in this story, set well after the war, is a former soldier. Like a number of other Kipling stories, "A Madonna of the Trenches" begins in a Masonic lodge where Strangwick the ex-soldier, in the middle of a dull lecture, suffers a relapse of shell shock. Dr. Keede, a member of the lodge, was attached to Strangwick's regiment during the war and treated him for his ailment when it first appeared. Keede believes that Strangwick is lying about the source of his trauma, which Strangwick claims is the creaking sound made by frozen corpses used to prop up the walls and floors of two French trenches, French End and Butcher's Row. Drugged with a "dark dose of something that was not sal volatile,"[71] Strangwick begins to relate a tale, not of the war, but of the home front. Strangwick's sergeant, John Godsoe, has died of carbon monoxide poisoning after being shut in a dressing station with two charcoal braziers. Godsoe, it turns out, was a close friend and neighbor to Strangwick's family.

Here the tale takes a strange twist. Strangwick admits to Keede that his Auntie Armine and John Godsoe, though both married to other people, had been lovers, a circumstance he only discovered right before Godsoe's death. Strangwick has relayed from his aunt a message telling Godsoe that "I expect to be through with my little trouble by the twenty-first of next month, an' I'm dyin' to see him as soon as possible after that date" (250). Strangwick believes her trouble was "a bit of a gatherin' in 'er breast," although he goes on to say that she never talked much about her body. Many critics, Edmund Wilson among them, believe the gathering is a euphemism for cancer and that Auntie Armine knows on what day she will die.[72] But when Strangwick sees his aunt at Christmas, she shows no signs of succumbing to cancer so soon, and he tells Keede of the message, "[t]he thing hardly stayed in my mind at all" (251). If, however, the gathering is not in her breast but elsewhere, as Tonie and Valmai Holt believe, Auntie Armine is pregnant and has scheduled an abortion for that date.[73] When Godsoe sees the apparition of Strangwick's aunt, he tells her, "this must be only the second time we've been alone together in all these years" (256). We may assume the first—and we will return to this moment—is the encounter that has set these events in motion. And Godsoe's response to Auntie Armine's note does not indicate that he expects her to die of cancer; it indicates a sense of relief. He says immediately that he will ask for leave and in Strangwick's words, "look[s] different all of a sudden—as if he'd got shaved" (252). Godsoe is in fact expecting to go on his leave and does not consider doing otherwise until, on the day in question, he learns that Strangwick has had a vision of his aunt, whose first name is Bella, in the trench called French End. Godsoe and Strangwick proceed there and together, see her again, beckoning to Godsoe who looks at her as if he "could 'ave et 'er" (256). Critics who view the story as a triumph of love over death wholesalely ignore Strangwick's response, which is a mixture of awe and disgust. He repeats several times, "An' she nearer fifty than forty an' me own Aunt!" (256). Bella's sexual aggression is neither expected nor appropriate behavior for a middle-aged madonna. And yet, Strangwick also asserts that "I didn't know such things was or could be!" (256). Bella is eager to have Godsoe join her. She tries to get him to use his rifle, but Godsoe says, "No! Don't tempt me, Bella. We've all eternity ahead of us. An hour or two won't make any odds" (256). And with that, shuts himself up in the dressing station with the apparition.

In *Something of Myself,* Kipling recounts an incident that occurred late in the summer of 1913 when he was participating in maneuvers with the Eighth Division. As the skirmish unfolded, the weather changed, and Kipling "conceived the whole pressure of our dead of the Boer War flickering and re-forming as the horizon flickered in the heat."[74] He even heard the clatter of a horse's hooves and a soldier's song from 1901–2. When the officers conducting the exercises heard of Kipling's vision, they called off maneuvers. Later, Kipling writes, he tried to fictionalize the moment, but "in cold blood it seemed more and more fantastic and absurd, unnecessary and hysterical."[75] After the war, he destroyed the story, claiming that, "there is a type of mind that dives after what it calls 'psychical experiences.' And I am in no way psychic."[76]

And yet, according to biographer Andrew Lycett, Kipling did maintain a fascination for "collective hallucination."[77] Bella's appearance in "A Madonna of the Trenches" is such a vision. The horror here is that the vision Godsoe and Strangwick have is a kind of La Belle Dame sans Merci. Godsoe and Bella have committed adultery, and Bella, who has paid with her life, lures Godsoe to his death as well. While Kipling may have been often accused of misogyny, the implications here go much deeper. In this perverted image of the madonna, we may find something of Mary Postgate. Given Kipling's hatred for the evils of the war brought on by Germany, and given the extent to which the home front is tainted by that war, we may see in Bella Armine another good but dull woman who has lost her sense of correctness. If, prior to the war, Bella Armine and John Godsoe have harbored squelched feelings for one another, it would not seem surprising for the two to act on those feelings before Godsoe shipped out to the front from which he might not return. Recall, he says they have only been alone together once. Without the war, John and Bella would have continued as "friends," but once again as Mary Postgate maintains, the war "did not stay decently outside England and in the newspapers, but intruded on the lives of people whom she knew" (423). An unlikelier Belle Dame sans Merci has undoubtedly never existed, but this is what Bella becomes under the tutelage of the savage Hun, just as Mary Postgate has become an unlikely sadist. Strangwick's shell shock, his psychic undoing, occurs because he is still bewitched by that look Bella gave John Godsoe. Twice Strangwick refers to the look, the first time before he tells Keede the whole story. When Keede asks if Strangwick has married his sweetheart, Strangwick replies, "No! . . . 'Fore it ended, I knew what reel things reelly mean" (250). Later, after the story has been aired, Strangwick tells Keede "not till I see that look on a face . . . that look. . . . I'm not taking any. The reel thing's life an' death. It *begins* at death, d'ye see" (259, italics Kipling's). Assuredly, Kipling does not mean for us to believe that love is best pursued in death. Love is only best pursued in death when those civilization-killing Huns have put things out of kilter. Even Strangwick's "shell shock" is a home front disease wrought by *Pestis teutonicus.*

Of all stories of World War I, Kipling's are perhaps the strangest. As Paul Fussell argues in *The Great War and Modern Memory,* World War I literature gave us our sense of irony. "Mary Postgate" and "A Madonna of the Trenches" lack irony but in turning to war fervor and to hatred as sources of psychic imbalance and misbehavior, they illustrate the peculiar sanity of war as soundly as any story of the greatest cynics.

Conclusion

After the war ended, Britain, France, America, and their allies experienced a jubilation the century had not seen since its beginning. But the joy of victory was tempered by the devastating influenza epidemic that began in the fall of 1918 and before it was over had taken in America alone more dead than the battles of World War I, World War II, Korea, and Vietnam.[1] The Spanish flu, as it was then called, killed the strong and healthy as well as the weak, and even today, scientists struggle to isolate the virus from bodies buried in permafrost in Alaska and Norway. The virus's DNA sequence, it seems, has been isolated, but no vaccine has to date been developed. And according to Gina Kolata, in her investigation of attempts to isolate the virus, no one is sure if the virus would return in exactly the same form it had in 1918.[2] Theories are also still unclear as to why the 1918 flu was so deadly. One theory holds that the 1918 virus was similar to a virus that appeared in 1890 and that victims of the 1890 flu developed antibodies against the virus which, when it struck again in 1918, attacked with such vengeance that white blood cells themselves caused the lungs to fill with fluid, thus suffocating the stricken victim. But without isolating the 1890 virus, this theory cannot be confirmed.[3]

Seen as a metaphor, this pandemic must have seemed to those who survived it as another kind of war, or a continuation of the war just ending, a force that demanded lives without regard for its victims. For a war-weary population, the flu must have appeared as a final apocalyptic sign of the terrors of the emerging century. Katherine Anne Porter, in her short novel *Pale Horse, Pale Rider,* describes in fiction her own bout with the flu. Dream sequences typical of Porter's style form much of the work. As she recovers with the knowledge of her own personal losses and of her near-death experience, she dreads the world into which she must emerge, a world where "all objects and beings [are] meaningless, ah, dead and withered things that believed themselves alive."[4] This inability to forget is a symptom also experienced by victims of shell shock.

As we know from more recent history, however, the true apocalypse was still to come. The seeds of a second world war were germinating, ready to spread almost as fast as the Spanish flu. After the second war ended in nuclear conflagration, and the escalating cold war threatened to provoke another more terrifying and perhaps final annihilation, daily life, at least in America, was pervaded with a sense of doom. Ordinary people built bomb shelters and mainstream ministers spoke in interviews of the second coming. As an adolescent, I nightly experienced apocalyptic dreams of planets standing still and the moon, much smaller than it is in reality, resting on the earth. During the Cuban missile crisis, along with many other Americans, I virtually bade my future goodbye.

The point of this self-revelation from a thirty-odd year perspective is to establish how pervasive is the taint of peculiar sanity, how far it has come since the days of the Great War. The uses and sources of propaganda, the linchpin of peculiar sanity, are infinite, the effects of rumor and gossip incalculable. The McCarthy hearings, which fed on lies and assumptions— the same kinds of lies and assumptions my mother feared in the early days of 1960—remain one of the black spots of the modern era. But the First World War looms at the beginning of the twentieth century as the defining moment for the way war would henceforth be waged, at least on the home front. The Great War's peculiar sanity is mythologized in its sheet music, its propaganda posters, and its literature. The peculiar sanity of the Purity Crusade, the Temperance movement, the flagging morality of the Victorian era, all led to the patriotic fervor that defined the war as an almost holy moment in history. H. G. Wells, who was the antithesis of the proper Edwardian, saw the war as the last war, the war that would forever end war. Perhaps the same naïveté that allowed Edward Ashburnham to believe in true love and the feudal system allowed Wells to coin the term we still use today to describe the war which began war rather than ended it.

Ford, Wells, Wharton, and many others wrote propaganda, not just promoting the interests of the Allies, but vilifying the enemy. Here, I might add, arises an interesting dilemma. There seems to be some agreement that the war could have been avoided if the appropriate political decisions had been made. But once Germany crossed into Belgium, the prospect for political solutions vanished, and ethnic hatreds, some of them stemming from the lengthy tussle over Alsace and Lorraine, emerged full-blown. It also seems likely that Germany would have annexed much of Europe had the Allies not fought back. There emerges then a fine line between "reasoned recognition of . . . peril" (*Fighting* 238) and war-mongering, and Wharton seems to have come closest to that reasoned recognition in the work she did for Frenchwomen who were unemployed because of the war.[5]

Much has been written lately on the Great War and its literature. Previously ignored, women's writing about the war has become important as a source of an alternative point of view. But at the beginning of the twenty-first century, looking back to what may be the defining moment of the twentieth is appropriate. While there may be some debate as to whether the Great War was the defining moment of the twentieth century, it is the purpose of this project to suggest that it was. So much horror has intervened since the 1918 Armistice, including recent ethnic cleansings in Serbia (where many locate the start of the Great War), it becomes easy to ignore those days of "Tipperary," and home fires, and white feathers, those days of seemingly endless innocence. But there was a dark side to every cheery anthem, a leering Hun, a handless Belgian baby lurking beneath—a gap between the reality and the perception of war. The real horrors of the trenches, of civilian bomb shelters, could not have decorated store fronts, could not have recruited, could not have enlisted civilians in the war to conserve sugar and flour, could not have supported what Wilfred Owen calls "the old Lie," that it is sweet and fitting to die in war.[6] It wasn't, and as the men and women who had experienced the war began to write about it, to explore the gap between myth and reality, literature took on a slightly different tone, that of despair and alienation. True, the foundations of literary modernism had been established before the war, but much of modernist literature revolves around that event or its aftermath. In addition, much of that literature, in its examination of the gap between myth and reality, reveals the war's peculiar sanity. Even *Mr. Britling Sees It Through,* which sold well in Britain and America during the war, reveals the tragedy and madness of war, and the fruits of warmongering.

Finally, the question arises as to what role peculiar sanity has in the diagnosis and treatment of shell shock, both military and civilian. Since the definition of madness is by nature subjective, as Foucault suggests, the definition of shell shock should also come under scrutiny. Perhaps the best example of the tragedy of shell shock lies in a 1998 debate before the British House of Commons. Families of men executed for desertion or mutiny, many of whom were underaged and shell-shocked, had petitioned for an across-the-board pardon. Armed forces minister John Reid declared "a deep sense of regret at this loss of life," but failed to endorse the pardon. The government's hesitation to grant the pardon was based on the notion that some of the men shot were cowards, an interesting piece of illogic, since deserters are generally shot. John Hipkin, veteran and spokesperson for the families called the shootings "the judicial murder of under-age boys, the shooting of shell-shocked men" and claimed that, "We know where the cowards are now, and they're not wearing khaki."[7] Shell shock was often perceived as cowardice, even when the men were relieved of duty and sent to hospitals. The accounts of treatment methods suggest that even the medical community saw the malady as one within the control of the patient's will. To be given electrotherapy, shocked, is one thing, but to be shot is another. Reid, in his address to Commons, remembered the last words of one young soldier: "What will my mother say?"[8]

Clearly, peculiar sanity declares these men cowards who should be shot. Peculiar sanity promotes treating shell-shocked patients as if they are bad children. Refusing to look beyond the clichés of war, people overcome with war mania fail to acknowledge that the human mind ultimately rebels at the act of war and shuts down, resulting not only in paralysis, memory loss, blindness and deafness, but also in the cynicism, loss of faith, and squelched emotions of the war's aftermath. And therein lies the true birth of the twentieth century, the true source of the despair and alienation that characterized literary modernism.

Sergeant Alvin York, an American from Kentucky fighting in the Argonne forest, singlehandedly killed twenty-eight Germans and captured 132 more. But York lost many of his friends in the battle and paid the price for his conquest. The next day he went back to the battle scene to look for wounded and found none. In his journal he wrote, "Everything destroyed, torn up, killed—trees, grass, men—. . . I was mussed up inside worser than I had ever been. I didn't want to kill a whole heap of Germans no how. I didn't hate them, but I done it just the same. I have tried to forget."[9] From York's tone, it is clear that he will never forget. Praised as a hero, York became one of the wounded of the war for doing his job. Never, of course, registered as a shell-shock victim, York and millions like him remain as the war's most tragic legacy.

Notes

Notes to Introduction

1. Joseph Conrad, "Heart of Darkness," *Youth* (New York: Doubleday, Page & Company, 1923), 116.

2. Paul Fussell, *The Great War and Modern Memory* (New York: Oxford Univ. Press, 1975), 29.

3. Ibid.

4. Ibid., 8.

5. Ibid., 23.

6. Ibid., 9. Italics Fussell's.

7. Ibid.

8. Sandra Gilbert and Susan Gubar, *No Man's Land: The Place of the Woman Writer in the Twentieth Century,* 3 vols. (New Haven: Yale Univ. Press, 1988–94), 2: 259.

9. Ibid., 260.

10. Ibid., 261.

11. Joseph Conrad, "Autocracy and War," *Notes on Life and Letters* (New York: Doubleday, Page & Company, 1923), 87.

12. Gilbert and Gubar, *No Man's Land,* 1:xiii.

13. Trudi Tate, *Modernism, History and the First World War* (Manchester: Manchester Univ. Press, 1998), 3.

14. Ibid., 5.

15. Trudi Tate has also edited two other volumes concerning war, *Women's Fiction and the Great War* with Suzanne Raitt, a collection of essays on World War One fiction, and *Women, Men and the Great War,* an anthology of short fiction from World War One. Tate is a feminist, but believes that "gender is only one aspect of subjectivity and of writing" (*Modernism* 4). I have also relied on three works by Samuel Hynes, *The Soldier's Tale* and *A War Imagined: The First World War and English Culture,* and *The Edwardian Turn of Mind,* which looks at prewar culture in ways that enable me to link it to wartime culture.

16. Claire Tylee, *The Great War and Women's Consciousness: Images of Militarism and Womanhood in Women's Writings, 1914–1964* (Iowa City: Univ. of Iowa Press, 1990), 55.

17. Peter Buitenhuis, *The Great War of Words: British, American, and Canadian Propaganda and Fiction, 1914–1933* (Vancouver: Univ. of British Columbia Press, 1987), 27.

18. James M. Beck, *The War and Humanity: A Further Discussion of the Ethics of the World War and the Attitude and Duty of the United States,* 2nd ed. (New York: Putnam, 1917), 221–2, italics mine.

19. Willa Cather, *One of Ours* (1922; reprint New York: Vintage, 1991), 194.

20.   Nor is it my purpose in any way to establish blame for the war as does Niall Ferguson in *The Pity of War* (New York: Basic Books, 1999).

Notes to Chapter 1

1. Lawrence LeShan, *The Psychology of War: Comprehending Its Mystique and Its Madness* (Chicago: Noble, 1992), 36.

2. Sam Keen, *Faces of the Enemy* (New York: Harper and Row, 1986).

3. Carl Jung, "Approaching the Unconscious," *Man and His Symbols,* ed. M.-L. Von Franz (New York: Dell, 1964), 73.

4. Konrad Lorenz, *On Aggression,* trans. Marjorie Kerr Wilson (New York: Harcourt, Brace and World, 1966).

5. Michel Foucault, *Madness and Civilization: A History of Insanity in the Age of Reason,* trans. Richard Howard (1965; reprint, New York: Vintage, 1988), ix.

6. Ibid., 64.

7. José Barchilon, introduction to *Madness and Civilization: A History of Insanity in the Age of Reason,* by Michel Foucault, v–viii.

8. Elmer E. Southard, *Shell-Shock and Other Neuropsychiatric Problems,* (1919; reprint, New York: Arno, 1973).

9. Joseph Conrad, "The Tale," *Tales of Hearsay* (New York: Doubleday, 1925), 61.

10. Joseph Conrad, "Autocracy and War," *Notes on Life and Letters* (New York: Doubleday, 1921), 87.

11. Martin Gilbert, *The First World War: A Complete History* (New York: Henry Holt, 1994), xv.

12. Samuel Hynes, *The Edwardian Turn of Mind* (Princeton: Princeton Univ. Press, 1968), 334.

13. Ibid., 3.

14. Scott Palmer, *Jack the Ripper: A Reference Guide* (Lanham, MD: Scarecrow Press, 1995.

15. Samuel Hynes, *The Edwardian Turn of Mind,* 4.

16. Martin Gilbert, *The First World War,* 13.

17. Ibid., 15.

18. Ibid., 13.

19. Ford Madox Ford, *The Good Soldier* (1915; reprint, New York: Vintage, 1989), 40.

20. Samuel Hynes, 5–6.

21. Walter E. Houghton, *The Victorian Frame of Mind, 1830–1870* (1957; reprint, New Haven: Yale Univ. Press, 1985), 430.

22. James Marchant, editor's note to *The Nation's Morals: Being the Proceedings of the Public Morals Conference held in London on the 14th and 15th July, 1910* (London: Cassell and Co., 1910), vii.

23. Samuel Hynes, *The Edwardian Turn of Mind,* 280.

24. Ibid., 282.

25. C. W. Saleeby, "Education for Parenthood," *The Nation's Morals,* 19. Italics Saleeby's.

26. Samuel Hynes says Marchant "coined the term" racial instinct in the 1909 pamphlet, *Social Hygenics,* but Saleeby, who founded the Eugenics Society, maintains that he has "been in the habit of using [the term] for some years" ("Education,"19). See *The Edwardian Turn of Mind,* 284–7.

27. Ibid., 287.

28. C. W. Saleeby, "Education for Parenthood," 22.

29. Edward died in 1910, but the peak of the Purity Crusade's activities spanned the entirety of his reign. We might wonder if, in part, the crusade took place because of his habits, but the evidence does not bear this out. Edward played the appropriate role publicly and since the public self was the one which remained under scrutiny, Edward remained as Hynes asserts, "popular with all classes" (*The Edwardian Turn of Mind,* 4).

30. James Marchant, editor's note to *Public Morals* (London: Morgan and Scott, 1908), 8.

31. Percy William Bunting, M. A., "Morality and Literature," *Public Morals,* 76.

32. William Alexander Coote, "Law and Morality," *Public Morals,* 64.

33. Percy Bunting, "Morality and Literature," 81.

34. James Marchant, editor's note to *The Nation's Morals,* viii.

35. H. Grattan Guinnes, M.D., "Men in Relation to the Problem of the Social Evil," *Public Morals,* 141–2. In his fifth commandment or commonsense means of maintaining purity, Guinness cautions his readers to "avoid evil literature" and goes on to maintain that "French realism is responsible for numberless sins. It is both the cause and product of a decadent morality" (143).

36. Samuel Hynes, *The Edwardian Turn of Mind,* 289.

37. Max Saunders, *Ford Madox Ford: A Dual Life,* 2 vols (Oxford: Oxford Univ. Press, 1996), 1: 415.

38. Ibid., 1:414.

39. Ibid., 1:415.

40. Ibid., 1:418.

41. Ibid., 1:436. Ford concludes his reminiscence *Return to Yesterday* with a trip to Berwick on the North Sea. When he arrives at the station, very far from London, he says, he buys a paper which among other things, reports "tucked away at the bottom of a page and headed minutely," the assassination of Archduke Ferdinand. Convinced still that war will never occur, Ford, his hosts, the Turners, and other guests read to each other. Ford chooses to read "the proofs from *Blast* of my one novel." Mrs. Turner reads from the work of a writer by the name of James Joyce, of whom Ford has never heard. Ford remembers that she read from *Ulysses,* but of course that work had not yet been written; Ford is hearing for the first time *Portrait of the Artist as a Young Man.* "So," he says, "for me Armageddon was bridged" (*Return to Yesterday* [New York: Liveright, 1932], 416–7).

42. A number of critics focus on the unreliability of Dowell as a narrator. See Patricia McFate and Bruce Golden ("*The Good Soldier:* A Tragedy of Self-Deception," *Modern Fiction Studies* 9 [1963]: 50–60) for arguments against Dowell's reliability. Others, including Norman Leer in *The Limited Hero in the Novels of Ford Madox Ford* (Lansing: Michigan State Univ. Press, 1966) join Arthur Mizener *(The Saddest Story: A Biography of Ford Madox Ford* [New York: World Publishing, 1971], ix–xxiii) and Max Saunders in looking at the question of duality in the novel. Mark Shorer, in his introduction to the Vintage edition of the novel (introduction to *The Good Soldier* [New York: Vintage, 1989], vii–xvii) focuses on character (he finds them all disagreeable), and John A. Miexner also looks at character with an eye toward Ashburnham's sentimentality ("The Saddest Story," *Ford Madox Ford: Modern Judgements,* ed. Richard A. Cassell [London: Macmillan, 1972], 70–96). Robert Green in *Ford Madox Ford: Prose and Politics* (Cambridge: Cambridge Univ. Press, 1981) examines Ford's work in terms of his own politics and the politics of the time, an interesting if limited view.

43. Robert Green, *Ford Madox Ford: Prose and Politics,* 103.

44. Arthur Mizener, *The Saddest Story,* xv–xvi.

45. Ford Madox Ford, *The Good Soldier,* 9. Further references will be cited in the text.

46. Max Saunders, *Ford Madox Ford,* 1:403.

47. Hynes, in his article "The Epistemology of the Good Soldier" (*Sewanee Review* 69 [Spring 1961]; 225–35) also addresses the question of passion and its conflict with convention. He argues that the "interaction" of the two produces the novel's catastrophes. According to Hynes's "Passion is the necessary antagonist of convention, the protest of the individual against the rules. It is anarchic and destructive; it reveals the secrets of the heart which convention exists to conceal and repress; it knows no rules except its own necessity" (233). Yes, and the repressive moral atmosphere of Edwardian England makes this all the more likely.

48. Max Saunders, *Ford Madox Ford,* 1:431.

49. Ibid., 1:404.

50. T. S. Eliot, introduction to *Nightwood,* by Djuna Barnes (1937; reprint, New York: New Directions, 1961), xv.

51. Samuel Hynes, "Epistemology," 229.

52. Ibid., 233.

53. Max Saunders, *Ford Madox Ford,* 1:421–2. As evidence, Saunders cites the passage in which Dowell says "both Edward and Leonora really regarded the girl as their daughter" and then corrects himself by saying "it might be more precise to say that they regarded her as being Leonora's daughter." Saunders believes this shift "repress[es] the horrendous possibility that she might be 'really regarded' as Edward's daughter" (422). Further evidence cited is the letter Nancy's mother writes in which she asks "How do you know that you are even Colonel Rufford's daughter?" For Saunders entire argument, see 1:420–7.

54. Joseph Conrad, "The Return," in *Tales of Unrest* (New York: Doubleday, Page & Company, 1923), 155. All further references are cited in the text.

55. Joseph Conrad, "Heart of Darkness," *Youth* (New York: Doubleday, Page & Company, 1923), 106. Further references are cited in the text.

56. Ruth Nadelhaft calls Hervey's comments on self-restraint "almost a parody of Marlow's commitment to 'restraint' and 'work' as the means of staving off anxiety and capitulation in the face of an indifferent universe" (*Joseph Conrad* [Atlantic Highlands, N J: Humanities Press International, 1991], 74).

57. Leon Edel, *Henry James: A Life* (New York: Harper and Row, 1985), 540, 539.

58. Walter E. Houghton, *The Victorian Frame of Mind,* 394–5.

59. Ibid., 404–5.

60. Leo Gurko, who calls all five of the stories in *Tales of Unrest* "flabbily mediocre," is among the harshest critics of "The Return" in *Joseph Conrad: Giant in Exile* (London: Frederick Muller Limited, 1965), 241. Lawrence Graver also looks at the story's shortcomings, its "lifeless dialogue, . . . unconvincing setting, and tiresome characters," all of which in his view render the story "extravagantly self-indulgent." (*Conrad's Short Fiction* [Berkeley: Univ. of California Press, 1969], 36.

Other brief treatments of "The Return" include those of Dwight Purdy who examines the story in terms of its biblical allusions (*Joseph Conrad's Bible* [Norman: Univ. of Oklahoma Press, 1984], 64–5), and Edward Said in *Joseph Conrad and the Fiction of Autobiography* (Cambridge: Harvard Univ. Press, 1966).

61. Zdzisław Najder, *Joseph Conrad: A Chronicle,* trans. Halina Carroll-Najder (New York: Quality Paperback Book Club, 1992), 208. Conrad's reactions against what Ian Watt refers to as "the complacency, insularity, and philistinism of English

bourgeois society" (*Conrad in the Nineteenth Century* [Los Angeles: Univ. of California Press, 1979], 23), are well chronicled, although many critics look elsewhere for the focus of "The Return." John Palmer, does not deny the "social irony" in the story, but does maintain that the story's focus is the "Jamesian psycho-moral difficulties of its protagonist"(*Joseph Conrad's Fiction: A Study in Literary Growth* [Ithaca: Cornell Univ. Press, 1968], 102).

62. *The Collected Letters of Joseph Conrad,* ed. Frederick Karl and Laurence Davies, 5 vols. (Cambridge: Cambridge Univ. Press, 1983–96), 1:387. Italics Conrad's.

63. *Collected Letters,* 1 394.

64. See Thomas Moser's *Joseph Conrad: Achievement and Decline* (Cambridge: Harvard Univ. Press, 1957), 71–8, and Bernard Meyer's *Joseph Conrad: A Psychoanalytic Biography* (Princeton: Princeton Univ. Press, 1967).

65. 7 January 1898, Collected Letters, 2:11.

66. The quotation is from Ted Billy, *A Wilderness of Words: Closure and Disclosure in Conrad's Short Fiction* (Lubbock: Texas Tech Univ. Press, 1997), 149. Daniel Schwarz calls "The Return" "Conrad's fullest satire of people in the urban wasteland until *The Secret Agent*" in *Conrad:* Almayer's Folly *to* Under Western Eyes (Ithaca: Cornell Univ. Press, 1980), 31. Dale Kramer also considers tone in his examination of "The Return." He argues that "[i]ts single tone is that of contempt, most frequently conveyed in an ironic manner." ("Conrad's Experiments with Language and Narrative in 'The Return,'" *Studies in Short Fiction* 25.1 [1988]: 3).

67. Ted Billy, *A Wilderness of Words,* 180.

68. Joseph Conrad, Author's Note, *Tales of Unrest,* x.

69. Ibid.

70. Joseph Conrad, "The Tale," *Tales of Hearsay* (New York: Doubleday, Page & Company, 1926), 61.

71. Ted Billy, *A Wilderness of Words,* 178.

72. This passage (and two others quoted below) echoes many in *Heart of Darkness* in which Marlow refers to lurking or concealed evils, such as the moment when, realizing Kurtz is near death, he defends Kurtz to the manager. Marlow thinks that "it seemed to me as if I also were buried in a vast grave full of unspeakable secrets. I felt an intolerable weight oppressing my breast, the smell of the damp earth, the unseen presence of victorious corruption, the darkness of an *impenetrable* night" (138, italics mine).

73. Jeremy Hawthorn, *Joseph Conrad: Narrative Technique and Ideological Commitment* (London: Edward Arnold, 1990), 265. Najder also notes similarities between "The Tale" and "The Return" (418).

74. Jeremy Hawthorn, *Joseph Conrad,* 265.

75. Dale Kramer is one of the few critics who believes Hervey "come[s]to terms with the need to achieve contact with something genuine" (7). Ruth Nadelhaft argues, and I agree, that Hervey's departure at the end of the story "constitutes cowardice on his part" (76). As we have seen, he cannot "stand" the uncertainty of his wife's behavior and prefers to retreat rather than put himself at the mercy of "real feelings" which are not governed by the rules. Deirdre David, who sees the story as a three act play, also acknowledges that Hervey does not change "from the way he had been at the beginning" ("Selfhood and Language in 'The Return' and 'Falk,'" *Conradiana* 8.2 [1976]: 142). While Conrad himself says in a letter to Garnett, "Another man goes out than the man who came in. T'other fellow is dead," we might speculate that he too sees the formation of a Kurtz-like hollowness (24 January 1898, *Collected Letters,* 2: 27). As Nadelhaft argues, Hervey's words lead us toward "the thoughts that must have

animated Kurtz, in *Heart of Darkness,* when he justifies to himself his departure from the empty injunctions of his Western morality" (74). Given the absence of the proverbial policeman on the corner, we might imagine Hervey, once his disillusionment sets in, to be Kurtz.

76. Nancy's exile to India, of course, places her in the care of another violent man, her father, Colonel Rufford whose violence toward his alcoholic wife has caused Nancy agony as a child. Sending her to him is only appropriate within the limitations of Edwardian culture.

Notes to Chapter 2

1. J. C. Furnas, *The Americans: A Social History of the United States 1587–1914* (New York: Putnam's Sons, 1969), 916.

2. Ibid., 915–6.

3. Laura Shapiro, *Perfection Salad: Women and Cooking at the Turn of the Century* (New York: Henry Holt, 1986), 4.

4. Ibid.

5. Herbert Hoover, "What I Would Like Women to Do," *Ladies' Home Journal,* August 1917, 25.

6. Ibid.

7. The United States Food Administration, *Food Saving and Sharing* (New York: Doubleday, 1918), v.

8. Thetta Quay Franks, *The Margin of Happiness: The Reward of Thrift* (New York: Knickerbocker, 1917), 3. Further references to the book will be cited in the text.

9. Willa Cather to Ferris Greenslet, 10 November, 1921, quoted in James Woodress, *Willa Cather, A Literary Life* (Lincoln: Univ. of Nebraska Press, 1989), 320.

10. Ibid., 284.

11. Woodress equates Red Cloud with two other famous and often fictionalized American small towns, Hannibal, Missouri and Oxford, Mississippi (44).

12. Sharon O'Brien, *Willa Cather: The Emerging Voice* (1987; reprint, Cambridge: Harvard Univ. Press, 1997), 100.

13. Ibid., 122.

14. Ibid., 124.

15. Ibid., 66.

16. James Woodress, *Willa Cather,* 304.

17. Ibid.

18. Ibid.

19. Sharon O'Brien also writes of One of Ours in "Combat Envy and Survivor Guilt: Willa Cather's 'Manly Battle Yarn.'" Here she also stresses the "dislike of Nebraska's constricted life and desire for escape" felt by both G. P. Cather and Willa herself. In France, O'Brien believes, Cather grants [Claude] the death of his old self and the birth of a new." In *Arms and the Woman: War, Gender, and Literary Representation,* ed. Helen M. Cooper, Adrienne A. Munich, and Susan M. Squier (Chapel Hill: Univ. of North Carolina Press, 1989), 189, 190.

20. Willa Cather, *One of Ours* (1922; reprint, New York: Vintage, 1991), 25. Further references will be cited in the text.

21. Dix McComas, writing about *One of Ours,* believes that Claude's eventual emotional release in the war connects with his negative relationship with Nat Wheeler. McComas asserts that "the urge to kill or be killed begins at home in a tormented

young man's incapacity to take a stand in his own behalf against a patently abusive father," that in fact, the enemy provides Claude with an opportunity to "strike back."
My assertion, however, is that Claude's father is only one aspect of the spiritually
stripped landscape from which Claude finally escapes. ("Willa Cather's *One of Ours*: In
Distant Effigy," *Legacy* 14.2 [1997]: 93–109.) For a slightly more forgiving interpreta-
tion of Claude's family life see Patricia Lee Yongue, "For Better and for Worse: At
Home and at War in *One of Ours,*" *Willa Cather: Family, Community, and History,* ed.,
John J. Murphy, Linda H. Adams, and Paul Rawlins (Provo: Brigham Young Univ.
Humanities Publications Center, 1990), 141–53.

22. Lou Klein and Harry Von Tilzer, "The Little Good for Nothing's Good for
Something After All" (New York: Harry Von Tilzer Music Publishing, 1918).

23. Sandra Gilbert and Susan Gubar, *No Man's Land: The Place of the Woman
Writer in the Twentieth Century,* 3 vols. (New Haven: Yale Univ. Press, 1988–1994),
2:299.

24. Ford Madox Ford, *The Good Soldier,* 40.

25. Joseph Conrad, "Heart of Darkness," *Youth* (New York: Doubleday, 1923),
117–8. Further references will be cited in the text.

26. Hannah Arendt, *The Origins of Totalitarianism,* new ed. (New York: Harcourt,
Brace & World, 1966), 189.

27. Ibid., 190.

28. Ibid.

29. Ibid.

30. Ibid., 189.

31. Ibid., 190.

32. Arendt's second chapter "Race and Bureaucracy" in fact refers repeatedly to
Kurtz and cites *Heart of Darkness* as "the most illuminating work on actual race experience in Africa" (185).

33. Sven Lindqvist, *Exterminate All the Brutes,* trans. Joan Tate (New York: New
Press, 1996), 36–9.

34. Adam Hochschild, in a more traditional historical account, also looks at the
colonization of Africa. Hochschild, in his book and in an article published in the *New
Yorker,* looks at Conrad's Africa and at the possible source of Kurtz, one Léon Rom,
from whom, Hochschild argues, Conrad may have gotten the idea for the pilloried
heads outside Kurtz's compound (*King Leopold's Ghost: A Story of Greed, Terror, and
Heroism in Colonial Africa* [Boston: Houghton Mifflin, 1998], 145).

35. Joseph Conrad, "Geography and Some Explorers," *Last Essays* (New York:
Doubleday, 1926), 17.

36. Zdzisław Najder, *Joseph Conrad: A Chronicle* (New York: Quality Paperback
Book Club, 1992), 140.

37. Ibid.

38. Marlow's need to tell his tale to the men on the Nellie also suggests a need for
absolution, or at least a need to soften his own guilt in the matter. Marlow's telling also
implicates his listeners, both on the Nellie and by extension, his readers, as Margot
Norris points out in her *Modern Fiction Studies* article on Francis Ford Coppola's film,
Apocalypse Now. In her words, Coppola captures "Conrad's genius for using both narration and narrative structure to create a textual performance of self-incrimination and
moral implication that ultimately extends to the reader and the viewer." ("Modernism
and Vietnam: Francis Ford Coppola's Apocalypse Now," *Modern Fiction Studies* 44.3
[Fall 1998]: 732).

39. Ruth Nadelhaft suggests that Alvan Hervey, once he learns that "morality is not a method of happiness," must experience the same thoughts as "the thoughts that must have animated Kurtz in *Heart of Darkness* when he justifies to himself his departure from the empty injunctions of his Western morality" (*Joseph Conrad* [Atlantic Highlands, NJ: Humanities Press International, 1991], 74).

40. Hunt Hawkins, responding to the charge that Conrad omitted from *Heart of Darkness* mention of the numerous revolts by Africans, asserts that Kurtz's madness itself stands as a paradigm for the insanity of imperialism, thus making unnecessary the naming of local pockets of resistance to its forces. *"Heart of Darkness* and the Erasure of African Resistance" (paper presented at the annual meeting of the Modern Language Association, San Francisco, December 1998).

41. Frederick R. Karl, *Joseph Conrad: The Three Lives* (New York: Farrar, Straus and Giroux, 1979), 473.

Notes to Chapter 3

1. Martin Gilbert, *The First World War: A Complete History* (New York: Henry Holt, 1994), 19.

2. Michael Coren, *The Invisible Man: The Life and Liberties of H. G. Wells* (New York: Atheneum, 1993), 129.

3. Joseph Conrad, "Poland Revisited," *Notes on Life and Letters* (New York: Doubleday, 1921), 149.

4. Joseph Conrad, "First News," *Notes on Life and Letters,* 178.

5. Henry James to Rhoda Broughton, August 10, 1914, *Selected Letters,* ed. Leon Edel (Cambridge, Mass: Belknap, 1974), 421. Italics James's.

6. Edith Wharton, *A Backward Glance* (New York: Appleton, 1934), 367.

7. Ibid.

8. Samuel Hynes, *A War Imagined: The First World War and English Culture* (New York: Atheneum, 1991), 4. Italics mine.

9. H. G. Wells, *Mr. Britling Sees It Through* (1916; reprint, London: Hogarth Press, 1985), 428.

10. Edith Wharton, *Fighting France*, vol. 3, of *The War on All Fronts* (New York: Scribner's, 1919), 3:236.

11. Ibid., 234.

12. Edith Wharton, *The Marne* (New York: Appleton, 1918), 11.

13. Ibid., 34.

14. Wharton, *Fighting France*, 237.

15. Shari Benstock, introduction to *A Son at the Front,* by Edith Wharton (1922; reprint, DeKalb: Northern Illinois Univ. Press, 1995), vii.

16. Wharton, *A Backward Glance,* 341.

17. Ernest Hemingway, *A Farewell to Arms* (1929; reprint, New York: Scribner's, 1957), 185.

18. Wharton, *The Marne,* 42, 27, 38. Italics Wharton's.

19. Edith Wharton to Sara Norton, September 2, 1914, *The Letters of Edith Wharton,* ed. R. W. B. Lewis and Nancy Lewis (New York: Scribner's, 1988), 335. Italics Wharton's.

20. Wharton, *The Marne,* 40.

21. Wharton, *A Backward Glance,* 351.

22. Ibid.

23. Wharton, *Fighting France,* 4.

24. Ibid., 6.

25. Benstock, introduction to *A Son at the Front,* ix.

26. Julie Olin-Ammentorp, "'Not Precisely War Stories': Edith Wharton's Short Fiction from the Great War," *Studies in American Fiction* 23:(2) (Autumn 1995), 154, 155.

27. Wharton, *A Backward Glance, 368.*

28. Edith Wharton, *A Son at the Front* (1922; reprint, DeKalb: Northern Illinois Univ. Press, 1995), 10. Further references will be cited in the text.

29. Wharton, *The Marne,* 21.

30. Wharton, *Glance,* 338–40.

31. Arthur Ponsonby, *Falsehood in War-time* (New York: Dutton, 1928), 103–4.

32. Ibid., 103.

33. While the Holocaust, which occurred twenty-five years later, has been documented by photographic evidence and extensive physical evidence, no evidence of the kind that substantiates that unspeakable horror exists for the rumors which proliferated in the Great War, although countless testimonials have been published. What seems to be important here, as we have seen, is the mythologization of atrocity stories, in many cases to deliberately inflame citizens against "ordinary" Germans. Some of the other rumors that we will examine later include that of the crucified Canadian, handless Belgian babies, and Nurse Grace Hume who was proven to be a figment of her "sister" Kate Hume's imagination. The story of Edith Cavell, who was indeed executed by the Germans, was used for propaganda purposes, even though her execution would have been legal and "justified" under the rules of war. The Allies, of course, did not shoot women and thus used Cavell's execution as propaganda.

34. In 1916 the British War Office published a report, *Alleged German Outrages,* collected by The Committee on Alleged German Outrages chaired by Viscount O. M. Bryce as an appendix to his official report on the subject and generally referred to as the Bryce Report. This report "documents" mutilations of babies. See *Evidence and Documents Laid Before the Committee on Alleged German Outrages: Being An Appendix to the Report of the Committee appointed by His Britannic Majesty's Government* (Ottawa: Government Printing Bureau, 1916). In America, The Committee on Public Information issued a similar report containing diaries and letters of German soldiers. Part I, "German War Practices," was published in January of 1918 and Part II, "German Treatment of Conquered Territory," appeared later that year. See United States, The Committee on Public Information, *German Treatment of Conquered Territory: Being Part II of German War Practices,* ed. Dana C. Munro, George C. Sellery, and August C. Krey (Washington, D.C.: GPO, 1918) and The Committee on Public Information, *German War Practices: Part I, Treatment of Civilians,* ed. Dana C. Munro, George C. Sellery, and August C. Krey (Washington, D.C.: GPO, 1918).

35. Robert Graves, *Good-Bye to All That* (1929; reprint, New York: Anchor-Doubleday, 1957), 183.

36. Ibid.

37. The Bryce Report includes stories of many murders of children, including the testimonial of a Belgian woman who claims to have seen a girl of seven or eight bayoneted because she could not walk fast enough (145).

38. Joseph Conrad, "Autocracy and War," in *Notes on Life and Letters* (New York: Doubleday, 1921), 87.

39. "The Great War: 1918," *The American Experience,* narr. Eric Sevareid, writ. and prod. Tom Weidlinger. WGBH, Boston. 31 Oct. 1989.

40. Alfred Bryan and Al Piantadosi, "I Didn't Raise My Boy to Be a Soldier" (New York: Leo Feist, 1915).

41. Mark Van Wienen writes extensively about the song and its importance to the pacifist movement in the U.S. Released simultaneously with the founding convention of the Women's Pacifist Party, the song sold, according to Van Wienen, 650,000 copies before the sinking of the Lusitania began to change American opinion. Van Wienen argues that "'I Didn't Raise My Boy to Be a Soldier' helped make the pacifist movement a hard, quantifiable political reality to be reckoned with." That the song also inspired a number of parodies, I believe, reiterates the ambiguous nature of its message. (*Partisans and Poets: The Political Work of American Poetry in The Great War* [New York: Cambridge Univ. Press, 1997], 57–9).

42. This passage echoes Mr. Britling's thoughts that there is a "creative and corrective impulse behind all hate." (H. G. Wells, *Mr. Britling Sees It Through* [1916; reprint, London: Hogarth Press, 1985], 296.

43. H. G. Wells to The Editor, *The Times,* 25 October 1914, *The Correspondence of H. G. Wells: 1904–1918,* ed. David C. Smith, 4 vols. (London: Pickering and Chatto, 1998), 2:393.

44. H. G. Wells, "Why Britain Went to War," *The War that Will End War* (New York: Duffield & Company, 1914), 14.

45. George Orwell, "Politics and the English Language," *Shooting an Elephant and Other Essays* (New York: Harcourt, Brace & Company, 1950), 88.

46. Ibid., 89.

47. Wells, *War,* 12.

48. Michael Foot, *The History of Mr. Wells* (Washington: Counterpoint, 1995), 150.

49. Sir Campbell Stuart, K.B.E., *Secrets of Crewe House: The Story of a Famous Campaign* (London: Hodder and Stoughton, 1920), 62.

50. Ibid.

51. Michael Coren, *The Invisible Man,* 131.

52. Wells, *War,* 12.

53. H. G. Wells to Lord Northcliffe, 17 July 1918, *Correspondence,* 557.

54. Ibid.

55. Mr. Britling offers his Belgian refugee, Mr. Van der Pant, a German wine at dinner and Van der Pant drinks it with the observation that the Moselle region will be a part of Belgium after the war (252–3).

56. Britling refers to the Bryce Report's "relentless array of witnesses, its particulars of countless acts of cruelty and arrogant unreason and uncleanness in Belgium and the occupied territory of France" (280). According to Ponsonby, The War Department understood the inflammatory effect of releasing this kind of information and deliberately did so to manipulate pubic opinion.

57. A Belgian refugee tells the story of a farmer who witnessed the decapitation of his baby who had been snatched from the breast of its mother who was then raped and mutilated by the German soldiers. When the farmer went mad and attacked the soldiers, the refugee escaped and was unable to say what happened to the farmer. The implication is that he also paid with his life (25–6). Posters immortalized these stories graphically.

58. H. G. Wells, *Mr. Britling Sees It Through* (1916; reprint, London: Hogarth Press, 1985), 125. All further references will be cited in the text.

59. Wilfred Owen, *The Collected Poems of Wilfred Owen* (1920; reprint, New York: New Directions, 1965), 67.

60. Paul Fussell, *The Great War and Modern Memory* (New York: Oxford Univ. Press, 1975), 25–6.

61. Ibid.

62. Ibid., 27.

Notes to Chapter 4

1. United States, The Committee on Public Information, "Spies and Lies," *Pictorial Review*, July 1918, 38.

2. Ibid.

3. Wharton, *Letters*, 335.

4. Conrad, "Heart of Darkness," 116.

5. Trudi Tate, *Modernism, History and the First World War* (Manchester: Manchester Univ. Press, 1998), 56.

6. Ibid., 52.

7. Ibid.

8. David M. Kennedy, *Over Here: The First World War and American Society* (New York: Oxford Univ. Press, 1980), 75.

9. Ibid., 76.

10. Ibid.

11. Ibid., 81, 82.

12. Ibid., 82.

13. Scott Nearing, introduction to *Bars and Shadows* by Ralph Chaplin (New York: Leonard Press, 1922), 5.

14. Ibid.

15. Ralph Chaplin, *Bars and Shadows*, 33.

16. Kennedy, *Over Here*, 68. Kennedy cites numerous examples of vigilantism and other forms of coercion that flourished in the short year and a half of American participation in the war.

17. Samuel Hynes, *A War Imagined: The First World War and English Culture* (New York: Atheneum, 1991), 80.

18. Ibid.

19. Ibid., 80–1.

20. Kennedy, *Over Here*, 68.

21. Robert Graves, *Good-Bye to All That* (1929; reprint, New York: Anchor-Doubleday, 1957), 68.

22. Max Saunders, *Ford Madox Ford: A Dual Life*, 2 vols. (Oxford: Oxford Univ. Press, 1996), 1:18.

23. Ibid., 1:486.

24. Ibid., 478.

25. Ford did not change his last name until after the war, and only then, according to Saunders, because of difficulties with Violet Hunt, who years before had caused scandal and lawsuits by calling herself Mrs. Hueffer. Hunt had also been drawing checks on Ford's bank account, as Sylvia Tietjens does to Christopher in *Parade's End* (2:71).

26. Saunders, *Ford*, 1:489.

27. Frank McShane, *Ford Madox Ford: The Critical Heritage* (London: Routledge, 1972), 125.

28. Ibid. Saunders also discusses this incident in *Ford Madox Ford*, 1:489.

29. H. G. Wells to G. K. Chesterton, early Autumn 1917, *The Correspondence of H. G. Wells: 1904–1918*, ed. David C. Smith, 4 vols. (London: Pickering and Chatto, 1998), 2:523.

30. Ibid., 1:476.

31. Jeffrey Meyers, *D. H. Lawrence: A Biography* (New York: Vintage, 1990), 180. Meyers's work as a biographer is generally considered suspect, hence his reliance on gossip as a source.

32. Ibid., 180–1.

33. H. D., *Bid Me to Live* (New York: Dial, 1960), 75.

34. Saunders, *Ford,* 1:478. For a full account of this incident from both perspectives, see Saunders, 1:476–8, and Meyers, 177–81.

35. Ibid., 1:473.

36. Ford Madox Ford, "The Scaremonger: A Tale of the War Times," *Women, Men and the Great War,* ed. and with an introduction by Trudi Tate (Manchester: Manchester Univ. Press, 1995), 268.

37. Saunders, *Ford,* 1:473.

38. Ibid., 1:471; Alan Judd, *Ford Madox Ford* (Cambridge: Harvard University Press, 1991), 246–7.

39. Ford Madox Ford, *When Blood is Their Argument: An Analysis of Prussian Culture* (London: Hodder and Stoughton, 1915), vii, viii.

40. American and British propaganda also attack "Prussianism," but in its most stereotyped, dehumanized form. An American Food Administration poster asks citizens to "Support Every Flag that Opposes Prussianism," and an ad in the 10 July 1917 edition of the Georgia newspaper *The Augusta Herald* contrasts "The American Way," which depicts neat homes, fathers with children, and busy factories where hatted workers cheerfully enter, with "The Prussian Way," which depicts pillage, plunder, and pickelhaube-sporting soldiers dragging off women and forcing men into factories at gunpoint. Ford's propaganda analyzes and debunks German institutions and language without mythologizing them.

41. Joseph Conrad, "Autocracy and War," *Notes on Life and Letters* (New York: Doubleday, 1921), 113–4.

42. Ford, *When Blood Is Their Argument,* 293.

43. Ibid.

44. Ford Madox Ford, *Between St. Dennis and St. George: A Sketch of Three Civilisations* (London: Hodder and Stoughton, 1915), 156.

45. Ibid.

46. Ford Madox Ford, *No Enemy* (1929; reprint, New York: Ecco Press, 1984), 9.

47. Ibid., 215, 216.

48. Ibid., 216–7. Ford qualifies his venom here with a footnote which as it continues becomes venomous itself. "Gringoire is too fond of this word [blackmailers]— which he uses in a special sense to indicate persons—mostly reviewers—who do not appreciate the work of himself and his school. In his conversation he introduced at this point a long denunciation of the ——— Literary Supplement, principally because, whilst purporting to be a literary paper, it devotes, according to him, 112/113ths of its space to books about facts, at the expense of works of the imagination. So he calls that respectable journal a blackmailing organ. Since, however, this is a topic that can hardly interest the nonliterary, and since the literary are hardly likely to read these pages, the compiler has taken the liberty of not reporting these sallies. It may be true that Pontius Pilate is more criminal than the crucified thieves—but it is *never* politic to say so" (217). Saunders believes Ford left this passage in *No Enemy* in spite of its "callous and bloodthirsty" tone, "as an impression of his state of mind when reading of Gaudier's death" (484).

49. Ibid., 216.

50. H. G. Wells to G. K. Chesterton, early autumn 1917, *The Correspondence of H. G. Wells: 1904–1918* ed. David C. Smith. 4 vols. (London: Pickering and Chatto, 1998), 2:523.

51. Ford Madox Ford to John Lane, 12 August 1915, *Letters of Ford Madox Ford,* ed. Richard M. Ludwig (Princeton: Princeton Univ. Press, 1965), 61.

52. Ford Madox Ford to Catherine Hueffer, 18 September 1915, quoted in Alan Judd, *Ford Madox Ford* (Cambridge: Harvard Univ. Press, 1991), 252.

53. Ford Madox Ford, *Parade's End* (1950; reprint, New York: Vintage, 1979), 161, 159. Further references to the novels will be cited in the text.

54. Tate, *Modernism,* 55.

55. Robie Macauley, introduction to *Parade's End,* by Ford Madox Ford, xiii.

56. Ibid.

57. Ibid.

58. Ford, *Good Soldier,* 270.

59. Joseph Conrad, "The Tale," *Tales of Hearsay* (New York: Doubleday, 1925), 60, 61. Further references will be cited in the text.

60. See Jeremy Hawthorn, *Joseph Conrad: Narrative Technique and Ideological Commitment* (New York: Routledge, 1990); Jakob Lothe, *Conrad's Narrative Method* (Oxford: Oxford Univ. Press, 1989); and William W. Bonney, *Thorns and Arabesques: Contexts for Conrad's Fiction* (Baltimore: Johns Hopkins Univ. Press, 1980).

61. Bonney, *Thorns and Arabesques,* 209.

62. Hawthorn, *Joseph Conrad,* 265.

63. Conrad, *Heart of Darkness,* 97.

64. Hawthorn, *Joseph Conrad,* 265. Italics mine.

65. Conrad, "The Return," 159–60, 185.

66. For a study that champions the development and use of American propaganda, largely by the Committee on Public Information, see George Creel, *How We Advertised America: The First Telling of the Amazing Story of the Committee on Public Information that Carried the Gospel of Americanism to Every Corner of the Globe* (New York: Harper and Brothers Publishers, 1920).

67. Arthur Ponsonby, *Falsehood in War-time* (New York: Dutton, 1928), 19.

68. Ibid., 20.

69. Ibid., 26.

70. Ibid., 27.

71. Conrad, *Heart of Darkness,* 51.

72. Ibid., 48.

73. Ibid., 162.

74. Hynes, *A War Imagined,* 88.

75. Jack Caddigan and James A. Brennan, "The Rose of No Man's Land" (New York: Leo Feist, 1918).

76. Graves, *Good-Bye to All That,* 228.

77. Ibid., 229.

78. Ibid.

79. Hawthorn, *Joseph Conrad,* 264.

80. Paul Fussell, *The Great War and Modern Memory* (New York: Oxford Univ. Press, 1975), 115.

81. Ernest Hemingway, "Soldier's Home," *The Complete Short Stories of Ernest Hemingway* (New York: Scribner's-Macmillan, 1987), 112.

82. Ibid.

83. H. G. Wells, *Mr. Britling Sees It Through* (1916; reprint, London: Hogarth, 1985), 280.

84. Ibid.

85. Ponsonby, *Falsehood*, 26.

86. Fussell, *The Great War,* 120–1.

87. Harry T. Moore, *The Intelligent Heart: The Story of D. H. Lawrence* (New York: Farrar, Straus and Young, 1954), 233.

88. Joseph Conrad to J. B. Pinker, October 1916, *The Collected Letters of Joseph Conrad,* ed. Frederick Karl and Laurence Davies, 5 vols. (Cambridge: Cambridge Univ. Press, 1983–96), 5:671.

89. Graves, *Good-Bye to All That,* 183.

90. Gaetano D'Elia, "Let Us Make Tales, Not Love: Conrad's 'The Tale,'" *Conradian* 12.1 (1987): 56.

91. R. B. Cunninghame Graham, preface to *Tales of Hearsay,* by Joseph Conrad (New York: Doubleday, 1925), xiii.

92. Zdzisław Nadjer, *Joseph Conrad: A Chronicle,* trans. Halina Carroll-Najder (New York: Quality Paperback Book Club, 1992), 418.

93. Joseph Conrad to J. M. Dent, 4 December 1916, *Collected Letters,* 682.

94. Wells, *Britling,* 297.

95. Michel Foucault, *Madness and Civilization: A History of Insanity in the Age of Reason,* trans. Richard Howard (1965; reprint, New York: Vintage, 1988), 9.

96. Ibid., 11. Italics mine.

97. Conrad, "The Return," 159–60.

Notes to Chapter 5

1. Joseph Conrad, "Autocracy and War," *Notes on Life and Letters* (New York: Doubleday, 1921), 83.

2. Hans Binneveld, *From Shell Shock to Combat Stress,* trans. John O'Kane (Amsterdam: Amsterdam Univ. Press, 1997), 138.

3. Ibid.

4. Ibid.

5. British Army Order of June 7, 1917, quoted in Binneveld, *Shell Shock,* 142.

6. Robert Graves also substantiates this argument in his treatment of the letter from the little mother cited in chapter 3.

7. Edwin Ash, M.D., *The Problem of Nervous Breakdown* (New York: Macmillan, 1920), 270.

8. Ibid., 273, 274.

9. Ibid., 279.

10. Ibid., 280.

11. Conrad, "Autocracy," 87.

12. Binneveld, *Shell Shock,* 108.

13. Ibid.

14. Lewis R. Yealland, M.D., *Hysterical Disorders of Warfare* (London: Macmillan, 1918), 113.

15. Ibid., 114.

16. Kaufmann uses the term *Überrumpelungsmethode,* which translates as "a surprise-attack method." According to Binneveld, "[h]e knowingly subjected his patients to an enormous psychological shock in the hope of being able subsequently to influence them for the better" (108).

17. Ash, *Nervous Breakdown*, 190.

18. Ibid. Italics mine.

19. Ibid., 191.

20. Virginia Woolf, *Mrs. Dalloway*, (1925; reprint, New York: Harcourt Brace & Company, 1981), 83. Further references will be cited in the text.

21. Binneveld, *Shell Shock*, 117.

22. W. H. R. Rivers, M.D. "The Repression of War Experience," *The Lancet*, 2 February 1918, 174.

23. Ibid.

24. Ash, *Nervous Breakdown*, 280.

25. Elmer E. Southard, *Shell-Shock and Other Neuropsychiatric Problems* (1919; reprint, New York: Arno, 1973), 462.

26. Ibid., 486.

27. Ibid., 487.

28. Carl Rollyson, *Rebecca West: A Life* (New York: Scribner's, 1996), 62.

29. Ibid., 59.

30. Ibid., 63.

31. Ibid., 69.

32. Rebecca West, *The Return of the Soldier* (1918; reprint, New York: Carroll & Graf, 1996), 29. Further references will be cited in the text.

33. Samuel Hynes, *A War Imagined: The First World War and English Culture* (New York: Atheneum, 1991), 212.

34. Ibid.

35. Rollyson, *Rebecca West*, 70.

36. West "reconsidered" her Socialist ideas during the war. Rollyson reports that West disagreed with the tendency of trade unions to see the war as a class struggle and to ignore the German invasion of Belgium and the threat to France and Great Britain. (63)

37. Ford Madox Ford, *Parade's End* (1950; reprint, New York: Vintage, 1979), 236. Further references will be cited in the text.

38. Tietjens's shell shock resembles that of Ford himself. After being blown up, according to Max Saunders, Ford lost three weeks of his life, during part of which he did not even know his name (2:2). The passages in *Some Do Not* which chronicle Tietjens's experiences parallel those of Ford.

39. Norman Fenton also briefly alludes to civilian shell shock in his chapter on the aftermath of the war. Fenton refers to civilians as part of a refutation of the claim that the Armistice had "cured" a large number of shell shock victims. This undoubtedly refers to the thought that soldiers became shell shocked to remove themselves from the front. (*Shell Shock and Its Aftermath* [St. Louis: C. V. Mosby Company, 1926], 149).

40. Ash, *Nervous Breakdown*, 276.

41. Vera Brittain, *Testament of Youth* (1933; reprint, New York: Penguin, 1994), 496.

42. Ibid., 496–7.

43. Sharon O'Brien, *Willa Cather: The Emerging Voice* (New York: Oxford Univ. Press, 1987), 384.

44. Winifred Holtby, *The Crowded Street* (1924; reprint, London: Virago, 1987), 120.

45. Ibid., 122.

46. Elizabeth Shepley Sergeant, *Shadow-Shapes: The Journal of a Wounded Woman* (Boston: Houghton Mifflin, 1920), 15.

47. Judith Guest, *Herself Defined: The Poet H. D. and Her World* (New York: Quill, 1984), 72–3.

48. Robert Spoo, introduction to *Asphodel* by H. D. (Durham: Duke Univ. Press, 1992), x.

49. Trudi Tate, "H. D.'s War Neurotics," *Women's Fiction and the Great War,* eds. Suzanne Raitt and Trudi Tate (Oxford: Clarendon Press, 1997), 248.

50. H. D., *Kora and Ka* (1934; reprint, New York: New Directions, 1996), 36.

51. Ibid.

52. Tate, "Neurotics," 250.

53. Ibid., 251.

54. H. D. *Bid Me to Live* (1960; reprint, Redding Ridge, CT: Black Swan Books, 1983), 12. Further references will be cited in the text.

55. Tate, "Neurotics," 257.

56. Guest, *Herself Defined,* 218.

57. Ibid., 278.

58. Ernest Hemingway, for instance, slept with a light on and wrote extensively on the subject of war wounds. Jake Barnes, like Christopher Tietjens and Chris Baldry, has been blown up and is impotent as a result. And in "A Way You'll Never Be," Nick Adams suffers from nervousness and intermittent memory loss, and also sleeps with the light on.

59. Rudyard Kipling to Herbert Baillie, 12 January 1916, *The Letters of Rudyard Kipling,* ed. Thomas Pinney, 4 vols. to date (Iowa City: Univ. of Iowa Press, 1999), 4:355–6.

60. See the editor's note in *The Letters of Rudyard Kipling,* 4:337–8. John's body was never actually identified, but he was believed to be buried in a cemetery north of Loos.

61. A. Michael Matin, "'The Hun Is at the Gate': Historicizing Kipling's Militaristic Rhetoric, from the Imperial Periphery to the National Center; Part Two: The French, Russian and German Threats to Great Britain," *Studies in the Novel* 32:4 (Winter 1999): 433.

62. J. I. M. Stewart, *Rudyard Kipling* (New York: Dodd, Mead & Company, 1966), 187–8.

63. Rudyard Kipling to Lionel Charles Dunsterville, 12 November 1915, *The Letters of Rudyard Kipling,* 4: 344.

64. See as an example Kipling to Edward Bok, 28 October 1914, *Letters,* 4: 263.

65. Rudyard Kipling, "Swept and Garnished," *A Diversity of Creatures* (New York: Doubleday, 1917), 416.

66. Peter E. Firchow, "Kipling's 'Mary Postgate': The Barbarians and the Critics," *Critical Essays on Rudyard Kipling,* ed. Harold Orel (Boston: G. K. Hall, 1989), 175; Norman Page, "What Happens in 'Mary Postgate'?" *English Literature in Transition* 29:1 (1986): 45–6.

67. C. A. Bodelsen, *Aspects of Kipling's Art* (New York: Barnes and Noble, 1964), 102. Perhaps because both stories end in rather brutal fashions, critics have tended over the years either to ignore the stories altogether or to ignore the brutality. Andrew Lycett, Kipling's most recent biographer briefly summarizes without comment "Mary Postgate," and limits his references to "A Madonna of the Trenches" to a reference to the Angel of Mons. (*Rudyard Kipling* [London: Weidenfield and Nicolson, 1999], 452, 453. Lord Birkenhead, who calls the resolution of "A Madonna of the Trenches" "a victory of love over death" while ignoring the implications of Strangwick's response, offers a treatment, if limited, of both stories. (*Rudyard Kipling* [London: Weidenfeld

and Nicolson,1978], 334. For other references see J. M. S. Tompkins, *The Art of Rudyard Kipling* (London: Methuen, 1959); J. I. M. Stewart, *Eight Modern Writers* (Oxford: Clarendon Press, 1963); and Bonamy Dobree, *The Lamp and the Lute: Studies in Six Modern Authors* (Oxford: Clarendon Press, 1929).

68. Rudyard Kipling, "Mary Postgate," *A Diversity of Creatures* (New York: Doubleday, 1917), 424. Further references will be cited in the text.

69. Martin Gilbert, *The First World War: A Complete History* (New York: Henry Holt and Company, 1994), 90, 110–1.

70. Firchow ("Kipling's 'Mary Postgate'") and Page ("What Happens in 'Mary Postgate'?") as well as J. I. M. Stewart (*Eight Modern Writers*) believe the German airman is a hallucination. Stewart and Page argue that since no one is summoned to retrieve the airman's body, he must be a figment of Mary's imagination. This is at best a highly illogical argument. Mary knows she is violating the rules of war by refusing to aid the wounded man, and she knows that Wynn would "leave everything to fetch help, and would certainly bring It into the house" (441). But in her own war fervor, Mary believes the German is less than human. He dies like an animal and like an animal, he is left to the elements. In death he is not worthy of the "decent earth" which will soon "hide" Edna Gerritt (440).

71. Rudyard Kipling, "A Madonna of the Trenches," in *Debits and Credits* (London: Macmillan, 1926), 243. Further references will be cited in the text.

72. Edmund Wilson, "The Kipling That Nobody Read," *The Wound and the Bow* (Cambridge: Riverside Press, 1941), 177. According to Wilson, in this story "cancer serves as a symbol for rejected or frustrated love."

73. Tonie and Valmai Holt, *My Boy Jack: The Search for Kipling's Only Son* (Barnsley, S. Yorkshire: Leo Cooper, 1998), 177. Their argument is strong until they assert that Strangwick and his Uncle Armine have murdered Godsoe, a highly implausible idea given Strangwick's story.

74. Rudyard Kipling, *Something of Myself: For My Friends Known and Unknown* (Garden City: Doubleday, Doran & Company, 1937), 231.

75. Ibid., 232.

76. Ibid.

77. Lycett, *Rudyard Kipling,* 453.

Notes to Conclusion

1. Gina Kolata, *FLU: The Story of the Great Influenza Pandemic of 1918 and the Search for the Virus That Caused It* (New York: Farrar, Straus and Giroux, 1999), ix–x.

2. Ibid., 306.

3. Ibid., 305.

4. Katherine Anne Porter, *Pale Horse, Pale Rider: Three Short Novels* (New York: Harcourt, Brace and Company, 1939), 259.

5. Edith Wharton, *Fighting France,* vol. 3, *The War on All Fronts* (New York: Scribner's, 1919), 238.

6. Wilfred Owen, "Dulce et Decorum Est," in *The Collected Poems of Wilfred Owen* (1920; reprint, New York: New Directions, 1965), 55.

7. Nick Thorpe and Carrell Severin, "If Some Were Found Wanting, It Was Not for Lack of Courage," *The Scotsman,* July 25, 1998.

8. Ibid.

9. "The Great War: 1918", *The American Experience,* writ. and prod. Tom Weidlinger, 60 min., WGBH, Boston, 1989, videocassette.

Works Consulted

Arendt, Hannah. *The Origins of Totalitarianism.* New York: Harcourt, Brace & World, 1966.

Ash, Edwin, M.D. *The Problem of Nervous Breakdown.* New York: Macmillan, 1920.

Barchilon, José. Introduction to *Madness and Civilization: A History of Insanity in the Age of Reason,* by Michel Foucault. Translated by Richard Howard. 1965. Reprint, New York: Random House, Vintage Books, 1988.

Barker, Pat. *Regeneration.* New York: Penguin Books, Plume, 1993.

Beck, James M. *The War and Humanity: A Further Discussion of the Ethics of the World War and the Attitude and Duty of the United States.* 2nd ed. New York: Putnam, 1917.

Benstock, Shari. Introduction to *A Son at the Front,* by Edith Wharton. DeKalb: Northern Illinois University Press, 1995.

———. *No Gifts From Chance: A Biography of Edith Wharton.* New York: Scribner's, 1994.

Billy, Ted. *A Wilderness of Words: Closure and Disclosure in Conrad's Short Fiction.* Lubbock: Texas Tech University Press, 1997.

Binneveld, Hans. *From Shell Shock to Combat Stress.* Translated by John O'Kane. Amsterdam: Amsterdam University Press, 1997.

Birkenhead, Lord. *Rudyard Kipling.* London: Weidenfield and Nicolson, 1979.

Bodelsen, C. A. *Aspects of Kipling's Art.* Reprint, New York: Barnes and Noble, 1964.

Bonamy, Dobree. *The Lamp and the Lute: Studies in Six Modern Authors.* Oxford: Clarendon Press, 1929.

Bonney, William W. *Thorns and Arabesques: Contexts for Conrad's Fiction.* Baltimore: Johns Hopkins University Press, 1980.

Brittain, Vera. *Testament of Youth.* 1933. Reprint, New York: Penguin, 1994.

Bryan, Alfred and Al Piantadosi. *I Didn't Raise My Boy to Be a Soldier.* New York: Leo Feist, 1915.

Bryce, Viscount, O.M., comp. *Evidence and Documents Laid Before the Committee on Alleged German Outrages: Being An Appendix to the Report of the Committee Appointed by His Britannic Majesty's Government.* Ottawa: Government Printing Bureau, 1916.

Buitenhuis, Peter. *The Great War of Words: British, American, and Canadian Propaganda and Fiction, 1914–1933.* Vancouver: University of British Columbia Press, 1987.

Bunting, Percy William. "Morality and Literature," in James Marchant, ed., *Public Morals.* London: Morgan and Scott, 1908.

Caddigan, Jack and James A. Brennan. *The Rose of No Man's Land.* New York: Leo Feist, 1918.

Campbell, Sir Stuart, K.B.E. *Secrets of Crewe House: The Story of a Famous Campaign.* London: Hodder and Stoughton, 1920.

Cather, Willa. *One of Ours.* 1922. Reprint, New York: Random House, Vintage Books, 1991.

Chaplin, Ralph. *Bars and Shadows: The Prison Poems of Ralph Chaplin.* New York: Leonard Press, 1922.

Coffman, Edward M. *The War to End All Wars.* Madison: University of Wisconsin Press, 1986.

Conrad, Joseph. "Autocracy and War," in *Notes on Life and Letters.* New York: Doubleday, Page, 1921.

———. *The Collected Letters of Joseph Conrad.* Edited by Frederick Karl and Laurence Davies. 5 vols. Cambridge: Cambridge University Press, 1983–96.

———. "First News," in *Notes on Life and Letters.* New York: Doubleday, Page, 1921.

———. "Geography and Some Explorers," in *Last Essays.* New York: Doubleday, Page, 1926.

———. "Heart of Darkness," in *Youth.* New York: Doubleday, Page, 1923.

———. "Poland Revisited," in *Notes on Life and Letters.* New York: Doubleday, Page, 1921.

———. "The Return," in *Tales of Unrest.* New York: Doubleday, Page, 1923.

———. "The Tale," in *Tales of Hearsay.* New York: Doubleday, Page, 1925.

Cooper, Helen M., Adrienne A. Munich, and Susan M. Squier, eds. *Arms and the Woman: War, Gender, and Literary Representation.* Chapel Hill: University of North Carolina Press, 1989.

Cooperman, Stanley. "The War Lover: Claude." *Critical Essays on Willa Cather.* Edited by John J. Murphy. Boston: G. K. Hall, 1984.

Coote, William Alexander. "Law and Morality," in James Marchant, ed., *Public Morals.* London: Morgan and Scott, 1908.

Coren, Michael. *The Invisible Man: The Life and Liberties of H. G. Wells.* New York: Atheneum, 1993.

Creel, George. *How We Advertised America: The First Telling of the Amazing Story of the Committee on Public Information that Carried the Gospel of Americanism to Every Corner of the Globe.* New York: Harper and Brothers, 1920.

D'Elia, Gaetano. "Let Us Make Tales, Not Love: Conrad's 'The Tale.'" *Conradian* 12:1 (1987): 50–8.

David, Deirdre. "Selfhood and Language in 'The Return' and 'Falk.'" *Conradiana* 8:2 (1976): 137–47.

Edel, Leon. *Henry James: A Life.* New York: Harper and Row, 1985.

Eliot, T. S. Introduction to Djuna Barnes, *Nightwood,* 1937. New York: New Directions, 1961.

Fenton, Norman. *Shell Shock and Its Aftermath.* St. Louis: C. V. Mosby, 1926.

Ferguson, Niall. *The Pity of War.* New York: Basic Books, 1999.

Field, Frank. *British and French Writers of the First World War.* Cambridge: Cambridge University Press, 1991.

Firchow, Peter E. "Kipling's 'Mary Postgate': The Barbarians and the Critics." *Critical Essays on Rudyard Kipling.* Edited by Harold Orel. Boston: G. K. Hall, 1989. 168–81.

Foot, Michael. *The History of Mr. Wells.* Washington: Counterpoint, 1995.

Ford, Ford Madox. *Between St. Dennis and St. George: A Sketch of Three Civilisations.* London: Hodder and Stoughton, 1915.

———. *The Correspondence of Ford Madox Ford and Stella Bowen.* Edited by Sondra J. Stang and Karen Cochran. Bloomington: Indiana University Press, 1992.

———. *The Good Soldier.* 1915. Reprint, New York: Random House, Vintage Books, 1989.

———. *Letters of Ford Madox Ford.* Edited by Richard M. Ludwig. Princeton: Princeton University Press, 1965.

———. *No Enemy.* 1929. New York: Ecco, 1984.

———. *Parade's End.* New York: Random House, Vintage Books, 1979.

———. *Return to Yesterday.* New York: Liveright, 1932.

———. "The Scaremonger: A Tale of the War Times." *Women, Men and The Great War.* Edited and introduced by Trudi Tate. Manchester: Manchester University Press, 1995. 268–74.

———. *When Blood Is Their Argument: An Analysis of Prussian Culture.* London: Hodder and Stoughton, 1915.

Foucault, Michel. *Madness and Civilization: A History of Insanity in the Age of Reason.* 1965. Translated by Richard Howard. New York: Random House, Vintage Books, 1988.

Franks, Thetta Quay. *The Margin of Happiness: The Reward of Thrift.* New York: Knickerbocker, 1917.

Freidel, Frank. *Over There.* Philadelphia: Temple University Press, 1990.

Fussell, Paul. *The Great War and Modern Memory.* New York: Oxford University Press, 1975.

Furnas, J. C. *The Americans: A Social History of the United States 1587–1914.* New York: Putnam, 1969.

Gabriel, Richard A. *The Painful Field: The Psychiatric Dimension of Modern War.* Westport: Greenwood, 1988.

Gilbert, Martin. *The First World War: A Complete History.* New York: Henry Holt, 1994.

Gilbert, Sandra and Susan Gubar. *No Man's Land: The Place of the Woman Writer in the Twentieth Century.* 3 vols. New Haven: Yale University Press, 1988–94.

Glad, Betty, ed. *Psychological Dimensions of War.* Newbury Park: Sage, 1990.

Goldman, Dorothy. *Women Writers and the Great War.* New York: Twayne, 1995.

Graham, R. B. Cunninghame. Preface to Joseph Conrad, *Tales of Hearsay.* New York: Doubleday, Page, 1925.

Graver, Lawrence. *Conrad's Short Fiction.* Berkeley: University of California Press, 1969.

Graves, Robert. *Good-Bye to All That.* 1929. New York: Anchor-Doubleday, 1957.

"The Great War: 1918." *The American Experience.* Narrated by Eric Sevareid, written and produced by Tom Weidlinger. PBS. WGBH, Boston. 31 Oct. 1989.

Green, Robert. *Ford Madox Ford: Prose and Politics.* Cambridge: Cambridge University Press, 1981.

Grinker, Lt. Col. Roy R., M.C. and John P. Spiegel, Major, M.C. *Men Under Stress.* Philadelphia: Blakiston, 1945.

Guest, Judith. *Herself Defined: The Poet H. D. and Her World.* New York: Quill, 1984.

Guinnes, H. Grattan. "Men in Relation to the Problem of the Social Evil," in James Marchant, ed., *Public Morals.* London: Morgan and Scott, 1908.

Gurko, Leo. *Joseph Conrad: Giant in Exile.* London: Frederick Muller, 1965.

H. D. *Kora and Ka.* 1934. New York: New Directions, 1996.

———. *Bid Me to Live.* New York: Dial, 1960.

Hawthorn, Jeremy. *Joseph Conrad: Narrative Technique and Ideological Commitment.* New York: Routledge, 1990.

Hemingway, Ernest. *A Farewell to Arms.* 1929. New York: Scribner's, 1957.

———. "Soldier's Home," in *The Complete Short Stories of Ernest Hemingway.* New York: Scribner's-Macmillan, 1987.

———. "A Way You'll Never Be," in *The Complete Short Stories of Ernest Hemingway.* New York: Scribner's-Macmillan, 1987.

———. *The Sun Also Rises.* 1926. New York: Scribner's, 1954.

Higonnet, Margaret R. et al., eds. *Behind the Lines: Gender and the Two World Wars.* New Haven: Yale University Press, 1987.

Hochschild, Adam. *King Leopold's Ghost: A Story of Greed, Terror, and Heroism in Colonial Africa.* Boston: Houghton Mifflin, 1998.

Holt, Tonnie and Valmai Holt. *My Boy Jack: The Search for Kipling's Only Son.* Barnsley, S. Yorkshire: Leo Cooper, 1998.

Holtby, Winifred. *The Crowded Street.* 1924. London: Virago, 1987.

Hoover, Herbert. "What I Would Like Women to Do." *Ladies' Home Journal.* August, 1917.

Houghton, Walter E. *The Victorian Frame of Mind, 1830–1870.* 1957. New Haven: Yale University Press, 1985.

Hynes, Samuel. *The Edwardian Turn of Mind.* Princeton: Princeton University Press, 1968.

———. "The Epistemology of The Good Soldier." *Sewanee Review* 69 (Spring 1961): 225–35.

———. *The Soldiers' Tale.* New York: Viking, 1997.

———. *A War Imagined: The First World War and English Culture.* New York: Atheneum, 1991.

James, Henry. *Selected Letters.* Edited by Leon Edel. Cambridge: Belknap, 1974.

Judd, Alan. *Ford Madox Ford.* Cambridge: Harvard University Press, 1991.

Jung, Carl. "Approaching the Unconscious," in *Man and His Symbols.* Edited by M.-L. Von Franz. New York: Dell, 1964.

Karl, Frederick. *Joseph Conrad: The Three Lives.* New York: Farrar, Straus and Giroux, 1979.

Keen, Sam. *Faces of the Enemy: Reflections of the Hostile Imagination.* New York: Harper & Row, 1986.

Kemp, Peter. *H. G. Wells and the Culminating Ape.* London: Macmillan, 1982.

Kennedy, David M. *Over Here: The First World War and American Society.* New York: Oxford University Press, 1980.

Kipling, Rudyard. *The Letters of Rudyard Kipling.* Edited by Thomas Pinney. Vol. 4. Iowa City: University of Iowa Press, 1999.

———. "A Madonna of the Trenches." *Debits and Credits.* London: Macmillan, 1926.

———. "Mary Postgate." *A Diversity of Creatures.* New York: Doubleday, Page, 1917.

———. *Something of Myself: For My Friends Known and Unknown.* Garden City: Doubleday, Page, 1937.

———. "Swept and Garnished." *A Diversity of Creatures.* New York: Doubleday, Page, 1917.

Klein, Yvonne, ed. *Beyond the Home Front.* New York: New York University Press, 1997.

Klein, Lou and Harry Von Tilzer. "The Little Good for Nothing's Good for Something After All." New York: Harry Von Tilzer Music Publishing, 1918.

Kolata, Gina. *FLU: The Story of the Great Influenza Pandemic of 1918 and the Search for the Virus That Caused It*. New York: Farrar, Straus and Giroux, 1999.

Kramer, Dale. "Conrad's Experiments With Language and Narrative in 'The Return.'" *Studies in Short Fiction* 25.1 (1988): 1–11.

Laski, Marghanita. *From Palm to Pine: Rudyard Kipling Abroad and At Home*. London: Sidgwick & Jackson, 1987.

LeShan, Lawrence. *The Psychology of War: Comprehending Its Mystique and Its Madness*. Chicago: Noble, 1992.

Leer, Norman. *The Limited Hero in the Novels of Ford Madox Ford*. Lansing: Michigan State University Press, 1966.

Lewis, R. W. B. *Edith Wharton: A Biography*. New York: Harper & Row, 1975.

Leys, Ruth. "Traumatic Cures: Shell Shock, Janet, and the Question of Memory." *Critical Inquiry* 20.4 (1994): 623–62.

Lindqvist, Sven. *Exterminate All the Brutes*. Translated by Joan Tate. New York: New Press, 1996.

Lorenz, Konrad. *On Aggression*. Translated by Marjorie Kerr Wilson. New York: Harcourt, Brace & World, 1966.

Lothe, Jakob. *Conrad's Narrative Method*. Oxford: Oxford University Press, 1989.

Lycett, Andrew. *Rudyard Kipling*. London: Weidenfield and Nicolson, 1999.

Macauley, Robie. Introduction to Ford Madox Ford, *Parade's End*. 1950. New York: Random House. Vintage Books, 1979.

Marchant, James, ed. *Public Morals*. Preface by the Right Rev. the Lord Bishop of Southwark (Edward Stuart Talbot, D.D.). London: Morgan & Scott, 1908. Published for the National Social Purity Crusade.

———. Note, *The Nation's Morals: Being the Proceedings of the Public Morals Conference held in London on the 14th and 15th July, 1910*. London: Cassell, 1910.

Marwick, Arthur. *The Deluge: British Society and the First World War*. New York: W. W. Norton, 1965.

Matin, A. Michael. "'The Hun Is at the Gate': Historicizing Kipling's Militaristic Rhetoric, from the Imperial Periphery to the National Center; Part Two: The French, Russian and German Threats to Great Britain." *Studies in the Novel* 32:4 (Winter 1999): 432–70.

McComas, Dix. "Willa Cather's *One of Ours:* In Distant Effigy." *Legacy* 14:2 (1997): 93–109.

McFate, Patricia, and Bruce Golden. "*The Good Soldier:* A Tragedy of Self Deception." *Modern Fiction Studies* 9 (1963): 50–60.

McShane, Frank. *Ford Madox Ford: The Critical Heritage*. London: Routledge, 1972.

Meixner, John A. "The Saddest Story," in *Ford Madox Ford: Modern Judgements*. Edited by Richard A. Cassell. London: Macmillan, 1972.

Meyer, Bernard. *Joseph Conrad: A Psychoanalytic Biography*. Princeton: Princeton University Press, 1967.

Meyers, Jeffrey. *D. H. Lawrence: A Biography*. New York: Random House, Vintage Books, 1990.

Mizener, Arthur. *The Saddest Story: A Biography of Ford Madox Ford*. New York: World, 1971.

Moore, Harry T. *The Intelligent Heart: The Story of D. H. Lawrence*. New York: Farrar, Straus and Giroux, 1954.

Moser, Thomas. *Joseph Conrad: Achievement and Decline*. Cambridge: Harvard University Press, 1957.

Nadelhaft, Ruth. *Joseph Conrad*. Atlantic Highlands, NJ: Humanities Press, 1991.

Najder, Zdzisław. *Joseph Conrad: A Chronicle*. Translated by Halina Carroll-Najder. Rutgers: Rutgers University Press, 1983.

Nearing, Scott. Introduction to Ralph Chaplin, *Bars and Shadows: The Prison Poems of Ralph Chaplin*. New York: Leonard Press, 1922.

Nelson, Robert J. *Willa Cather and France*. Urbana: University of Illinois Press, 1988.

Norgate, Paul. "Shell-Shock and Poetry: Wilfred Owen at Craiglockhart Hospital." *English*. 36.1 (1987): 1–35.

O'Brien, Sharon. *Willa Cather: The Emerging Voice*. New York: Oxford University Press, 1987.

———. "Combat Envy and Survivor Guilt." *Arms and the Woman: War, Gender, and Literary Representation*. Edited by Helen M. Cooper, Adrienne A. Munich, and Susan M. Squier. Chapel Hill: University of North Carolina Press, 1989. 184–204.

Olin-Ammentorp, Julie. "'Not Precisely War Stories': Edith Wharton's Short Fiction From the Great War." *Studies in American Fiction*. 23:2 (Autumn 1995): 153–72.

Onions, John. *English Fiction and Drama of The Great War, 1918–1939*. London: Macmillan, 1990.

Orwell, George. "Politics and the English Language," in *Shooting an Elephant and Other Essays*. New York: Harcourt, Brace & Company, 1950.

Owen, Wilfred. *The Collected Poems of Wilfred Owen*. 1920. New York: New Directions, 1965.

Page, Norman. "What Happens in 'Mary Postgate'?" *English Literature in Transition*. 29:1 (1986): 41–7.

Palmer, John. *Joseph Conrad's Fiction: A Study in Literary Growth*. Ithaca: Cornell University Press, 1968.

Palmer, Scott. *Jack the Ripper: A Reference Guide*. Lanham, Maryland: Scarecrow Press, 1995.

Ponsonby, Arthur. *Falsehood in War-time*. New York: Dutton, 1928.

Porter, Katherine Anne. *Pale Horse, Pale Rider: Three Short Novels*. New York: Harcourt, Brace and Company, 1939. 179–264.

Purdy, Dwight. *Joseph Conrad's Bible*. Norman: University of Oklahoma Press, 1984.

Rivers, W. H. R., M.D. "The Repression of War Experience." *The Lancet*. February 2, 1918. 173–7.

Rollyson, Carl. *Rebecca West: A Life*. New York: Scribner's, 1996.

Said, Edward. *Joseph Conrad and the Fiction of Autobiography*. Cambridge: Harvard University Press, 1966.

Saleeby, C. W. "Education for Parenthood." *The Nation's Morals: Being the Proceedings of the Public Morals Conference held in London on the 14th and 15th July, 1910*. London: Cassell, 1910. 17–24.

Saunders, Max. *Ford Madox Ford: A Dual Life*. 2 vols. Oxford: Oxford University Press, 1996.

Schwarz, Daniel. *Conrad:* Almayer's Folly *to* Under Western Eyes. Ithaca: Cornell University Press, 1980.

Sergeant, Elizabeth Shepley. *Shadow-Shapes*: The Journal of a Wounded Woman. Boston: Houghton Mifflin, 1920.

Shapiro, Laura. *Perfection Salad: Women and Cooking at the Turn of the Century*. New York: Henry Holt, 1986.

Shorer, Mark. Introduction to Ford Madox Ford, *The Good Soldier*. New York: Random House, Vintage Books, 1989.

Sinclair, May. *A Journal of Impressions in Belgium.* New York: Macmillan, 1915.

Southard, Elmer E. *Shell-Shock and Other Neuropsychiatric Problems.* 1919. New York: Arno, 1973.

Spoo, Robert. Introduction to H. D., *Asphodel.* Durham: Duke University Press, 1992.

Stevens, Anthony. *The Roots of War: A Jungian Perspective.* New York: Paragon, 1989.

Stewart, J. I. M. *Eight Modern Writers.* Oxford: Clarendon, 1963.

———. *Rudyard Kipling.* New York: Dodd, Mead and Company, 1966.

Stuart, Sir Campbell, K.B.E. *Secrets of Crewe House: The Story of a Famous Campaign.* London: Hodder and Stoughton, 1920.

Tate, Trudi. "H. D.'s War Neurotics." *Women's Fiction and The Great War.* Edited by Suzanne Raitt and Trudi Tate. Oxford: Clarendon, 1997. 241–62.

———. *Modernism, History and the First World War.* Manchester: Manchester University Press, 1998.

Thorpe, Nick and Carrell Severin. "If Some Were Found Wanting, It Was Not for Lack of Courage." Edinburgh: *The Scotsman.* July 25, 1998.

Tompkins, J. M. S. *The Art of Rudyard Kipling.* London: Methuen, 1959.

Tylee, Claire. *The Great War and Women's Consciousness: Images of Militarism and Womanhood in Women's Writings, 1914–1964.* Iowa City: University of Iowa Press, 1990.

Van Wienen, Mark. *Partisans and Poets: The Political Work of American Poetry in the Great War.* New York: Cambridge University Press, 1997.

United States. The Committee on Public Information. *German Treatment of Conquered Territory: Being Part II of German War Practices.* Edited by Dana C. Munro, George C. Sellery, and August C. Krey. Washington: GPO, 1918.

———. The Committee on Public Information. *German War Practices: Part I, Treatment of Civilians.* Edited by Dana C. Munro, George C. Sellery, and August C. Krey. Washington: GPO, 1918.

———. The Committee on Public Information. "Spies and Lies." *Pictorial Review.* July, 1918. 38.

———. The United States Food Administration. *Food Saving and Sharing.* New York: Doubleday, Page, 1918.

Watt, Ian. *Conrad in the Nineteenth Century.* Los Angeles: University of California Press, 1979.

Wells, H. G. *The Correspondence of H. G. Wells: 1904–1918.* Edited by David C. Smith. Vol 2. London: Pickering & Chatto, 1998.

———. *Mr. Britling Sees It Through.* 1916. London: Hogarth, 1985.

———. "Why Britain Went to War." *The War That Will End War.* New York: Duffield, 1914.

———. *The World Set Free: A Story of Mankind.* London: Macmillan, 1914.

West, Rebecca. *The Return of the Soldier.* 1918. New York: Carroll & Graf, 1996.

Wharton, Edith. *A Backward Glance.* New York: Appleton, 1934.

———. *Fighting France.* New York: Scribner's, 1919. Vol. 3 of *The War on All Fronts.*

———. *The Letters of Edith Wharton.* Edited by R. W. B. Lewis and Nancy Lewis. New York: Scribner's, 1988.

———. *The Marne.* New York: Appleton, 1918.

———. *A Son at the Front.* 1923. DeKalb: Northern Illinois University Press, 1995.

Wilson, Edmund. "The Kipling that Nobody Read." *The Wound and the Bow.* Cambridge: Houghton Mifflin, Riverside Press, 1941.

Winter, Jay, and Jean-Louis Robert. *Capital Cities at War: Paris, London, Berlin 1914–1919.* Cambridge: Cambridge University Press, 1997.

Wolff, Cynthia Griffin. *A Feast of Words: The Triumph of Edith Wharton.* 1977. 2nd ed. Reading, MA: Addison-Wesley, 1995.

Woodress, James. *Willa Cather: A Literary Life.* Lincoln: University of Nebraska Press, 1989.

Woolf, Virginia. *Mrs. Dalloway.* 1925. New York: Harcourt Brace & Company, 1981.

Yealland, Lewis R, M.D. *Hysterical Disorders of Warfare.* London: Macmillan, 1918.

Yongue, Patricia L. "For Better and for Worse: At Home and at War in *One Of Ours.*" Willa Cather: Family, Community, and History. Provo, Utah: Brigham Young University Press, 1990.

Index